REFERENCE GUIDES TO RHETORIC AND COMPOSITION
Series Editor, Charles Bazerman

Reference Guides to Rhetoric and Composition
Series Editor, Charles Bazerman

The Series provides compact, comprehensive and convenient surveys of what has been learned through research and practice as composition has emerged as an academic discipline over the last half century. Each volume is devoted to a single topic that has been of interest in rhetoric and composition in recent years, to synthesize and make available the sum and parts of what has been learned on that topic. These reference guides are designed to help deepen classroom practice by making available the collective wisdom of the field and will provide the basis for new research. The Series is intended to be of use to teachers at all levels of education, researchers and scholars of writing, graduate students learning about the field, and all who have interest in or responsibility for writing programs and the teaching of writing.

Parlor Press and The WAC Clearinghouse are collaborating so that these books will be widely available through low-cost print editions and free digital distribution. The publishers and the Series editor are teachers and researchers of writing, committed to the principle that knowledge should freely circulate. We see the opportunities that new technologies have for further democratizing knowledge. And we see that to share the power of writing is to share the means for all to articulate their needs, interest, and learning into the great experiment of literacy.

Revision

History, Theory, and Practice

Edited by Alice Horning and Anne Becker

Parlor Press
West Lafayette, Indiana
www.parlorpress.com

The WAC Clearinghouse
http://wac.colostate.edu/

Parlor Press LLC, West Lafayette, Indiana 47906

© 2006 by Parlor Press and The WAC Clearinghouse
All rights reserved.
Printed in the United States of America

SAN: 254-8879

Library of Congress Cataloging-in-Publication Data

Revision : history, theory, and practice / edited by Alice Horning, Anne Becker.
   p. cm. -- (Reference guides to rhetoric and composition)
   Includes bibliographical references and index.
   ISBN 1-932559-75-2 (pbk. : alk. paper) -- ISBN 1-932559-76-0 (hardcover : alk. paper) -- ISBN 1-932559-77-9 (adobe ebook)
   1. Editing. I. Horning, Alice S. II. Becker, Anne, 1944- . III. Series.
   PN162.H61 2006
   808'.027--dc22
                                             2006006625

Series logo designed by Karl Stolley.
This book is printed on acid-free paper.

Parlor Press, LLC is an independent publisher of scholarly and trade titles in print and multimedia formats. This book is available in paperback, cloth, and Adobe eBook formats from Parlor Press on the World Wide Web at http://www.parlorpress.com. For submission information or to find out about Parlor Press publications, write to Parlor Press, 816 Robinson St., West Lafayette, Indiana, 47906, or e-mail editor@parlorpress.com.

The WAC Clearinghouse supports teachers of writing across the disciplines. Hosted by Colorado State University's Composition Program, it brings together four journals, three book series, and resources for teachers who use writing in their courses. This book will also be available free on the Internet at The WAC Clearinghouse (http://wac.colostate.edu/).

Contents

PREFACE *xi*

1 INTRODUCTION AND OVERVIEW *3*
Catherine Haar and Alice Horning *3*

2 DEFINITIONS AND DISTINCTIONS *10*
Catherine Haar

    Revision Defined by Scholars *11*
    Revision Defined in Practice *14*
    Revision as Correction *15*
    Revision as Development and Discovery *17*
    Revision as Rhetorical Goal-Setting
        and Function *18*
    Revision as Assertion of Identity *19*
    Students and Revision *20*
    Crucial Role for Teaching Revision Well *23*

3 A REVIEW OF WRITING MODEL RESEARCH BASED ON COGNITIVE PROCESSES *25*
Anne Becker

    Early Models—Basic Processes and Their
        Key Sub-Categories *26*
    Task-centered Models—Assessing the Role of
        Reading and Memory in Revision *31*
    Recent Research—Continued Analysis and
        Testing to Validate Revision Models *34*
    Instructional Techniques *39*
    Computers and Their Impact on
        Writing Model Research *44*
    Implications for Classroom Instruction *46*

4 Basic Writers and Revision 50
Alice Horning and Jeanie Robertson

    Defining Basic Writers 50
    Awarenesses and Basic Writers 53
    Skills and Basic Writers 58
    A "Pivotal Moment:" Some Suggestions and Recommendations 61

5 Revision and ESL Students 63
Kasia Kietlinska

    History of the Discipline 64
    Diversity of the ESL Student Population 65
    Revision Attitudes of ESL Students 67
    Revision Patterns of ESL Students 68
    Revision Effectiveness of ESL Students 69
    Revision Feedback by Teachers 71
    Timing of Revision Feedback 75
    Most Effective Techniques of Revision Feedback 77
    Peer Revision Feedback 78
    Alternative Strategies to Support Revision 83

6 What's in a Textbook? 88
Robert Lamphear

    Handbooks 89
    Revision Focused Textbooks 97
    Readers 99
    Appendix: A Listing of Books from Major Composition Publishers 100

7 Revising with Word Processing/Technology/Document Design 102
Douglas Eyman and Colleen Reilly

    Scholarship about Computer Applications and Revision 102
    Basic Computer Applications and Revision Strategies 104
    Cut and Paste 105
    Font Formatting 105

Textual Analysis Tools   106
Track Changes   107
Highlighting and Commenting   109
Other Applications for Peer Review   110
Remediation, Redesign, and Revision   112
Conclusion   115
Appendix: Directions for Using the Track Changes Tool in Microsoft Word   115

8 PROFESSIONAL WRITERS AND REVISION   117
Alice Horning

Awarenesses and Skills: A Summary   117
   Professionals' Awareness   118
   Professionals' Skills   119
Methodology for the Case Studies   121
   Case studies: Writing Teachers Revising   122
   Background Questionnaire for Subject A   122
   Task Questionnaire for Subject A   124
   Observation of Subject A   125
   Analysis of Revising: Subject A   127
   Background Questionnaire for Subject B   130
   Task Questionnaire for Subject B   131
   Observation Report for Subject B   132
   Analysis of Revising: Subject B   134
Cross-Case Analysis   136
Pedagogical Suggestions: A Summary   138
Appendix A: Background Questionnaire on Writing and Revising Strategies   139
Appendix B: Questionnaire for Revising Session   140
Appendix C: Practice Passage for Think Aloud.   141

9 CREATIVE WRITERS AND REVISION   142
David Stephen Calonne

Creativity and Revision   143
Writers on Revision   147
Revision and Computers   161

The Role of Collaborators and Editors 164
Revision of Proofs and Galleys 165
Revision after Publication 168
Scholars Study Revision: Process Criticism 171
Wordsworth, Parallel Texts, Nabokov,
  Poststructuralism, Hypertext
  and Beyond 174

10 Best Classroom Practices 177
Carol Trupiano

Introduction 177
Peer Review 178
Writing Centers and Other Writing
  Support Programs 185
Portfolios 188
Teacher and Student Conferences 190
Group Review Exercise 193
  Modeling Exercise #1 194
  Modeling Exercise #2 194
  Role-Playing Exercise #1 195
  Role-Playing Exercise #2 195

11 Practical Guidelines for Writers and Teachers 197
Cathleen Breidenbach

Revision: A Complex, Intuitive, and
  Elusive Process 198
The Dangers of Practical Strategies 199
Revision's Secret Identity 199
The Fallacy of the Natural Writer 200
The Difference between Deep Revision
  and Final Editing 202
The Ants-at-a-Picnic Metaphor 203
Breaking Old Habits: Colorizing
  Comments 204
Including Good News with the Bad 204
Building Time into the Process 205
If It's Not a Draft, It's a Revision 206

Risk-Free Revision   207
Divide and Conquer—Clusters of
   Consideration   208
   *Content: Argument, Logic, Narrative,
      Organization*   208
   *Rhetorical Decisions: Purpose, Genre, Audience,
      Tone, and Point of View*   210
Visualizing Henrietta   211
Style   214
Voice   216
Mechanics   218
This Much We Know Is True—Writing
   Teachers Who Write   218

GLOSSARY   220
   Cathy McQueen

ANNOTATED BIBLIOGRAPHY   223

WORKS CITED   232

INDEX   245

CONTRIBUTORS   255

Preface

Revision holds a special place in writing research, practice and pedagogy. As a highly visible, public, and craft-like aspect of the writing process, revision early became associated with writing skill in a way that appealed to teachers and writers of all levels and approaches to writing. Working with existing text and improving it has a substantial and finite quality that defines it in ways that elude the more evanescent and complex invention, as reviewed in the first volume in this series. Nonetheless, revision moves beyond narrow issues of correctness, associated with editing and error based evaluation, to engage some of the complexity and subtlety of the writer's craft. Revision is something that published writers could attest to and literary archives could reveal in the multiple drafts of famous works. In composition pedagogy revision is a key focus of individual student-teacher conferences, discussing how a student paper could be improved. In revision one can concretely help students in a focused way that matches their levels of skill and learning as well as their expressive motives. As tutorial labs emerged, revision was a natural site of work, as it also became for small peer groups—for it was a task that students could provide useful help to each other.

For those whose pedagogy emphasizes expression and creativity, the security of having well developed revision opportunities and support later in the process frees students in the earliest stages of writing to turn off the censor; nonetheless, this postponement of craft work until text has emerged to work on provides concrete focus and motive for attention to language. For those concerned with development of specific elements of student writing, such as detail, or argument structure, or sentence clarity and variety, revision makes those issues substantive and immediate. More formally-minded writers and instructors can turn to issues of correctness and well-formedness at a moment when students could see the attention as helpful and formative rather than evaluative and punitive. For those concerned with ESL writers, revision is a site to help students formulate their ideas into communicative English and to recognize the patterned interferences introduced by their first language. Similarly, for teachers of basic writers focus on revision provides opportunities for students to develop their first ideas into fuller statements, expanding their range of expression. Revision offers something for every kind of student and every pedagogic stance. We see some of these many elements in the chapters of this book.

Yet for all its defined activity and craft, revision contains a mystery: How can this seeing again, this re-visioning come about? How can one see one's words fresh in a deep way, opening up and evaluating alternative ways of developing and expressing one's thoughts? People seem to be deeply attached and committed to the words they initially come up with through hard struggles. The words seem their own, and were their best solution at the moment to the problem of saying what they want to say. How can it be said any differently without losing its essence? This attachment to first formulations seems to be true both for the struggling beginner grasping onto any words produced and the more accomplished writer proud of his or her style and ideas.

As teachers we have developed many tricks to help students to see the writing freshly, to get them outside their words, to give them leverage on texts. We suggest putting texts aside and sleeping on them to get the distance of time. We find ways to enlist others to provide another perspective—through simply having students read their texts aloud to listeners who provide an account of what they got from reading the text, to peer editors providing full scale revision comments of their own. We offer specific heuristic questions for students and revision groups to use to interrogate the texts. Yet no matter what device we use one of the most robust research findings is that students tend to revise essays shallowly, following only very concrete revision suggestions or working only on minor phrasal adjustment and sentence correctness. Even when as word processing has facilitated the moving of text, the substitution of phrasing, even the marking up and transfer of drafts, still that ability to see one's own text with fresh eyes remains elusive.

Revision: History, Theory and Practice, the third volume of the Reference Guides to Rhetoric and Composition reviews the research, practice, and pedagogy on revision and places it within the broader concern for process. In so doing it identifies and explores more recent work on the kinds of awareness that make one able to view one's writing through fresh eyes: a writer's awareness of his or her self as a writer using particular writing processes; a strategic awareness of one's personal ways of recognizing difficulties and eliciting support; and a well developed awareness of the way language works and what alternatives are possible to have different effects. These kinds of awareness suggest that we need to teach our students something beyond the writing process itself, to develop the underlying knowledge and awareness that need to be brought to bear in revision. It is my hope that this synthesis will mark the beginning of a new period in revision research and pedagogy that opens up new issues of writer's knowledge and craft, and that is sensitive to the variety of tasks and situations writers engage in. The issues raised by revision can open fresh looks at writing process, through the lens of how writers come to know, understand, and develop themselves as individuals and writers engaged within particular writing situations. And the issues raised here about revision can open up more precise analyses of what it is writers can most usefully understand about language, and how different knowledges about language can facilitate different kinds of writing.

—*Charles Bazerman*

Revision
History, Theory, and Practice

1 Introduction and Overview

Catherine Haar and Alice Horning

While revision is consistently included as a topic in any writing handbook or rhetoric, it doesn't have a well-developed history of theorizing and study. A search for works on revision turns up personal discussions of revision practices embedded in writers' memoirs and accounts of their craft; advice and prescriptions for students about revision; some scholarly studies of how particular groups, mainly young people, approach revising; style books in which revision is cast mainly at the level of the sentence and the word; and a few rhetoric and composition works by scholars like Peter Elbow and Donald Murray, who explore revision extensively. Writing teachers have much to gain from investigating all these various trails, but need as well a synthesis of current theory and practice, which this book provides.

Revision's importance seems so self-evident that it takes a minute to marshal support for the premise. Students ought to come out of writing classes able to write under the new conditions of other college classes or graduate school, employment, and community. If students can revise, it means they can measure their writing against the needs of an audience, a purpose, a set of disciplinary constraints, and expectations. Society as a whole deserves carefully-wrought, precise prose, not just pleasing to read but ethically written, to clarify issues, decisions, and tasks like filling in income tax forms.

Teachers ought to be able to present revision not just as the way to an "A" grade but as the way to individual satisfaction and social usefulness. These functional understandings of revision stand alongside ethical and aesthetic ones. Writers, whether student or professional, may continue to wrestle until a meaning is fully explored, developed and nuanced; they ask themselves "how true is this writing?" Or writers may continue to work until their aesthetic responses to the cadences and patterns of language are more nearly satisfied. Understanding successful revision might result from exploring the role of creativity in re-imagining a document with a new visual image or architectural design; from rhetorical analysis; from studying the role of partnerships and mentoring, both in a classroom and outside.

In general, mature, experienced writers are better at revising than younger people. In *Revision Revisited,* Alice S. Horning explores the extensive repertoire of revising practices that professional writers use. Student writers occasionally revise extensively too, but are more likely to stick to surface correction and small changes. If we study the differing practices of students and professionals, teachers can note, first, that some aspects of revising are lifelong skills, the result of self-knowledge, ambition rooted in a career and a discipline, and even the rewards of a salary or a significant entry on a resume. We include here in various chapters studies related to the maturity of our students as writers, the roles of procrastination and writers' blocks at the revision as well as the starting stage: psychology's contribution to our grasp of revision. It is clear that revision touches every part of the writing process, so we explore it not only as a starting point but also as woven into all aspects of writing, a first chief goal of this collection. Our second major objective here is to survey new research on writing processes and strategies that yields insights into the nature of revision. Current findings on creativity, on the impact of technology and on other aspects of writing enhance our understanding of writing and revising.

A pedagogy that not only supports revision but shows how it might be done is central. Mina Shaughnessy and David Bartholomae, among others, point out that in creating text, the students we call "basic writers" encounter confusing messages and impulses as they attend to their own ideas along with what they know of the academy's rules and expectations. Not just basic writers but all learning writers must attempt to reconcile personal goals and institutional expectations, and the revision process is fraught with these conflicts. A first step in teaching document-level revision may be to acknowledge these issues.

A further step includes assessing teaching and classroom practices for their support or their undermining of revision. For example, heavy grammar and style comments on a student's early draft may carry the message that the surface matters most. Trained to find mistakes, students sometimes notice a symptom of a problem, like an obtrusive repetition of a word, but rather than deal with the underlying coherence and sequence-of-ideas problem, they replace the offending word with a synonym here and there. If a passage seems disconnected, rather than seek out the idea-basis of the connection, they'll add in a transition word like moreover or however. Untrained peer reviewers in a classroom peer review session may produce impressionistic and vague responses on whether a topic per se is interesting and use badly-understood and vaguely conceived terms of criticism (as in "does the paper flow?").

The challenge of teaching revision is to do it with appropriate expectations and goals. Real revising is more a habit of mind, an openness to further consideration, a willingness to keep at it. And revision for students shouldn't result in blandness and flattening of the students' language nor the imposition of teachers' phrases and insights. Our hope for students is that they understand the conventions of the writing situations they find themselves in, while at the same time maintaining the freedom to change the situation in response to principle or passion. Following is a brief overview and summary of the chapters of the text.

In Chapter 2 on "Distinctions and Definitions," Catherine Haar explores what "revision" currently means, and who subscribes to the meaning given. In the growth and development of composition studies, have assumptions about revision changed suddenly or gradually? Are there competing meanings? To answer these questions, a first step in synthesizing work on revision includes charting the appearances, changes in, and assumptions about the term "revision." Metaphors for revision signal both understandings and misunderstandings. Students sometimes want to "polish up" a paper, restricting what they do to the surface features (like waxing the car but forgetting the tune-up, body work, or need for trade-in). Students assert they're "fixing" their essay, thus repairing what's broken.

Teachers sometimes read a "diagnostic" essay, suggesting illness to be cured. Metaphors of development liken revision to organic things which grow, while metaphors of readiness link writing to other performances like musical concerts or presentations of plays or poetry. Distinctions between revising—holistic, macro or discourse-level considerations—and editing—at the sentence and word level—have their uses but limitations as well (since discourse attains coherence and connectedness as it moves through a sequence of sentences).

In her review of the recent literature, Anne Becker reviews major books and other research reports published within the last five years, along with the relevant background from earlier theoretical proposals. This section summarizes the major models of revision processes that have been proposed recently. In addition, new programs and classroom applications are included. This chapter builds on the detailed review of the literature in Horning's *Revision Revisited*, which reviews all of the major work on revising published from 1975 to 2000.

Turning to basic writers, in the fourth chapter Alice Horning and Jeanie Robertson examine the diverse approaches to composing and revising found in this group of students, using the framework of the awarenesses and skills set up in *Revision Revisited*. Beginning with a definition of the wide range of types of writing students who are categorized as basic writers, the exploration compares and contrasts their strategies to those of professional writers. Basic writers' diversity creates a complex environment for teaching and learning revising. This chapter studies what happens and what doesn't happen when basic writers take beginning drafts, often viewed by the writer as "finished" or "done," and move to revisions that enhance meaningful communication. The chapter explores reasons for these perceptions and practices. Revision, particularly for basic writers, is not a "one size fits all" process. This part of the book offers ways instructors and student writers can more clearly understand and utilize the revision process on an individual, personalized level.

The ESL student population presents its own challenges with regard to revision, as discussed by Kasia Kietlinska, who was herself a student of English as a second language. Her discussion in the fifth chapter examines the common features of ESL writing and specific needs of ESL students in approaching the revision process. Revision work for non-native speakers of English is complicated by both the linguistic challenges of writing in a second language and the underlying cultural assumptions about text, the presentation of ideas and the larger character of writing. Strategies for revision for students and for the teaching of revision for teachers are both reviewed.

Robert Lamphear's discussion of "What's in a Textbook?" in Chapter 6 focuses on the approaches taken by the major English handbooks currently in publication. The review of textbook approaches will include an understanding of the trends and theories displayed in these texts. In addition, the chapter will offer a brief analysis of the effectiveness of techniques and exercises in each text. The discussion will demonstrate how each textbook attempts to aid students with the revision process. This chapter also includes a review of several books that focus exclusively on revision practices intended for student writers, such as Donald Murray's classic *The Craft of Revision*.

Just as revision touches every part of the writing process, so, too, does the impact of the computer affect every aspect of revision. In "Revising with Word Processing/Technology/ Document Design" Douglas Eyman and Colleen Reilly show how the development of word processing and other computer-based technologies has changed the nature of writing and the writing process. In Chapter 7, the impact of technology on revision processes and strategies is examined. The features of typical word processing programs that facilitate revision are discussed, along with ways in which technology can sometimes interfere with substantive revision in writing, such as with grammar-checking programs that lead writers astray. Power Point, Web pages and document design strategies and their impact on revising are discussed with detailed examples.

"Professional Writers and Revision" summarizes the research and findings in *Revision Revisited*. For that project, the revision processes of nine professional writers were studied through interviews on their writing habits and revision practices, through think-aloud protocols, and through their reviews of the descriptions of their work. The case studies show that professional writers use three kinds of awareness of themselves as writers and four kinds of skills to revise successfully. Detailed examples of the work of two of the contributors to this volume provide some new convincing data. In general, teachers of writing spend plenty of time building the skills that the experts have, but not nearly enough time helping student writers develop an awareness of themselves as writers.

Turning to creative writing, in the ninth chapter "Creativity and Revision," David Stephen Calonne takes up the process of revision and its role in the psychology of creativity, examining insights from literary theory, psychological investigations, and depth psychology. The chapter reviews interviews and personal accounts of such writers as Vladimir Nabokov, Robert Graves, Aldous Huxley, Henry Miller, William Faulkner, and Jorge Luis Borges. The chapter concludes by considering the role of revision in "creative" work and seeks to determine whether there is any fundamental difference between "literary" revision and the revising process for university composition students.

The tenth chapter on current views reviews the literature to discover what preferred approaches, methods, and activities are being used to help students revise their writing. Carol Trupiano focuses on three areas: teachers, peers, and tutors. Within each of these areas, the chapter explores a variety of questions. For example, how helpful are written comments on student papers, student conferences, and the use of portfolios? What types of training and/or tools do students need in order to participate in peer reviews? What are the different tutoring programs (writing centers, online tutoring, others), what are their strengths, and how can they become part of a writing assignment? Trupiano then discusses how students can effectively use what they have learned from feedback as they revise their writing. It includes practical steps that teachers can use to help students go through the necessary process of reflection and understanding. For example, after a peer review session a student might write a response discussing what issues were addressed during the session, what changes he or she decided to implement, and what impact these changes had on the revised paper. This chapter includes several sample activities and step-by-step instructions illustrating the various methods and approaches.

The final portion of the book, "Practical Guidelines for Writers and Teachers," includes Cathleen Breidenbach's ideas about lessons and assignments to help students understand their options as writers and to practice deep revision with emphasis on rhetorical strategies. Chapter 11 dispels fallacies of the "natural writer" and clarifies the difference between deep revision and editing. "Practical Guidelines" challenges the perception that revision, by its nature, is tedious drudgery and argues instead for a creative approach to revision as a discovery process. In a lighthearted discussion, the chapter advises teachers to break old habits of grading and to expand their comments on papers to include a broader range of rhetorical issues and options. It justifies building more time into the revision process. The proposed divide and conquer strategy breaks down the complicated, recursive process of revision into four areas of consideration to help students realize and experiment with their choices as writers. The discussion includes definitions and suggested lessons and assignments to focus on content (argument, logic, narrative, organization), rhetorical decisions that writers make (purpose, genre, audience, tone, and point of view), style (with advice about how to teach "writing by ear"), and lastly mechanics. Focusing on the choices writers make helps students break down and clarify the complicated process of composition and appreciate the way multiple threads entwine as a piece of writing come to life

The book closes with a glossary and annotated bibliographic essay, both assembled by Cathy McQueen with help from all the contributors. The bibliographic essay include important and generative works in the area, as well as introductory material, controversial books and articles, useful materials, exercises and related work.

All the writers who contributed to this project have come away from it with a deep awareness of how complex and integral the revision process is to the creation of successful written texts. Their work presents some of the new research on writing that helps explain how revision functions in the writing process. The preparation of the chapters showed all the contributors just how revision bears on all parts of writing, from inspiration to final draft, a continuous thread that winds through all parts of the book. Readers can follow this thread in all of the areas explored here and will ultimately find that it binds the book together into the unified fabric of teaching and learning effective writing through revising.

2 Definitions and Distinctions

Catherine Haar

Revision might be defined quite straightforwardly as the act of making changes to a written document to make it better. In writing classrooms, students have other students to work with and a teacher to guide the revision process. Both the companionship and the help ought to smooth the way for student revisers. But teachers' experiences offer caution to this uncomplicated description. How do writers make the changes? What does "improve" mean? What roles do peers, teachers, readers, and writers themselves play? These questions, which are just the most obvious ones, show that seeking a definition of revision means grabbing the tiger's tail, and with it the whole of composition theory and writing instruction. In a 1982 monograph on revision, *Revising: New Essays for Teachers of Writing,* the editor, Ronald A. Sudol, makes precisely this point, noting that "when we examine revising as teachers and researchers, we find it to be related to almost everything else we know about writing" (ix).

Understanding the scholarly work on revision prepares teachers to assist college writers in their everyday writing challenge: to revise not just as an abstract, repeatable, predictable procedure, but to revise in the face of increasingly complex intellectual and rhetorical tasks. By keeping in mind the increasing complexity of the circumstances in which college writers revise, teachers will avoid oversimplifying and overgeneralizing their pedagogy on revision. They will recognize that student writers can benefit from thoughtful explanations of many aspects of revision and classroom practices which encourage energetic, active, intellectually vital revising. In this chapter I'll consider scholarly definitions of revision, some common understandings which develop in classroom practice, and students' efforts to understand and define revision.

Revision Defined by Scholars

Along with reporting results of studies and articulating precise descriptions of revision, scholars offer vivid images and metaphorical language to assist their definitions. Unlike casual metaphorical language captured in a phrase like "clean up my writing," however, the metaphors of scholars are deliberately wrought. The scholars' definitions lay out extensive, ambitious ground for what revising might mean and raise significant questions about the nature of revisers and revising.

Composition scholars and writers often think in metaphors and images to explain revision. Some of these suggest movement or location in physical space, and they frequently consist of paired, contrastive terms. For example, Donald M. Murray discussed and contrasted "internal" and "external" revising in his essay, "Internal Revision: A Process of Discovery," published in the 1978 volume *Research on Composing: Points of Departure*, edited by Charles R. Cooper and Lee Odell. For Murray, the revising writer is paying attention both to the outside demands of correctness, forms, and appropriateness and to internal voices suggesting discoveries about structure, focus, and language (91). For internal revision, he says, "The audience is one person: the writer" (91).

Anne Lamott's *Bird by Bird: Some Instructions on Writing and Life*, introduces two contrasting terms and a third, humorous kicker: "A friend of mine says that the first draft is the down draft—you just get it down. The second draft is the up draft—you fix it up. And the third draft is the dental draft (25–26). Since the "dental" draft is the fine points, the "up draft" must mean everything a writer has to do to assess the writing as a totality. Wendy Bishop, revision scholar and editor of a recent book on revision called *Acts of Revision: A Guide for Writers*, imagines the job as "revising out," or extending and developing ideas as much as possible, then "revising in," cutting and pruning with the confidence that you've given yourself lots to work with: "Revising out allows for revising in and often helps a writer as a result produce a better text because all investigations—of ideas, words, sentences, style, shape, and tone—are instructive to the interested writer" ("Revising Out and Revising In" 14).

Linda Flower's cognitive model of revision also uses contrastive terms and movement. She sees revision as a turn, a change of direction or attention, a step, a transformation from a writer-centered to a reader-centered mode of writing. Her 1998 book *Problem-Solving Strategies for Writing in College and Community* (a new edition with significant new sections and reworkings of her 1981 book *Problem-Solving Strategies for Writing*) presents several examples of writer-based prose, characterized by "narrative organization and an egocentric focus," reworked into reader-based prose, which has "more issue-centered hierarchical organization" (218). According to Flower, writers would be better off writing for readers from the start, but in the middle of complex writing tasks, can't always manage. She offers four key points for doing this sort of revision, including formal organization "around a problem, a thesis, or a purpose"; a clear hierarchy which "distinguish[es] between your major and minor ideas, and make[s] the relationship between them explicit to the reader"; directly stated conclusions; and deliberate use of cues to point the way (220).

Compositionist Peter Elbow devotes several chapters to revision in his 1981 book *Writing with Power*. Instead of metaphor, he uses time references to quick revising (32–37) and thorough revising (128-138). The role metaphor plays for Elbow in this book is as a source of generative questions which stimulate revision. In *Being a Writer: A Community of Writers Revisited,* which Elbow wrote with Pat Belanoff, the scholars use two interrelated metaphors, levels and organic structures, to organize their thinking on revision. These levels include, in the authors' words:

1. Reseeing or rethinking: changing what a piece says, or its "bones."

2. Reworking or reshaping: changing how a piece says it, or changing its "muscles."

3. Copyediting or proofreading for mechanics and usage: checking for deviations from standard conventions, or changing the writing's "skin." (124)

As the scholar who introduced and popularized freewriting, Elbow's conceptions of revision emphasize the time task for writers and the organic, interrelated nature of texts.

Though mainly literal, the definition of revision offered by scholar Jill Fitzgerald contains a submerged metaphor of a gap to be bridged. In an article called "Research on Revision in Writing," she says, drawing on a number of other works:

Definitions and Distinctions

> Revision means making any changes at any point in the writing process. It involves identifying discrepancies between intended and instantiated text, deciding what could or should be changed in the text and how to make desired changes and operating, that is, making the desired changes. Changes may or may not affect meaning of the text, and they may be major or minor. Also, changes may be made in the writer's mind before being instantiated in written text, at the time text is first written, and/or after text is first written. (484)

Fitzgerald's definition includes thinking, comparing, deciding, and choosing, then taking action. It is broadly inclusive, in that it accepts changes at any point in composing, including changes which occur in the mind, and it applies to any sort of change, significant or less so. What's important is the writer as agent; the actual changes, as well as their effect on the document, are less important.

Sometimes revision is conceived as attention to craft. Compositionist and linguist Alice S. Horning, in *Revision Revisited*, presents "weaving as a metaphor for the revision process writers follow" (1). Like weaving, composing and then revising text involve both the starting shape or warp, and the artistry of weft, all coming together: "To create the tapestry of a text, then, just pursuing this metaphor, the revisions made become the seamless, solid fabric of the complete document" (2). Extending from her metaphor is Horning's descriptive definition of revision, "the interaction of conscious and unconscious choices writers make in a draft as they weave readable writing for readers, drawing on a balance of several kinds of self-awareness and on specific skills to produce the finished fabric of a readable text" (5).

Craft is also the heart of Joseph Harris's recent definition of revision in the article, "Revision as a Critical Practice," published July 2003 in *College English*. Working with students on academic writing, Harris suggests "some ways of imagining revision as a practice of making stronger use of the work of others and of more clearly articulating one's own project as a writer" (591). In these two criteria, Harris provides measurable ways of ascertaining improvement in a reviser's work. He notes "the appeal of rooting our teaching in the actual labor of drafting, revising, and editing texts. And as in teaching someone to farm or sew, our job in teaching writing is to help students gain more control over their work" (591). A craft depends on laboring. Accepting Harris's analogy, students are less likely to insist that some people can write and others can't. Rather, revising is a matter of learning how to work at it.

Stepping back from this selected group of scholarly definitions, one notices the frequency and importance of metaphorical thinking. Revision means movement: turning from self to reader; drafting both up and down, out and in; heeding interior and exterior voices. These images of movement witness to the active, fluid thinking of revision, its creativeness, and its multiple, interconnected tasks. Metaphors of craft signal high standards, whether in achieving a smooth weave or successful academic writing which comes through efforts similar to those of a farmer or a gardener. No magician's wand here, but rather a rake, hot sun, a bandanna for sweat, and a sun-up to sun-down work ethic. Another important idea is increasing control. Writers come to know their ideas fully and control the ways they extend and elaborate them in documents.

The definitions suggest some ways to measure success. Using Flower, one looks for a hierarchy of ideas and cues for readers. Using Horning, one expects the absence of unplanned irregularities. Using Harris, one values thesis control and competent integration of the work of others. Nevertheless, for students, knowing when revising is necessary and what steps will truly improve a document remain problematic.

REVISION DEFINED IN PRACTICE

Some collective understandings of revision have emerged from the major trends of composition history. While the trends have a historical dimension, they overlay each other as well. Using the terms of James A. Berlin, composition scholar and historian, "This diachronic diversity in rhetoric is matched by a synchronic one" (*Rhetoric and Reality* 3). Consult Anne Becker's chapter for an extended explanation of historical aspects. The theories and trends of composition comprise a large, sprawling, and diverse family over a period of time. Members come and go, some are powerful and some have ordinary status, some seem revolutionary but their influence wanes as decades pass. Despite differences between family members, cohesion develops out of a common enterprise. The analogy to a large family suggests that composition teachers strive to understand how they have been "brought up" as writing teachers, and what their students and they themselves say about revising.

Four aspects of revision are familiar in classrooms: (1) revision as correction; (2) revision as growth, development, and discovery; (3) revision as rhetorical goal-setting and function; (4) revision as assertion of identity, whether personal, political, or aesthetic. These conceptual pictures can be inferred from listing off some common metaphors for and statements about revising. We say "polish it up," "clean it up," "fix it," "play with it some more," "go in depth," "make it sound better." Writers sometimes talk about being "all over the place" or "lost" in their drafts, with revision directed at achieving better organization or "focus" (another common metaphor). Sometimes writers present the revision challenge as getting a particular job done, or opening up what they think or wish to say, or standing up for beliefs. These common statements reveal received wisdom, the methods and practices of teachers, and the assumptions of students.

Revision as Correction

Students and teachers alike might think of revision mainly as correcting previous mistakes, the "fix-it-up" plan. In secondary school, some of us revised essays by writing the correct forms for misspelled words or grammatical goofs on the same copy of the paper, right above the teacher's correction symbol. Students may still think of revising this way, depending on their high school experiences. The emphasis on correcting mistakes has its roots in "current-traditional" rhetoric, a set of assumptions that developed in the mid-nineteenth century and held sway for a century. Drawing on other scholars, revision scholar Jill Fitzgerald tells us that this emphasis on surface correction goes all the way back to Aristotle ("Research on Revision in Writing" 481–82). Current-traditional rhetoric has led to the dominance of the five-paragraph theme and modes of writing, and "[c]orrecting themes becomes the teacher's primary, if not exclusive, concern," according to W. Ross Winterowd, whose 1994 book, *A Teacher's Introduction to Composition in the Rhetorical Tradition*, provides an eight-point overview of the main consequences of this instructional plan (31). As Robert J. Connors observes in *Composition-Rhetoric: Backgrounds, Theory, and Pedagogy*, it's very easy to turn current-traditionalism into a straw-man or villain to argue against (4–7). At the same time, one must understand the implications of a corrections-only view of revising.

Often, under current-traditional assumptions, the idea of correction occurs in a vague or absent context. Correct is simply correct; English is English. But students taught not to use acronyms will have trouble with upper-level papers for specialized engineering or computer-science courses, where acronyms occur constantly. Journalists don't write like historians, or the reverse. In reality, "correct" needs to be defined in a context and for a particular purpose, without the comfort of solid, unvarying rules.

Another drawback of current-traditional assumptions comes from a coding of mistakes. I remember my father railing at the ignorance of someone who said, "Where are you at?" In the unneeded "at," he inferred class distinctions, perhaps moral distinctions, even though he understood the speaker perfectly well. When students make mistakes, or use nonstandard terms or dialect, it's important not to let that signify some sort of general ignorance or unfitness. Thus, writing instruction today tries to balance a respect for students' own language, drawing from a 1972 resolution at the Conference on College Composition and Communication called "Students' Right to Their Own Language" and reaffirmed in 2003, while at the same time helping students understand the conventions of academic writing and speech.

Current-traditional assumptions blur the useful distinction between revising and editing. Full scale revising may include major new sections of text or even a substantially new try at a document, while editing involves spelling, grammar, mechanics, word-usage, and other local concerns. In blurring the distinction, students and teachers alike overlook conceptual revision. Whatever the person drafted the first time becomes the end point, and major rethinking or reassessing isn't a serious option.

Someone should put in a good word for correction, as long as it doesn't take over all other aspects of revising. Sometimes, when teachers reexamine students' papers, a second look leads to correcting an overall impression of a student, reconsidering one's own marginal comments, and changing strategies with assignments. Students who misread assignments have the benefit of a second try and can deal with slips in word-usage, punctuation, even what "saved" version of a word-processed document they've submitted. In a relatively forgiving framework where not everything has to be nailed down exactly on the first try, correction helps everybody manage day-to-day matters in the classroom.

Revision defined as correction becomes problematic when it asserts one single, acceptable form of English language to which every writer must conform and for every purpose, and when it gives the teachers marking the corrections too much clout. Revision as correction also squeezes out conceptual revision, because surface correction implicitly pairs with stipulated models or formulas in current-traditional pedagogy. Keith Hjortshoj, in *The Transition to College Writing*, likens the five-paragraph essay to a "footstool," a simple piece of furniture that the craftsperson must soon move beyond. When students have little power to make choices, when they sense the limited range of a closed, predictable form, and when they are not part of the decision-making process about how and when to revise, they lose interest and passion. They regard revision as that tedious effort demanded by teachers as a condition for raising grades.

REVISION AS DEVELOPMENT AND DISCOVERY

Students who say they need to go in depth when they tackle an essay again, flesh out ideas, or find their voice often are speaking as learners in a process-centered classroom. Since the process revolution in writing instruction, which started in the 1960s and gained momentum through the 1970s, writers of all ages have gotten familiar with writing workshops, peer editing, brainstorming techniques, and multiple drafting. Developing at roughly the same time as process pedagogy, word-processing changed the landscape of revising dramatically. Instead of the torture endured by the amateur typist, forced to retype whole pages to fix a crucial mistake, there's instant and easy repair with a few keystrokes of word-processing. Adding became easy, so much so that some scholars began to observe a discrepancy between some students' professional-looking word-processed texts and the casual additions to create length or an illusion of completeness. Despite this critique, for most writers it's a joy to add, to create, as composition scholar Wendy Bishop calls it, a "fat draft" and to draft "generously," with more than the writer will ever need ("Revising Out and Revising In" 16). The process movement brought writing back into the classroom, students occupying themselves with drafting, conferencing, revising, and moving around in the room and also moving around in the writing process, or processes.

A process orientation blurs the distinction between composing and revising, usefully so. In a word-processed document, layers of drafts don't exist unless a writer makes a special effort to keep printing them out. Meticulous writers, who often perfect each sentence as they compose, revise on the screen. In classrooms, the existence of a revising stage results not only from writers' decisions but also from the syllabus and the teacher's schedule of reading and returning essays.

Process theorists shifted from a stage model of composing (writing happens in clear stages, one after the other, like baking brownies), to a recursion model (writers jump around in the process, restructuring in big bold steps, then fussing with a paragraph or sentence, then rereading a source and introducing a quotation, etc.). This recursion model brings in cognitive psychology. Investigating how thoughts and words team up leads to thinking about revision as not just happening to a page of text but something happening within the cognitive apparatus of the writer. And just as at a certain point it seemed incomplete to study psychology without learning about the brain, and putting behavior and brain function together, likewise, writing scholars began to ask questions about the mental processes that underlie revision. Anne Becker's chapter takes up these questions in much more detail.

The process movement led to defining revision not just as changes to a text but to events related to work habits and actions and mental events. The writer plays an active role and peers come in as friendly compatriots. Development, extension, and growth, as well as reflection, are the hallmarks of revision as a process-centered event.

Revision as Rhetorical Goal-Setting and Function

As composition gained recognition as a discipline, the new status generated upper-level writing courses, specialized courses, programs in writing across the curriculum, and first-year courses with a clearly rhetorical focus and design. Teachers assigned documents in a variety of genres in addition to essays in the traditional sense, and classroom investigations centered around the function and work of documents. Students who thought about revisions in terms of what work the document accomplished or its function for a particular discourse community were learning in classrooms structured around rhetorical analysis. Instead of seeking their own authentic tone, writers thought about appropriate roles or personae. They read academic and popular writing to detect appropriate lexicon and register for their purposes, which might change from one writing task to another. This rhetorical emphasis in some sense follows process, but also subsumes it. W. Ross Winterowd's discussion of "Neo-Classical Rhetoric" and "New Rhetoric" (*A Teacher's Introduction* 30–51) provides a useful primer to composition's return to the concepts of rhetoric starting from the mid-1970s and on.

Students who learned to assess their writing for the work it might do in a real, often public environment, who wrote collaboratively, and who understood conventions as enabling structures and not just constricting ones, found themselves well-prepared for both academic and non-academic writing projects, and for specialized kinds of writing. If the rhetorical approach has a limitation, it may be that it pays too little attention to joyfulness and play in writing. My favorite teachers explained the conventions and showed how to use them, but also showed how much fun it was, on occasion, to play against them or with them. If the reviser understands how to balance risks and benefits, the functional quality of writing becomes just one measure, not the only one.

Revision as Assertion of Identity

Writers don't just write to fit in, to become part of a group. They write to stand up, stand out, speak up, depart from the group, and many of our most memorable writers, from Henry David Thoreau to Shirley Brice Heath to students whose words still echo in our heads, have a vision of truth or beauty which dominates their work. There's a timeless quality to the urge to perfect one's writing; writers labor over their words to create powerful, moving, original discourse. See Chapter 9 by David Calonne for an investigation of revision in the work of literary writers. Revision as an assertion of identity also connects to postmodernism, which has opened up nonstandard forms for writing and a space for non-mainstream groups and insights.

Nancy Welch, author of *Getting Restless: Rethinking Revision in Writing Instruction,* questions "ways of talking in classrooms about revision that, despite the displacements of post-modernity, continue to posit the ideal of a stable, clear, and complete text" (137). Her work calls into question "this continued insistence on words like *clarity, consistency,* and *completeness* [Welch's emphasis] at a time when other cherished and problematic goals have given way" (137). In a chapter called "Revising a Writer's Identity," Welch discusses "revision as strategy for intervening in the meanings and identifications of one's life" (55). The important question for Welch about teaching is, "How do we facilitate the recognition and revision of what we're identifying with, who we are imitating—and what's being denied, suppressed or perpetuated in the process?" (56).

Revision sometimes means undermining and challenging assumptions, philosophies, or practices and then remaking them. This interpretation brings to mind texts that explode the idea of revision and carry it to large scale reimaginings, for instance Sharon Crowley's *Composition in the University: Historical and Polemical Essays,* or Eleanor Kutz's and Hepzibah Roskelly's *An Unquiet Pedagogy: Transforming Practice in the English Classroom,* or *Writing and Revising the Disciplines,* edited by Jonathan Monroe. These works take up, respectively, the place of the composition course in a university education, the mood and workings of the composition classroom, and the place and use of writing as part of the definition of academic disciplines. With such works, revision blurs into reformation or revolution.

Intentional, motivated writers may care deeply about their ideas, philosophy, and declaration of self, and as individualists they can construct the reader or readers their art requires. Teachers have a responsibility to question to what extent writing classrooms should radicalize or politicize students. As teachers, do we revise society or do we revise texts? For individual writers, what's the balance between a writer's idiosyncratic wordings and readers' access to texts?

Most would agree that instruction on revision properly takes up correcting, discovering, rhetorical strategizing, and asserting identity and individual meanings. Chapters that follow on best practices by Carol Trupiano and on the practical side of revision by Cathleen Breidenbach explore in detail how these understandings ought to be pursued and in what combinations and balances.

Students and Revision

One subject for revision research has been the differences between the revision strategies of mature writers and novice writers. Compositionist Nancy Sommers, in a 1980 essay titled "Revision Strategies of Student

Writers and Experienced Adult Writers," found significant differences both in what each group worried about and what each group did: "But unlike the students, experienced writers make changes on all levels and use all revision operations. [. . .] Unlike the students the experienced writers possess a nonlinear theory in which a sense of the whole writing both precedes and grows out of an examination of the parts. (126) Sommers calls on metaphor to explain the thinking strategies of mature writers. She says, "The experienced writers describe their primary objective when revising as finding the form or shape of their argument. Although the metaphors vary, the experienced writers often use structural expressions such as 'finding a framework,' 'a pattern,' or 'a design' for their argument" (125).

In Alice Horning's *Revision Revisited*, what mature writers do is defined and differentiated into two sets: awarenesses and skills. According to Horning, "writers balance their awarenesses and skills to weave readable texts through revision. To fully understand revision, we must examine both awarenesses and skills" (10). Consult Horning's chapter in this volume for an enumeration and explanation of awarenesses and skills.

Both Sommers and Horning would say that when students don't revise very much, or revise with limited success, it's because they don't see what to do or see paths to follow to do it. Although one might consider students' lifestyles, psychological stage, or motivation, writing teachers probably need to concentrate on students' inexperience with revision. Nancy Sommers says, "The evidence from my research suggests that it is not that students are unwilling to revise, but rather that they do what they have been taught to do in a consistently narrow and predictable way" (123). In responding to papers, teachers have an opportunity to do more than mark errors. Teachers' suggestions ought to focus on the important tasks of revising and also give some idea of how to go about it. Since the time Sommers did her work in 1980, teachers have more resources, notably Donald M. Murray's *The Craft of Revision*, 5th edition, and Wendy Bishop's edited collection of essays on revision for students, *Acts of Revision: A Guide for Writers*, both published in 2004.

Even students who have some awareness of what's needed may not carry through. Wayne C. Peck has studied this problem in "The Effects of Prompts on Revision: A Glimpse of the Gap Between Planning and Performance," published in the 1990 collection *Reading to Write:*

Exploring a Cognitive and Social Process. Peck's study shows that while some students have limited intentions, others have solid, ambitious intentions for revision which they can explain well; what's missing is follow-through. It may not be enough to ask students for a revision plan; perhaps teachers also should ask for a specific description of the revision, with text references and comparisons.

The terror of the blank page is commonplace. In its own way, revision could be just as overwhelming, especially for anyone seeing the gap between intended and instantiated text, in Fitzgerald's terms, but not seeing the means to close the gap. Brock Dethier speaks of "Revising Attitudes" in Bishop's *Acts of Revision*. Much of his advice is for students with negative attitudes about revision and how to overcome them. But there's advice for teachers too. He says, "Practiced revisers can work almost simultaneously on scores of processes, from checking homophones to rethinking theses. But I find that simple, step-by-step approaches can best open writers' eyes to the value of revision and lead us to make major changes without thinking, 'I'm revising'" (10). Novice writers may be less aware of revising practices and possibilities and at the same time more aware of revising as a looming difficulty, as they worry about how to make their documents satisfactory. While teachers can glory in the free movement and creativity of revising, novice writers may do better in a classroom which provides a protected space for comfortable yet still challenging learning.

Keith Hjortshoj, a social sciences researcher and a director, at one time, of writing across the curriculum and writing center activities at Cornell, has done interesting work on writing blocks. Blocks occur at times of rapid change and jumps in the level of difficulty, he says in *Understanding Writing Blocks*. While most would maintain that we are doing our jobs as college writing teachers if we present students with increasingly difficult intellectual challenges and new rhetorical situations, we also need to understand the danger of overload and breakdown.

Recently, I asked students in a first-semester college composition class to tell me if they liked revising. Their responses were instructive. While some students might be unsure how to revise, or sense what to do but not carry through, or feel overwhelmed as they combine disparate tasks, students can also be quite pragmatic, as mine were. One said because no one's going to use the paper again, what's the purpose of revising? One student said she actually liked revising, implying that her answer went against expectation. One gave qualified approval of revising, that it's okay as long as you don't have to re-do the whole paper and worth it if you can raise your grade. In fact, quite a few students said they liked revising because you could raise your grade, but the downside was that it was time-consuming. Several said revising helps you understand your writing better so you can improve. According to one student, college writing classes offer teachers who take revising seriously, thus resulting in more interesting possibilities for students at the revision phase.

By and large, these students were practical-minded, regarding revision partly as a learning tool, partly as a negotiation about grades. I like to think I build revision into my whole course, and that in peer groups and read-alouds and conferences, we're always talking about how to revise, yet when my students answered this question they thought about "revision" mainly as a discrete step listed in the syllabus. They also tended to think of it in connection to a grade, although it wouldn't need to be. Thus a major incongruity develops around the function of revision, whether the reward is a grade, standing outside the work, or improved writing, an implicit reward. A second incongruity is in the placement of revision, whether in one place quite late in the writing of a paper, as students often think, or embedded and recursive as writing professionals present it.

Crucial Role for Teaching Revision Well

To teach revision well, teachers must present techniques and skills and remember what it feels like to be a novice. As a case in point, advanced mathematics is a mystery to me. I couldn't give you a list of what and why; instead, it's an undifferentiated, confusing, threatening blob. Students may have this reaction to revising, and thus teachers must take the time to untangle the processes, coach awarenesses and skills, and do revision exercises in class.

Beyond skills, however, students need intrinsic and valid reasons for trying. Revising can be key to understanding one's own thinking as well as the subject thought about. A measure of success concerning revising comes in what's been learned. By developing systematic habits for reading and then revising their own work, students may learn to appreciate themselves as writers. Thus, students develop important awarenesses about themselves as writers (see Alice Horning's chapter in this volume for a brief summary and *Revision Revisited* for extensive explanation). Not everyone writes quickly, in a flash of brilliance, but many know how to get seriously to work on something. Exerting the same sort of honest labor, student writers will have a solid sense of accomplishment.

Scholar and culture critic Gerald Graff, in an essay called "Disliking Books at an Early Age," (presented to first-year writing students by Wendy Bishop in her *On Writing: A Process Reader*, 137–45) explains that until he was introduced to a critical vocabulary and active, dynamic discussions about readings, he was without a point of entry or way to engage with texts. The necessary critical framework came first, the enjoyment next. There was no naïve, holistic immersion in the text for Graff, who needed to learn how to read interpretatively before he could read with concentration and focus. His teachers helped him make sense of reading. It's likely that some students could resemble Graff not only in their reading but in their writing as well, so that as they learn to inspect their drafts closely, to consider their readers, to discover and complicate their meanings, and to work towards an architectural or gestalt-level view of their text, they'll invest more in composing and writing generally.

There's perhaps no natural appetite for acts of revision in writing. Professionals, who revise as a matter of course, have years of training informing their practice. Even at the college level, students may resist revising, dislike it, or do it in perfunctory or desultory ways. Yet many students both acknowledge reasons for revising and command considerable resources for achieving results. Although students may teach themselves to revise, especially in groups of supportive friends, and although people outside formal teaching environments also find means and methods to become revisers, the writing teacher can help writers become revisers. It might be our most important job.

3 A Review of Writing Model Research Based on Cognitive Processes

Anne Becker

Faced with many different levels of writing proficiency, composition instructors know all too well the extreme variations in ability between students. Typically inexperienced or novice writers do not take much time to develop detailed plans before writing, and when confronted with the need for revision, they consider any rewriting as punitive. This negative attitude toward correcting their text often means they focus on surface errors only, or if they do global revision, often it is less effective than their original text. Professional or expert writers, on the other hand, incorporate revision into every aspect of the writing process, looking at it as a positive opportunity for discovery as they write and rewrite. Since they view creating written text as a recursive activity, their revisions are typically global in scope.

Given this constant disparity between novice and expert writers, as well as the complexity of revision, over the last twenty-plus years composition researchers have tried to parse the process through different writing models. In 1980 Linda Flower and John Hayes proposed a shift from the traditional linear sequence models being used to describe various steps taken during writing to process-based models. By placing cognitive actions in a hierarchical format that reflected the recursive nature of writing, they initiated a new and highly productive approach to composition research. Dividing their model into three main parts, "the task environment, the writer's long-term memory, and the writing processes," Flower and Hayes hoped this basic cognitive model would lead to a clearer understanding of the key steps and thought patterns that occur throughout the writing process (369). With this knowledge, they hoped composition researchers might then discover the most effective ways to instruct novice writers so that they could more easily learn and then use strategies that foster better overall revision, thereby developing writing expertise. To better understand what progress has been made in understanding the cognitive processes used in writing, and in particular in revision, it is helpful to review the key writing models that have evolved over the last twenty years. With a clearer understanding of how various cognitive abilities interact during the writing process, especially the role that evaluation skills and working and long-term memory play, it becomes much easier to determine what kinds of instruction techniques will help novice writers develop effective revision strategies, and therefore, writing fluency.

Early Models—Basic Processes and Their Key Sub-Categories

During the 1980s, researchers refined their analysis of the basic elements of the composing process model, in an attempt to discover how to help basic writers develop into more proficient writers by improving their revision strategies. Throughout the 1980s, Flower and Hayes continued to rework the components of their writing model to better understand why expert writers were better than novice writers in constructing effective global-based review of their texts, with the hope of helping inexperienced writers learn how to revise more effectively. The first reconfiguration of their initial model was made in 1981. In this model, three main processes of planning, translating and reviewing operate through a monitor function that allows access not only to these three activities but also the writer's long-term memory. Reviewing is divided into two sub-categories: 1) evaluation, which provided for specific appraisal of the written text, and 2) revision, which referred to the actual changes.

To better represent the recursive nature of revision, Carl Bereiter and Marlene Scardamalia expanded the evaluation and revising process suggested by Flower and Hayes in 1981 by developing a compare, diagnose and operate (CDO) planning stage in their 1983 model, which they later refined in 1985. Since most writers read their own mental version of what they planned to write, rather than the actual text on the page, Bereiter and Scardamalia theorized that when revising, writers first "compare" their mental text with what they have

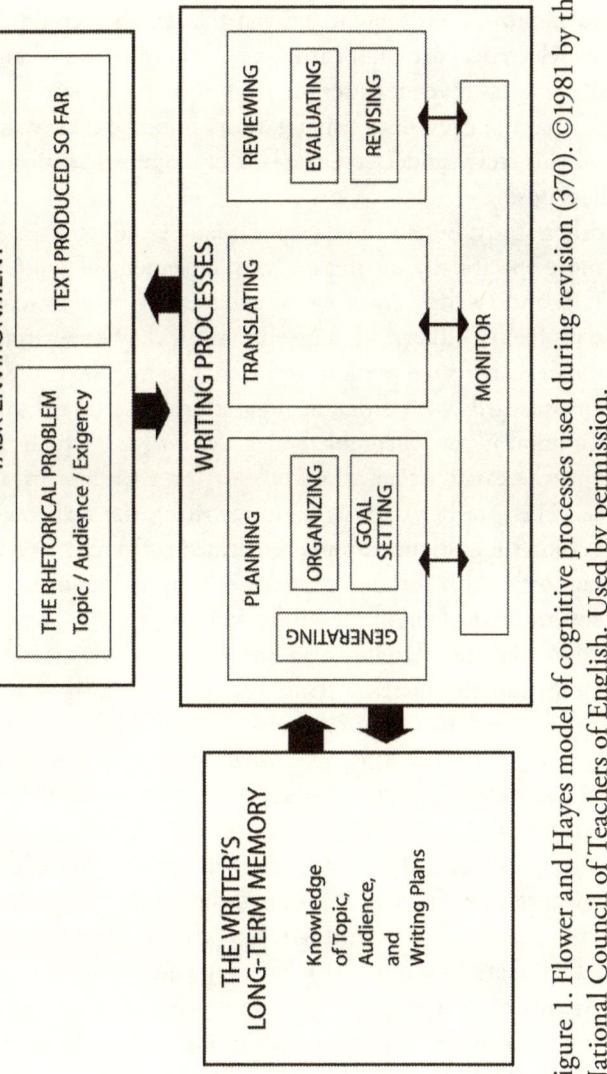

Figure 1. Flower and Hayes model of cognitive processes used during revision (370). ©1981 by the National Council of Teachers of English. Used by permission.

written. Then if they see a problem, they "diagnose" what needs to be changed and, after considering revision options, "operate" on the text to complete the revision. In one study, Bereiter and Scardamalia asked elementary-aged children to follow the CDO process as they first wrote and then reviewed their sentences. The children next decided if there were any problems with their text, by using a set of diagnostic cards, some offering evaluative comments, others revision suggestions.

The third step included doing any rewriting the children thought necessary to improve their sentences. Even though they couldn't explain why they selected a particular card, 74 percent of the children thought the CDO process made it easier for them to write. However, it should be noted that their revisions usually didn't improve their writing. The results of this study underscore the lack of diagnostic skills most novice writers possess.

Another study Bereiter and Scardamalia conducted in 1983, focused more specifically on the diagnostic element of the CDO process. Sixth and twelfth graders evaluated essays by color-coding any *detected* problems, either with a green mark if they knew exactly what the problem was or a red mark if they were unsure. Next students used 13 diagnostic cards with different suggestions, like "Hard to tell what the main point is" or "Incomplete idea," to *diagnose* which tactic best applied to the essay, either as a whole or for a specific paragraph or sentence. Then, rather than actually rewriting the text, students offered revision suggestions. Results confirmed that students do increase their diagnostic skills through support techniques that offer evaluative comments or tactical cues for revision work.

Scardamalia and Bereiter also tracked how advanced planning might help students increase their reflective thinking. Focusing on how students used planning cue cards, whether self selected or proposed by an experimenter or peer, Scardamalia and Bereiter hoped to discover what writing tactics worked best and when these methods had the most productive effect on the writing process. In order to do this, as students planned and then wrote essays, they were handed cue cards whenever they paused. Some cues, the "go-on" ones, encouraged students to expand their planning ideas, while others, the "reflective" ones, led students to reconsider what they had already decided to do (317). Again, while the quality of the writing itself didn't improve, there was an increase in reflective thinking, especially when experimenters gave cue cards to students. The results of Bereiter and Scardamalia's CDO-based studies helped to demonstrate just how complex the reviewing process really is, and in addition, to highlight the need for further research in how various cognitive processes function, especially in relation to detection and diagnosis, within the basic writing model.

To further augment this focus on the diagnostic operations that occur during revision, Flower, et al. in 1986 and Hayes, et al. in

1987 modified their writing models to include two new sub-stages: 1) processes, which involved reading to evaluate, selecting a strategy, and executing the revision; and 2) knowledge, which included task definition, criteria for planning and text, problem representation, and revision procedures. In this way, they tried to represent more specific cognitive paths followed during the evaluation and revision processes. For the first time, the writer's knowledge and intentions are both included in the model. In addition, reading takes on added importance, as it becomes the key to discovering text problems, which in turn leads to revision, whether on a local or global level. During revision, in the 1987 model writers read the written text to evaluate whether it matches their intended purpose. If they detect or diagnose a problem, then they decided what strategy to use for correcting the situation.

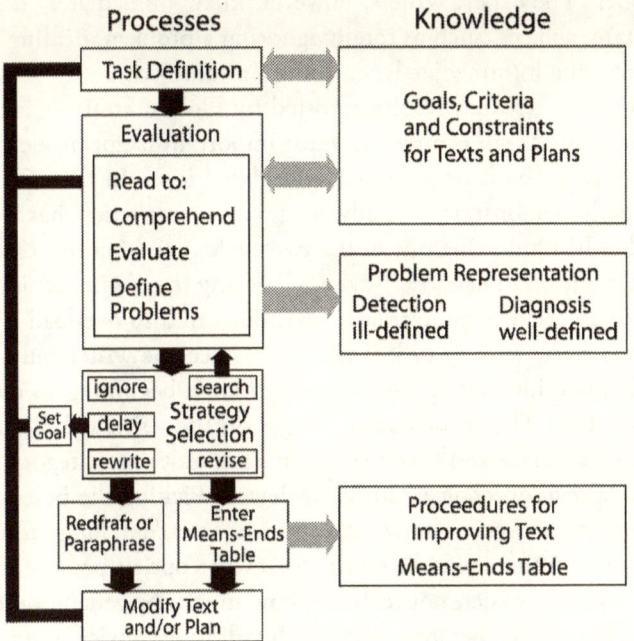

Figure 2. Flower, et al. model of key interactions between processes and knowledge used during revision (24). © 1986 by the National Council of Teachers of English. Used by permission.

In an effort to specifically track where and how detection and diagnosis facilitate or block the revision process, Flower, et al. designed a study which compared revising approaches implemented by students, teachers and professional writers when confronted with a revision task—to create a freshman student handout from a letter dealing with college sports participation written by a college coach for a colleague. While the expert writers only detected 58 percent of the "planted problems," when their revisions were completed, 91 percent of these problems had disappeared (39). Flower, et al. attributed this to one of two rules: 1) precedence, where once a global problem is discovered, it becomes the main priority so the search for other errors stops; and 2) density, where once a great deal of problems surface, it becomes more efficient to merely rewrite everything. The students in this study had more difficulty detecting the "planted" problems, even adding many new problems as they tried to rewrite the letter, pointing to weak detection skills—especially as they tried to determine what key intentions to focus on for planning and then selecting appropriate revision strategies. The expert writers, however, knew immediately that they had many choices, such as totally ignoring a problem, dealing with it later, revising it immediately, or doing a total rewrite.

From the research results reported by Flower, et al. it is evident that diagnostic skill is often the most important factor in successfully revising texts, both on a surface and global level. In fact, Flower, et al. clearly demonstrate the advantage an expert writer has over the novice, when following one of the two basic reviewing strategies: Detect/Rewrite and Diagnose/Revise. Choosing the rewrite option is the simplest solution to problematic text, but can also overload working memory if the writing task is complex, since the writer must juggle various planning and translating ideas before beginning to compose any new text. The revise option hinges on the writer's ability to first recognize an error and then place it in an appropriate category so that workable revision choices can be reviewed. Picking the best solution depends on the writer's knowledge, which is stored in long-term memory. Novice writers tend to select the rewrite option because they assume it will be easier, not realizing how much the generation of new text will tax their memory capacity. In addition, novice writers don't have the ability to categorize problems—"to see a problem in the text as a meaningful, familiar pattern" (48)—like more experienced writers. To help illustrate this point, Flower, et al. noted that in a study analyzing how chess players plan their moves, "[t]he masters planned no further ahead than normal players—they simply made better plans; they planned the *right* moves" (47). This kind of ability also separates novice writers from expert writers. Since they have a large repository of past writing experiences stored in their long-term memory, expert writers can implement "a rapid interplay of conscious and automatic processes" as they revise, without overloading either their working or long-term memory capacity (48).

As researchers began to better understand how knowledge worked with intentions throughout the revision process, working memory and long-term memory capacity became an integral piece in explaining why novice writers usually attempt surface corrections, instead of more challenging globally-oriented revisions preferred by most expert writers. Psychologist Alan D. Baddeley facilitated this shift in focus in 1986, when he formulated the first model of working memory, which includes the central executive function, and two slave systems: the visuo-spatial sketchpad and phonological loop. By analyzing what kinds of knowledge and types of activities are done in working memory, especially automatic ones that then help to ease the cognitive load that writing requires, researchers now hoped to track differences in how novice and expert writers used these processes. Throughout the 1980s, composition researchers analyzed how cognitive processes interacted during writing. The results of their studies expanded the initial three-part Flower and Hayes model of planning, translating and reviewing, shifting the focus so that more emphasis was devoted to the reviewing process, especially detection and diagnosis strategies.

Task-centered Models—Assessing the Role of Reading and Memory in Revision

The 1990s saw a shift in focus, as new models were developed to further in-depth analysis of working memory and long-term memory and their role in writing proficiency, in addition to addressing social and motivational aspects of the writing process. Three new models developed by Ronald T. Kellogg, John Hayes, and Huub van der Bergh and Gert Rijlaarsdam are presented in *The Science of Writing: Theories, Methods, Individual Differences, and Applications*. Kellogg concentrated on adapting Baddeley's working memory model to the overall writing process, Hayes focused on developing more detailed sub-processes used during revision in his task schema model, and van der Bergh and Rijlaarsdam inserted the element of time into their writing model.

Kellogg, in his essay "A Model of Working Memory in Writing," reinterpreted the basic parts of the writing model setting up three processes that operate in conjunction with the working memory functions, the visuo-spatial sketchpad, central executive and phonological loop. His first process, formulation, involves planning and translating rhetorical goals into text. The second, execution, is comprised of actually creating the text, either by writing it out by hand or word processing it. In the final process, monitoring, reading and editing are used to evaluate and then revise text. According to Kellogg, these processes operate simultaneously and, depending on the tasks involved, affect the capacity of working memory, especially the central executive, since it is activated during most of these activities. Claiming that writing fluency, but not necessarily quality, is affected by different skill levels, Kellogg analyzes six areas researchers have studied in relationship to writing models and working memory: output modes, planning strategies, capacity differences, irrelevant speech, simultaneous articulation, and loading of the central executive. Most of these studies show that expert writers usually have better overall memory capacity, because they have more developed skills needed to effectively compose or revise texts which operate automatically, thereby easing any overload on their central executive as they write. Students, on the other hand, often get stuck as they try to revise their writing because they have weak skill levels, in addition to minimal practice in planning or translating their ideas into words, which in turn affects the over all capacity of both their working memory and long-term memory capacities.

Hayes, too, was interested in how a writer's skills affected fluency and quality of text. Focusing on the evaluation of text in the reviewing stage in his essay "A New Framework for Understanding Cognition and Affect in Writing," he devised a task schema with two main categories: 1) fundamental processes, which include text processing, reflection and text production; and 2) resources, which are stored either in working or long-term memory. During revision, once a problem is discovered through fundamental processes like critical reading or reflection, writers select an appropriate resource stored in their long-term memory and activate it in their working memory. Hayes stresses the importance of critical reading skills in his schema, focusing on three key areas: content comprehension, task definition, and text revision. Because expert writers have stronger reading skills, have more audience awareness, and have a better understanding of their writing topic, they produce more successful texts as they draft/revise to meet their rhetorical goals, probably because they utilize their working memory capacities more effectively than novice writers.

Neither Hayes nor Kellogg include the element of time in their writing models, an omission van der Bergh and Rijlaarsdam feel is an integral part of writing that must be accounted for in any writing model. To incorporate time into the writing process, they designed a model in 1994, refining it in 1999, for monitoring when various cognitive activities occur. According to van der Bergh and Rijlaarsdam, in "The Dynamics of Composing—An Agenda for Research into an Interactive Compensatory Model of Writing: Many Questions, Some Answers," cognitive activity is initiated through four interrelated functions: 1) the writing assignment, 2) rereading written text, 3) translation of meaning into text, and 4) generation of ideas. Activation of any of these activities, which may happen at any time during the writing process, increases the likelihood of additional discovery for generating writing.

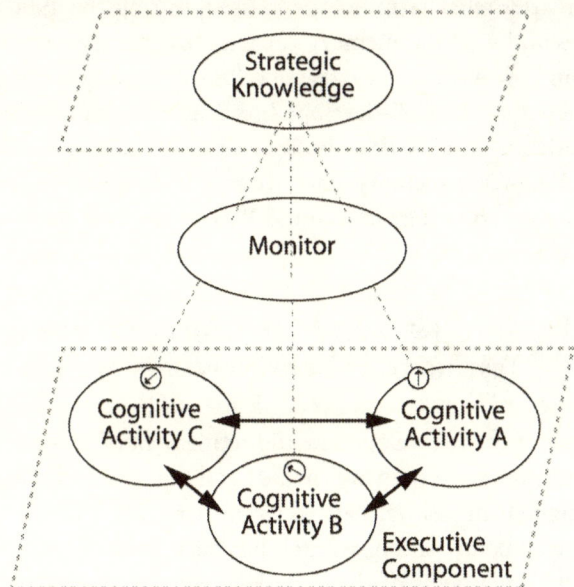

Figure 3. Writing model developed by van der Bergh and Rijlaarsdam to incorporate the element of time into the writing process (Levy and Ransdell 108). Used by permission.

Placing the most emphasis on the role cognitive strategies play during the writing process, van der Bergh and Rijlaarsdam's model has three basic modules: the executive component, monitor and strategic knowledge. The executive component module includes basic writing activities such as organizing content, generating text or evaluating ideas; the monitor module manages the transfer of knowledge domains; and the strategic knowledge module stores cognitive strategies that can be summoned by the monitor module when needed by the executive component during the writing process. In this model, memory of different cognitive strategies is contingent on different learning activities done in the executive component module. Writing activities can be based on three different approaches: trial and error, specific instructions or self-construction. The act of writing increases a writer's ability to learn different cognitive strategies. As writers gain more writing skills, they learn how to transfer them in a productive way when faced with an unfamiliar writing task. Because of this capacity to adapt skills over time, van der Bergh and Rijlaarsdam make distinctions between weak and good novices, rather than novice and expert writers.

No matter what terminology is used, during the 1990s cognitive strategies and working memory capacity became the central focus for analyzing how writing expertise develops. It became very apparent to researchers that the well-developed reading ability and extensive writing experience expert writers possess expands working memory capacity and long-term memory knowledge. However, more research was still necessary to better understand how to increase these capabilities in novice writers.

Recent Research—Continued Analysis and Testing to Validate Revision Models

As a result of the redevelopment and refinement of so many cognitive-based writing models during the 80s and 90s, research data based on well-designed studies was needed to confirm their validity. Therefore, much recent composition research has been devoted to not only analyzing the key aspects of these models, but also devising studies that can effectively measure the cognitive activities that novice and expert writers use as they write/revise texts, to see if the models accurately predict what happens from initial planning of the writing task assignment to the completion of the written text.

In *Through the Models of Writing,* Denis Alamargot and Lucile Chanquoy present an exhaustive review of cognitive writing models to determine exactly how writers can develop expertise in writing, concluding that expertise comes with maturity and practice. Dividing their discussion into three main parts, they first review cognitive writing-model designs and then closely analyze how planning, translating and revising processes function in these models. Part II follows with an examination of how cognitive processes are controlled, how working memory operates within the key writing models, and how writers develop into expert writers. In conjunction with their main conclusion that maturity and practice are the two key components that lead to better writing ability, Alamargot and Chanquoy offer several points for further study, as they analyze the different mechanisms implemented during the writing process, looking specifically at implications created by differences in working memory capacity between inexperienced and expert writers. Capacity is affected by how knowledgeable writers are about the subject matter, in addition to their ability to activate appropriate linguistic resources and rhetorical strategies. Being more familiar with topic data enables writers to more easily select ideas from long-term memory and organize them into an effective structure; this results in less working memory capacity being expended on the planning and translating processes. Expanding linguistic resources enables writers to become more fluent, since their selection of lexical and syntactical structures becomes more automatic, while increasing the range of rhetorical strategies allows writers to construct texts that address overall goals more quickly, again because their increased knowledge frees up working memory space.

While most recent writing models seem to indicate that working memory capacity improves as writers mature or gain writing experience, Alamargot and Chanquoy suggest that this narrow focus may be too restrictive. The two commentaries offered by Kellogg and Hayes in Part III of *Through the Models of Writing* reinforce this point. Kellogg suggests that the highly interactive nature of writing processes places extensive demands on working memory capacity, that these complex tasks indicate the need for a multicomponent model of working memory, and that the time expended during writing tasks may be just as important as the working memory load. Hayes comments on the importance of analyzing how writing ability develops in children, of learning how to increase metacognition, of continuing to develop means for expanding awareness of task, audience, and persona. He also calls for continued efforts to connect research results with practical applications, so that theory and practice can produce a clearer understanding of cognitive strategies.

In this vein, based on results from their 2001 study of writing fluency in students who are learning a second language, John Hayes and N. Ann Chenoweth propose a new version of the 1996 task schema that includes three levels: control, process and resource. While the control level is identical in both models, the process level, designated as the fundamental processes in the 1996 version, is now divided into two main components, to underscore the importance repertoire of writing strategies and long-term memory capacity play in writing fluency. First, there is external; this includes the written text, the audience for the writing task, and any materials used to draft/write the text, from reference texts like dictionaries or style books to notes or peer comments. The second component is internal; it may initiate four possible actions: 1) proposing, 2) translating, 3) revising, and 4) transcribing. In order to create text, any of these internal actions may activate working memory, long-term memory, or critical reading, the three components stored in the final resource level. With this model, then, at the process level, various internal actions work with specific external elements, calling on stored resources as needed to complete the writing task goals. Since the results of their study showed increased language skills facilitated writing fluency, Chenoweth and Hayes recommend that teachers give students ample opportunity to practice writing in order to increase their lexical and strategic proficiency, so that retrieval of these skills becomes more automatic. Any kind of writing task that helps students increase their ability to use new writing strategies will increase their fluency. Chenoweth and Hayes favor assignments that will not be interrupted by revision, so students can practice "the strategy of 'write it down, even if flawed, and revise it later'"(96). This kind of writing practice not only helps students expand their repertoire of writing strategies, but also increases their long-term memory capacity, necessary task schema components for building better fluency.

Alice S. Horning, in her 2002 book *Revision Revisited,* also focuses on writing fluency, but her study analyzes the processes nine expert writers from various professions use as they revise text. She suggests that writing expertise, especially revision, is contingent on well-developed metarhetorical, metastrategic and metalinguistic awareness, in addition to four basic writing skills: 1) collaboration, 2) genre, 3) text and context, and 4) tools. These categories of awareness are em-

Writing Model Research Based on Cognitive Processes 37

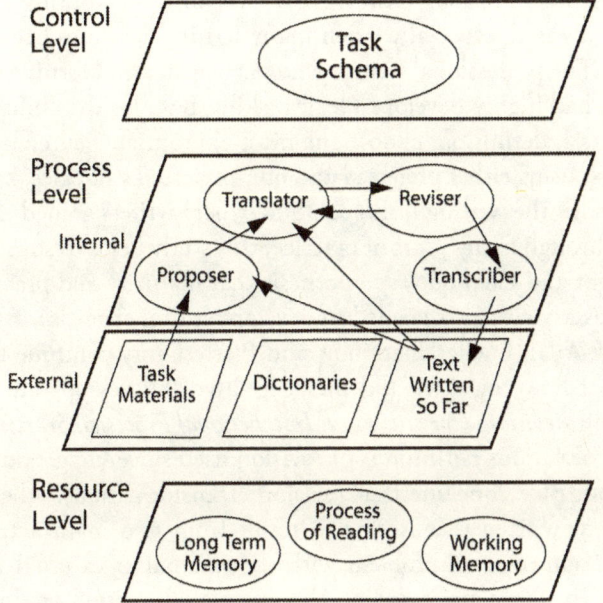

Figure 4. Chenoweth and Hayes model of four basic writing actions (84). Used by permision.

bedded in various writing models, especially when the task schema is considered. Starting with the 1987 Hayes, et al. model, metarhetorical, metastrategic and metalinguistic awareness would encompass the process of text evaluation and strategy selection, when the need for revision is detected. The four writing skills would be equated with the writer's knowledge. Specifically, collaboration and genre would parallel task definition; genre would also parallel criteria for plan and text; text and context would parallel problem representation; and procedures for fixing text problems would parallel tools. In the most recent 2001 Chenoweth and Hayes model, metarhetorical, metastrategic and metalinguistic awareness would be part of the internal process, activated when writers propose, translate, revise or transcribe text, while the collaboration, genre, text and context, and tools would operate as part of the external process.

Horning's contention that expert revision often employs unconscious knowledge of the three kinds of awareness she defines, along with conscious knowledge or activation of the four basic skills, underscores the role working and long-term memory play during the writing process. With extensive resources for both technical skills and cognitive awareness stored in long-term memory, the load on working memory capacity is eased, especially when many writing activities become automatic. The professional writers who participated in Horning's study, not only had highly developed lexical skills, but also the ability to assess the task definition, choose the most appropriate genre, and then create text using either preferred and non-preferred strategies, based on what best fit the writing task/goal. Since these writers gained their expertise through many years of practice, this study helps to substantiate Alamargot and Chanquoy's hypothesis that maturity and practice are two necessary elements needed to develop writing expertise.

Linda Allal, Lucile Chanquoy, and Pierre Largy continue the discussion of how cognitive and metacognitive abilities operate during revision in *Revision: Cognitive and Instructional Processes*. Starting with a review of various definitions of revision used since Fitzgerald's 1987 definition, they conclude that revision "transformations," the actual changes to written text, seems to result from two main actions: 1) the detection of some problem with the internal or external text, or 2) some discovery made during the process of envisioning and then creating written text. Because of this key difference in how revision is initiated, Allal, Chanquoy, and Largy suggest that studying various instructional techniques to determine how they increase cognitive processing might help writing instructors assist novice writers in gaining appropriate skills needed to revise on both a local and global level.

Serving as an introduction to the studies Allal, Chanquoy, and Largy include in Volume 13, the most recent addition to the *Studies in Writing* series, Hayes introduces the question of how novice writers detect the need for revision by reviewing the basic cognitive writing models. Since most novice writers have difficulty finding problems, especially on a global level, he suggests that more research is needed to determine how students can expand the their criteria for evaluating written text, especially since many of the traditional instruction methods, like teacher comments on drafts or the use of models, fail to help novice writers successfully revise their writing.

This situation recalls Flower, et al.'s work with detection and diagnosis during the mid-1980s; however, almost twenty years later, the use of computer technology has helped refine data collection and analysis. For example, in order to study the relationship between revision and low- or high-working memory capacity, Annie Piolat, et al. monitored undergraduate psychology students as they worked with three versions of a psychology magazine article, to which various spelling, syntactical or coherence problems had been added. This computer-based experiment was done in two stages. In the first session students were evaluated on how well they read and then answered questions about the text content. Depending on their responses, students were then divided into two groups based on whether they exhibited low or high working memory capacity. The second session involved having students detect problems, find solutions, and then revise the problematic text. Piolat, et al. determined that cognitive effort does not seem to be affected by working memory capacity, because no matter what the level of working memory, participants took whatever time was needed to resolve the revision problems. However, this study did show that reading text for basic understanding is much less taxing on working memory than reading to discover problems that may require revision. Here then, the results reflect research data reported by Flower, et al. in 1986, where detection of a problem becomes the key determiner for the direction any revision work might take.

Instructional Techniques

Since this kind of highly demanding cognitive activity is not easy to learn, many of the other studies included in Allal, Chanquoy, and Largy's book focus on various instructional techniques. For example, David Galbraith and Mark Torrance monitor two basic methods of drafting: one where the writer plans his or her text by creating an outline *before* writing, the other where the writer begins to write, developing his or her text through discoveries made *during* the writing process. In their study, they track four drafting strategies: 1) organized sentences, similar to rough drafting; 2) unorganized sentences, like multiple drafting; 3) organized notes, equated to outlining; and 4) unorganized notes. While their results confirm Kellogg's research that developing an outline before writing yields the most successful text, they suggest that individual differences might influence successful use of these four strategies, a hypothesis Horning raises in *Revision Revisited*, as she illustrates how personality type influences implementation of various metastrategies during writing.

While a writer's personality may dictate writing strategy choices, for novice writers, the need for additional instruction in a number of other basic writing skills plays a far greater role in increasing their ability to make effective revisions. Learning to understand text from the reader's perspective, for instance, can help writers view text more globally, leading to better revision. David R. Holliway and Deborah McCutchen created a study where fifth and ninth grade writers wrote and evaluated descriptions of tangram figures in three ways: 1) giving feedback only; 2) giving feedback plus a rating; and 3) giving feedback by assessing how successful the descriptions were from a reader's perspective. The results of this study indicated that peer response work is most effective when there is a real purpose for the written text. In addition, if peer responses are based on very specific evaluation criteria, then the peer reviewers are much more likely to apply these skills to their own writing.

Similar results were reported by Angela Conner and Margaret R. Moulton when they attempted to increase eighth grade students' revision and editing skills by having them publish two genres of writing for two different audiences. First, students created research-based booklets and poetry books for the sixth grade students. Then they wrote a short story, news article or poem as part of a local writing competition. While the students did increase their writing ability, Conner and Moulton were disappointed in the extent of the improvement. Their realization that they needed to more actively teach editing and revision skills underscores the importance that task schema resource knowledge plays in developing writing expertise. However, because these students had closer contact with their readers, especially the sixth graders, they were much more motivated to do revision work. Also, because of the positive feedback they received, they increased their self-confidence, viewing themselves as better writers. Charles A. MacArthur, Steve Graham and Karen R. Harris reported similar conclusions about the need for well-developed evaluation criteria in their study of writers with learning disabilities. Their results showed that working with peers can offer motivation by adding a social element, but there is still need for fairly specific instructions, as well as help in selecting what kinds of cognitive strategies will work best.

Increasing linguistic fluency also seems to play a major role in effective revision. Amos Van Gelderen and Ron Oostdam look at this aspect of revision by first reviewing the fundamental task schema model and then proposing a four-level revision process model. The first level, proposed text, is where the specific form of the words is reviewed; the second, local externalized text forms, is where editing is done to fix form errors; the third, local externalized text meaning, is where the meaning of the proposed text is checked against text already written; and the fourth, global externalized text meaning, is where proposed text content is compared to the entire piece of writing. Noting that each level increases the cognitive cost, especially for novice writers, Van Gelderen and Oostdam offer some recommendations for how to increase skill levels in the classroom, in particular using exercises that offer both implicit and explicit practice in identifying both linguistic forms and content meaning.

Since peer responses have proven to be beneficial in helping students revise their writing, recently more attention has been directed to assessing the use of integrated sociocognitive (IS) instruction. Allal compares the IS approach to the componential skills (CS) method to see if the type and sequence of writing tasks affect instruction, and in particular if one format is more beneficial in helping second and sixth graders gain better writing skills. In this two-part study, students first initiated their prewriting work by defining the specific writing task. Then, after looking at models and analyzing basic elements like genre, purpose, and so forth, students worked in groups to facilitate sharing ideas about content, which in turn helped generate some guidelines for the assigned writing task. The second part of the process involved on-line revision, based on help from teachers or peers, with text transformations made either during the actual writing process or delayed to another writing session. In addition, some of the skill instruction work involved explicit, separate exercises that were not part of the writing process, while others were implicit, embedded in the various writing activities connected to the writing tasks.

Allal's study pointed to three key effects IS has on student revision. First, it increased the number of transformations made on students' drafts. Second, fewer errors were found in drafts, especially for students who were better at translating their ideas into concepts or had more skill in revising as they word processed text. Third, since most of the revisions dealt with form and organization and not semantics, most of the revision work done by novice writers was still made at the local level. Based on her findings, Allal concludes that many children enter high school with few writing strategies to address revision needs. Therefore it is important for these beginning writers to get more practice using a combination of instruction techniques, from the explicit exercises used in CS to the implicit learning that results when IS instruction is integrated into the classroom.

The last two studies presented in Allal, Chanquoy, and Largy's book focus on the collaborative element found in IS instruction. By analyzing how children interact while revising narratives, Pietro Boscolo and Katia Ascorti determined that these beginning writers use two typical methods that teachers also rely on to help students revise. The first involves the collaborator *requesting* a change in the text to make the writer more aware of the reader's understanding of the narrative. The second entails *suggesting* concrete ideas to make the text more reader-oriented. Peers tended to suggest more than request when the narrative was based on fact, apparently feeling that this kind of writing needed to be accurate unlike a totally invented story, and therefore it was their responsibility as collaborators to help make sure the narrative fulfilled their expectations as readers. Not only does this kind of directed revision, where collaborators are given a specific task to analyze, activate the use of more cognitive processes, but it also encourages students to analyze their own writing in light of the same kinds of suggestions they make about their fellow students' narratives.

Yviane Rouiller also finds collaborative revision to be very effective for novice writers, because it leads to more transformations, both in spelling and ordering of idea content. It also increases student motivation. When students take a more positive view of revision and feel that they have equal roles in the revising process, they usually view their revision tasks more globally, and also show better cognitive awareness since they can describe what they are revising and why it needs to be changed. To help novice writers improve their collaborative revision skills, Rouiller suggests four teaching approaches. First, it is important to have students work collaboratively on more than one assignment. It is also helpful to vary the make-up of the pairs or peer groups, so that students interact with as many different students as possible, allowing them to discover a wide range of individual differences in revision strategies. Second, to help students understand these different strategies, it is necessary for them to have enough time to fully discuss everyone's ideas so that they can adequately compare the strengths and weaknesses of each approach. Repeating this kind of activity also increases students' metacognitive skills, by enabling them to be less sensitive when a particular method they might have used to revise their writing is critiqued by their peers. Third, it is important to carefully structure this kind of interactive work so that students receive optimum benefit from this kind of interaction. Well-designed group activities can lead to more productive cooperation among peers, better motivation and growth in self esteem. It can also encourage students to be more responsible in a group setting. And finally, collaborative revision can allow the teacher greater flexibility on whether individual or group instruction is implemented in the classroom.

One interesting teacher-based activity suggested by Christyne A. Berzsenyi might be used in conjunction with peer collaborations. She designed her "Comments to Comments" system to help technical writing students better understand feedback on their papers. This method involves an instructor writing comments that prompt revision needs—either local or global—by asking questions about the problematic text. Students then must respond to the issues raised by explaining their reason for using a particular strategy/construction, etc. This comment technique helps to activate the planning function in the task schema, by having the students explain in detail what their reasons were for various choices they made as they planned and then wrote their text. As students revisit the task assignment and their earlier planning steps, in order to justify their choices to the instructor, they discover why certain strategies solve their revision needs better than others. In addition, since this sets up a positive dialogue between the instructor and student, revision is not viewed in a negative way, with the student merely correcting mistakes to please the teacher.

In the final section of Allal, Chanquoy, and Largy's book, Gert Rijlaarsdam, Michel Couzijn and Huub van den Bergh present an overview of revision—how it should be defined, why it continues to be a central focus of composition research, and how instructors can use revision activities to help novice writers gain more writing expertise. They note that since revision does not necessarily improve a written text, it may actually point to deficiencies in the cognitive abilities needed to use appropriate writing process strategies. In addition, revision can activate any number of cognitive processes following no set pattern and these actions can occur at any time, in many combinations through the entire writing process. Improved revision is also directly affected not only by how familiar revisers are with a particular writing task, but also by how capable they are at implementing the basic writing model processes of planning, translating and reviewing. To explain the highly complex process of revision, Rijlaarsdam, Couzijn, and van den Bergh offer the following definition:

> The (co)author or revisor reviews (part of) the already-written text, to reach a certain goal (communication goal, learning goal), at a certain text level, at a certain moment (i.e., draft, final copy), with a certain effect (i.e., improvement, neutral, weakening effect), at a certain level (text, plan, learning), and with a certain cognitive cost. (193)

Here, then, revision involves *re-seeing* the entire writing process.

COMPUTERS AND THEIR IMPACT ON WRITING MODEL RESEARCH

The second question Rijlaarsdam, Couzijn, and van den Bergh consider deals with why so much research attention has been devoted to revision. One reason they suggest has to do with how easy it is to track text transformations. Today writing activity can be tracked by using S-notation, Trace-It, JEdit and LS graphing, and when combined with think-aloud protocols, these methods give researchers a fairly accurate record of what writers do as they write or revise. As this kind of measurement is perfected, researchers hope to validate theoretical hypotheses about how cognitive processes operate in writing models. As early as 1996, C. Michael Levy and Sarah Ransdell documented some of the first computers techniques used in research, by analyzing keystrokes in order to track when writers added text, paused to reread text, deleted text, in addition to where they paused—within a word, sentence, or paragraph.

One of the most extensive reviews of present computer-based techniques available is Olive and Levy's 2002 book *Contemporary Tools and Techniques for Studying Writing*. Of particular note is Thierry Olive, Ronald Kellogg and Annie Piolat's successful use of the triple task technique to study how a writer's knowledge, planning abilities, writing methods and cognitive resources affect the writing process. By measuring the reaction time (RT) made by study participants to variable auditory signals while composing different writing tasks, Olive, Kellogg, and Piolat were able to monitor both the RT and capacity load on working memory. They reported on three basic areas that affect writing expertise. The first is writer-specific and includes domain-specific knowledge plus working memory capacity. The second is situation-specific and involves pre-writing activities like outlining, and so forth. The third area includes both linguistic knowledge and the method used to produce text. Their results demonstrate that the amount of cognitive effort and the length of processing time needed to create text are affected most by the writing situation and the linguistic ability of the writer.

Similar results are reported in a recent study done by Chanquoy, where third and fifth graders were given an opportunity to revise their writing first as they composed the text, and second, after they had completed the text, in order to see whether postponing revision would lead to more in-depth revisions. Chanquoy assumed that with more time, there would be less of a load on working memory, and as a result the children would be able to make more content-based changes. While delaying revision work did lead to more revisions, most of them were surface corrections rather than extensive reworking of text meaning.

Another promising technique, S-notation, is presented by Py Kollberg and Kerstin S. Eklundh. Here computers track any changes made to a text, noting the sequence of the changes and also where they are made—at the word, sentence, or paragraph level. When this kind of record is combined with think-aloud protocols, a very representative picture of external writing processes can be traced, in particular the complex patterns that occur during revision work.

LS graphing, based on S-notation, is yet another way to monitor writing processes that Eva Lindgren and Kirk P.H. Sullivan recommend. Using keystroke-tracking software programs like JEdit, a computer file log of every keystroke action, whether it is an addition or deletion, can be created. Another software program, Trace-it, then allows writers to analyze their actions during a writing session. Here two windows are used, with one displaying the S-notation text, the other every change made during the entire writing session. By combining the information gathered using JEdit and Trace-it, an LS graph can be created which records variables, such as how many strokes have been made, when they were made, and so forth. This method allows researchers, teachers and writers to see various writing activities represented together in one LS graph, making it easier to compare actions that occur during a writing session. For example after a revision session, novice writers might reflect on why they made text changes when they did, and then determine whether their planning was adequate. They might also review their LS graph with their instructor to open a dialogue about specific problems in their text related to prewriting work. Another option would be to compare their LS graph with one made by an expert writer completing the same writing task, in order to see what other kinds of activities were used, and to reinforce that fact that there is no one correct way to revise. Whether it is used to make a specific diagnosis or to initiate a dialogue among writers, LS graphing offers an opportunity for close analysis of the task schema external writing processes, helping to indicate concrete differences between novice and expert writers.

While all of these computer-based technologies offer researchers promising methods for gathering data, Rijlaarsdam, Cousijn, and van den Bergh still question what specific information there is beyond the transformation act itself. In Allal, Chanquoy, and Largy's book, the results of van der Bergh and Rijlaarsdam's 2001 study based on monitoring keyboard activity during writing sessions, first presented at the 2001 International IAIMTE Conference in Amsterdam, are summarized. As they tracked transformations, they noted that no matter how/where revisions were made, they usually occurred after some evaluative activity; but more often than not, whatever the nature of the evaluative activity, there was still little actual revision made to texts. Basically, then, tracking text transformations doesn't lead to many valid conclusions about how the revision processes operate before, during and after this activity. However, implementing more detailed tracking of cognitive activity did reveal more specific correlations between transformation behavior and the quality of the text, as well as when various writing processes occurred. As more research is done using computer tracking of transformations along with writing-aloud protocols, it will become easier to determine not only how the writing process is organized, but also when and why cognitive processes are activated over time.

Implications for Classroom Instruction

Since research has already shown that novice and expert writers employ different patterns throughout the composing process, more focused research with these aspects will lead to the development of writing instruction specifically tailored to the needs of the writer/reviser. This leads to the third question raised by Rijlaarsdam, Couzijn, and van den Bergh—how does the study of revision benefit classroom instruction? Dividing their discussion into three parts, they first look at writing, then at how writing develops as a learning process, and finally at how revision instruction aids in the teaching of writing.

Rijlaarsdam, Couzijn, and van den Bergh suggest that since most children start to write by sharing stories, as they begin to create text there is little need for revision. Writing is seen as an enjoyable task. But soon mere story telling is changed as teachers begin to use classroom writing to develop basic skills. Now these novice writers need to not only think about their narrative content, but also whether they have spelled words correctly, used proper grammatical forms, and so on. At each grade level, new demands are made so that within a few years, writing tasks are used as multi-leveled teaching instruments—no longer easy and fun to create, but instead difficult, time consuming and cognitively demanding. Even though this is true, it is important to help students view revision as a starting point for generating communication with their readers, rather than a punishment for bad writing.

When the purpose of writing shifts from an explicit form of story telling to a mixture of explicit and implicit instruction used for learning different cognitive skills, students are confronted with a very demanding task that requires both productive and reflective ability. According to Rijlaarsdam, Couzijn, and van den Bergh, these difficulties arise for a number of reasons. First, these beginning writers need to devote much of their working memory capacity to producing the written text, because they are not practiced writers. Second, they have weak rhetorical skills so they are often not able to select the most appropriate pattern through which to present their content. Third, novice writers lack experience in understanding reader's needs, and thus remain very writer-oriented as they review their text. As a result, peer feedback is central to effective revision, because it provides students with a sense of audience, as well as increasing their motivation. More controlled feedback criteria that concentrate on a specific aspect also enables peers to offer better evaluative comments. In addition, commentary from a number of peers, especially when it is written down, helps writers gain a broader perspective of how different readers react to drafting strategies. This feedback then needs to be used in a constructive way, so that the information learned from peer responses can be applied to a writing task—either as the basis for revising the evaluated text or for starting a new piece of writing. In this way, the writer gains needed experience in practicing the new skill, the first step in making it become a more automatic activity for future composing.

Research results, derived from tracking how the writing process operates within the task schema of the different cognitive writing models, have helped shed light on what type of emphasis instructors should place on planning, translating and reviewing as they work with novice writers. Even though half of the composing process is usually devoted to translating, it requires the least cognitive effort. Therefore most of the differences in process between novice and expert writers occur during planning and revising, both highly controlled activities. The more adept writers are at planning, especially in developing outlines for the writing task, the less stress there is placed on working memory. The more feedback writers receive throughout the writing process, the more aware they are of rhetorical considerations. Because peer commentary motivates writers to reevaluate both the form and content of their written text, feedback encourages them to implement additional planning activities, followed by translating these new ideas into revised text, thereby setting up the critical cyclical interaction that occurs within task schema models.

While planning and feedback operations are integral components of revision, genre also has a major effect on cognitive effort. Narrative writing, for instance, takes the least amount of effort, probably because writers at every ability level have practiced this genre since they started to write. In fact, the more practice a writer has with a genre, the less working memory capacity is taxed. Veteran journalists, as an example, may actually compose a news story text while still gathering information, since the inverted pyramid format stored in their long-term memory is easy for the central executive function to activate in their working memory. Because they are so well versed with this genre, they need little time for planning their final article, and therefore spend more time translating their ideas into text. On the other hand, beginning journalism students have no experience with the inverted pyramid genre, so they expend more cognitive effort deciding what fact is most important to the story and therefore should become the lead. Since their main focus is directed toward planning, once they have decided how to organize the information, they are able to translate their ideas into words fairly easily. Whatever the writing task, then, the more knowledgeable writers are—in content, in genre, in linguistic skills, and so forth—the less effort they need for the planning process. Therefore, increasing planning skills seems to be one of the most important elements of the task schema for novice writers, with feedback being one of the best resources for promoting effective planning choices.

A bit more than twenty years ago revision was seen as a fairly simple task of reviewing which occurred at the end of the writing process. However, through the development and study of how cognitive models function, revision has proved to be a highly complex operation, now viewed as a starting point. Revision is an essential activity that initiates discovery, builds skill levels, and over time, as writers gain maturity through practice, creates writing expertise.

4 Basic Writers and Revision

Alice Horning and Jeanie Robertson

Students usually referred to as Basic Writers (hereafter BWs, used for both Basic Writing and Basic Writers) in a college context confront more difficulties than do well-prepared college students. For all writers, revising bears on every part of the writing process, from planning and organizing to drafting and editing. Because BWs are not strong writers to begin with, they find revising especially challenging. What they do when asked to revise is closer to editing and cleaning up than to making substantive changes to content, organization, development and related areas of their writing. Current research shows that to move beyond the focus on errors and correction, BW teachers can offer students a fuller understanding of the nature of revising and specific strategies to learn effective writing and revising, albeit at a developmental or beginning level.

The opening chapter of this volume sets up a broad definition of revising as change or modification of text, using those awarenesses and skills as writers may apply to create a finished text. Before moving to a discussion of these awarenesses and skills that professional or experienced writers bring to the revision process, a definition of BWs is in order. Any number of definitions and measures seem to describe students labeled as BWs, so the definition provided here is meant as a general guideline. The general definition will provide the framework for an exploration of BWs' revising and their need for more systematic instruction in how to revise successfully.

Defining Basic Writers

Defining BWs presents a significant challenge. Students may be so designated by a particular college or university based on a variety of criteria. For example, at Oakland University, a medium-sized state university of about seventeen thousand students where most authors of this book teach, students placed in our developmental course are those whose ACT English score is at 15 or below, one kind of definition. This example is not presented because it is an exemplar of a perfect system of defining or placing BWs. Rather, it shows how BWs are commonly defined: procedurally rather than in more appropriately descriptive and substantive ways. Charles Bazerman points out that "the institutional procedures carry the theoretical baggage of the evaluative procedures—no more and no less, though they are taken as indicators of something substantive about the students as learners and writers" (Bazerman).

We chose the ACT cutoff more or less arbitrarily years ago after a study of our writing placement procedures showed that our reading of students' impromptu writing samples did not place students any better than did the use of the ACT score. The ACT is a multiple choice test, of course, and not a direct sample of writing. So we have created several mechanisms for students to offer direct samples of their writing. These include a Placement Packet which asks students to prepare, on their own, two samples of their writing for our review in response to specific prompts; a second option is for students to present their results on the high school writing portion of Michigan's required MEAP test (Michigan Educational Assessment of Progress, a state-wide test in most subject areas administered in 4th, 7th and 11th grades); finally students can submit their scores on either of the Advanced Placement English exams to attempt to place differently in our program. Ours is just one example of a procedural definition of BWs.

Other definitions of BWs have been presented by leading researchers in this area, such as Marilyn Sternglass. Her landmark, award-winning longitudinal study of BWs, *Time to Know Them,* examines the writing development of nine students at City College of City University of New York. As she makes clear at the outset, BWs are difficult to define as a group because so many factors affect their placement in writing programs and their abilities. They may be diverse racially and in terms of ethnic background. Some will not be native speakers of English, or they may not be speakers of Standard English (Sternglass 4–7). Some will be members of the group now described as Generation 1.5, students who may or may not have been born in the United States, who speak some other language as their native language in addition to English, and who are graduates of American high schools (Harklau).

BWs whose native language is not English have their own distinct issues with respect to revising, treated elsewhere in this volume in Chapter 5 on ESL and revising. Horning has argued elsewhere that learning to write in formal academic English is for many of these students like learning a whole new language (Horning, *Teaching*). These points provide some sense of the issues involved in defining BWs.

Probably the classic study and survey of the characteristics of BWs is Mina Shaughnessy's *Errors and Expectations*, published in 1977. Shaughnessy saw, from her seminal study of hundreds of placement essays of open admissions students, again at City College in New York, the range of difficulties that BWs face, including handwriting and punctuation, syntax, common errors in verb and noun forms and agreement, spelling, vocabulary, and issues of organization and development. Ultimately, Shaughnessy's book made such a huge impact on our understanding and treatment of BWs for two reasons. First, she demonstrates that BWs cannot be defined solely as writers who make lots of errors in their writing. Second, she shows that BWs must be understood as writers whose work *is* rule-governed. Shaughnessy's findings reshaped the definition of BWs significantly.

One final point about definitions of BWs comes from the recent work of Linda Adler-Kassner and Susanmarie Harrington. Like Shaughnessy, Sternglass and other scholars, they make the point that too much of the research on BWs has focused on errors and problems, treating these writers as disembodied and separated from the contexts from which they come and in which they live and work and write. This point was raised in a study of BWs in two-year and four-year institutions done by Lynn Quitman Troyka ("Defining"). In her study, Troyka found much variation in definition through an examination of BWs from differing institutions. Her study shows that those who are considered BWs changes with the context in which their writing is being evaluated. Adler-Kassner and Harrington, who also consider context pertinent to the issue of definition, suggest a more productive alternative approach:

> Exploring fundamental assumptions typically carried in basic writing classes (about what students are like, what abilities they have, and how and why they interpret things as they do) raises important questions about the "commonsensical" notions about how stu-

dents in basic writing courses, and the work of those courses, should be defined. (29)

The resulting questions, they say, arise from scholars who have conceptualized BWs much more broadly and move BW to a different realm:

Taking into consideration the interaction among language, ideology, and contexts defines the work of basic writing classes and teachers differently. Here, definitions of students no longer rest on delineating and classifying problems manifest in writing. [. . .] Rather than asking what strategies can most effectively facilitate students' "fluid" movements from one discourse to another, researchers ask how basic writing classes can become sites for investigating the contexts and ideologies associated with a range of literacy practices, particularly students' and those in the academy (and even the basic writing class itself). Such questions shift attention away from trying to classify writers' (cognitive or cultural) characteristics, and reorient the work of the basic writing class toward collaborative action with teacher and student (Adler-Kassner and Harrington 30–31).

Many contemporary scholars working on BW, then, are trying hard to move the definitions away from a focus on error and toward helping writers develop their ability to probe and express their ideas effectively in writing. Consistent with this shift in focus, the use of an analysis of BWs' awarenesses and skills in revision provides broader view of who BWs are and how they might approach this work.

Awarenesses and Basic Writers

Revision Revisited argues that revising in the very sophisticated form carried out by professional writers entails three kinds of awareness (metarhetorical, metastrategic and metalinguistic) and four kinds of skill (collaboration, genre, text and context, and tools). Professional writers, then, have metarhetorical awareness, which is the awareness of one's self as a writer, including typical strategies and approaches to writing and revising, both successful and not. This is the "I always do this and change it later" part of skilled writers' awarenesses. They know the strategies that work for them as well as the ones they use with an eye toward revision at a later time. (See Chapter 8 for fuller detail.)

Basic writers can fairly be described as lacking in metarhetorical awareness, chiefly because they are novices. Because BWs don't see themselves as writers, this first kind of awareness has a substantial impact of their ability to revise effectively and warrants extended discussion. Experienced BW teachers are familiar with this characteristic. One of us has had students respond to discussions about writing activities with statements like "I am not a writer" or "I don't think of myself as a writer." The development of metarhetorical awareness comes in part from direct instruction in writing courses, but arises chiefly as a by-product of extensive writing experience, one thing most BWs lack. As early as 1981, Ann Berthoff pointed out in the *Journal of Basic Writing* that most writing instruction focuses on skills and not on awarenesses, and this claim is as true of BW instruction as it is of writing instruction in general. Her observation of a graduate student attempting to begin writing suggested to her that this writer did not "understand how writing gets written" (143); Berthoff noticed that the grad student she watched by chance seemed to have the same problem as her BWs.

Research shows clearly that BWs can develop metarhetorical awareness and that doing so leads to more substantive and more effective revising. A key study of such development, reported in 1985 by Matsuhashi and Gordon, entailed having BWs respond to several different kinds of prompts to revise their work. Instead of focusing on correctness, the experimenters asked students to make specific kinds of changes; they were told either to revise or to add five things while reading through their writing, or to list five things on the back or on a separate sheet, not looking at the text, and then to review the text to locate insertion points for the new ideas. Both of the prompts to add to the text produced significantly more changes to BWs' content and development, particularly the prompt to add to the unseen text. BWs, then, are capable of becoming more aware of themselves as writers and can use this kind of awareness to revise in a substantive way.

A similar finding is reported in a longitudinal study done at Pepperdine University in California. While not focused on BWs, Lee Ann Carroll continues the kind of study pioneered by Marilyn Sternglass. Carroll found that the twenty students she followed through their undergraduate years used their writing portfolios to develop metarhetorical awareness. She notes that the students in the two semesters of first-year composition at Pepperdine

> valued having a record of their college experience in the form of their paper and, later, digital portfolios.

> These students [. . .] became more aware of their own development as they examined their own work and verbalized what they felt they were learning. Such metacognitive awareness helps promote further learning. (Carroll 123)

The students' portfolio work entails reviewing and revising work done over the whole of each semester of the course as well as adding to the portfolio writing done in other courses through their entire undergraduate careers. The use of portfolios in this way can contribute significantly to the development of metarhetorical awareness.

Portfolios and the reflective writing often requested with them, then, may not produce the kind of metarhetorical or metacognitive awareness teachers hope for in setting up such a task, especially for BWs. Laurel Bower found this problem in her study of portfolio cover letters written by BWs and reported in 2003. BWs often do not write about their writing processes but use the letter as an opportunity to complain about the course or their grades. If students have been given some direct instruction in reflective writing, Bower suggests, the letters they write for their portfolios might address issues in revision and other process matters more directly (62–63). Like other writers, then, BWs need instruction in order to develop the awarenesses and skills that expert writers have.

Some strategies for building metarhetorical awareness as well as metalinguistic awareness and use of writers' toolbox skills are described by Sandra Schor, yet another City University of New York writing teacher. In her work with BWs at Queens College, Schor moved away from ordering students to simply revise and toward having them work as professional writers do. In her use of what she calls "fastwriting" (50) and interruptions to do other kinds of writing, such as defining the terms students are using in their essays, Schor makes the case for building BWs metarhetorical and metalinguistic awarenesses. By doing separate work defining "authority" for an essay on challenging authority, she gives BWs additional material that can later be integrated into their essays. Her assignments also require BWs to focus on grammatical elements as part of the content of the task. An essay on a turning point in students' lives requires them to reflect on their situation before and after the turning point and thus requires them to focus on verb tenses as they move from past to present or more recent descriptions (Schor 53). Knowledge of the grammatical structures involved raises BWs' metalinguistic awareness and may lead them to develop skill in the use of tools such as grammar handbooks.

BWs also lack a second kind of awareness found among the professional writers studied in *Revision Revisited,* metastrategic awareness (Horning). This awareness entails writers' understanding themselves as people and in terms of their personality preferences as described, for example, by the Myers-Briggs Type Indicator. About half of the professional writers studied in *Revision Revisited* were aware of their personality preferences and type results and used this information to build flexible strategies for writing. They knew when their writing approaches worked and when they did not, and in the latter case, were able to shift to non-preferred tactics to resolve writing problems.

BWs lack the knowledge and experience to have this metastrategic awareness. They simply have not done enough writing to have developed a sense of what approaches to writing have worked for them and which ones have not. Like most students, they are also unlikely to have had any exposure to personality type theory or to have taken the MBTI, an instrument that analyzes and reports individuals' personality preferences. While discussions of personality type preferences may not be practical for the BW classroom, an understanding of type preferences can be helpful to BW teachers, especially insofar as type preferences shape student learning styles. Knowledge of the impact of type can be very helpful in any classroom, including the BW classroom (Lawrence). In addition, the work of rhetorician George Jensen and psychologist John DiTiberio in *Personality and the Teaching of Composition* (141–53) reports on the writing and revising strategies of a variety of writers including BWs, and their findings show that BWs are diverse in terms of personality type: they do not uniformly prefer extraversion or sensing any more than do other groups of students.

While there are no specific studies on the impact of the development of type awareness among BWs, Muriel Harris' discussion of the impact of type on writing center work gives a clear indication of how helpful metastrategic awareness can be for teachers or others working with BWs, especially in tutoring. When she teaches peer tutors in training about personality type, Harris shows them that writers choose their strategies for and approaches to writing largely as a function of their type preferences. When tutoring then, or more generally, when working with BWs and others learning to write, it is important for teachers and tutors to be aware of their own and others' metastrategic awareness and to use it in a helpful way:

This does not mean that tutors can't share their strategies with their students, but they have to do so with the awareness that such strategies may or may not help, depending on how similar the student is to them. In short, descriptions of writing strategies become suggestions, not instructions (Harris 93).

Understanding and being able to use metastrategic awareness, the awareness of personality type preferences, can be extremely helpful to BWs, since it opens up the possibility of a more flexible approach to writing and can allow them to build on strengths deriving from their preferred approaches to writing. If teachers can convey this perspective, they can change BWs' understanding about the nature of writing from "right" and "wrong" to a range of options in terms of writing and revising, moving them toward the skilled writing and revising of expert writers.

Metalinguistic awareness, an awareness of language *per se*, is a third kind of awareness found among professional writers. These writers are fully familiar with the language itself and use that knowledge of language to evaluate their writing and revise it. By contrast, as Mina Shaughnessy's study shows, BWs have little knowledge of the nature of written language. Partly of course, this lack of awareness about the nature of written language arises because BWs have little reading experience, especially with the formal written language of academic prose, as Horning has argued elsewhere ("The Connection" and "The Trouble"). The result is writing that is filled with technical errors, often severe enough to limit writers' ability to convey meaning. So, while teachers must address language conventions, current research shows that this focus is most helpfully concentrated in discussions of writers' use of the toolbox for revision, a skill discussed later in this chapter.

Other research shows that a lack of metalinguistic awareness is a significant problem in terms of BWs' revision. Much of what happens when BWs revise focuses on language *per se* is amply illustrated in Sondra Perl's 1979 study of five unskilled college writers "The Composing Processes of Unskilled College Writers." Perl's report on Tony, one of the writers in the group she studied, shows that he mostly focused on editorial issues in his revisions, making 210 of his 234 changes to his texts on form, including spelling, punctuation and other linguistic issues. The changes he made, like many changes made by BWs in editing, are attempts to create writing that is correct. A different focus that would lead to more substantive changes beyond correctness is that described by Horner and Lu as they work with non-native speakers of English (176–79). They work with BWs on metalinguistic awareness but in the context of conveying the ideas they have in mind, not just getting writing "right." The findings on professional writers suggest that they use their metalinguistic awareness not to correct their writing but to address stylistic concerns and clarity of expression; BWs, too, need help to develop this kind of metalinguistic awareness in order to revise holistically, for substance, beyond being correct.

Skills and Basic Writers

The research reported in *Revision Revisited* shows that in addition to awarenesses of themselves as writers, successful professionals also have four kinds of skills that they apply to their revising, skills with collaboration, genre, text and context and tools. These skills provide a frame through which to view the challenges BWs face when it comes to successful revision. The first of the skills of effective revision, collaboration, appears when expert writers turn to others for substantive help with their texts. The work on this chapter provides a clear example. In addition to having the second author, a highly experienced teacher of BWs, read and contribute to the text, we sent it to a respected professional who is not part of our authors' group. This colleague has edited the *Journal of Basic Writing;* she is also an experienced BW teacher. We sent the chapter to her knowing that we would get excellent editorial help, but more importantly, substantive commentary on the content of the chapter.

BWs do not have the kind of writing experience that allows them to use substantive collaboration. As novices, they can begin to respond to the writing of others in a BW class and get reactions to their own work. This kind of classroom work is often limited, and experience shows that in both giving and receiving feedback in a collaborative framework, BWs have difficulty. Studies of BWs trying to collaborate on writing show that the kind of "collaborative action" of student and teacher advocated by Adler-Kassner and Harrington and discussed above is more successful than superficial error correction. One example of how collaboration can be demonstrated and used successfully appears in Gregory Shafer's exploration of the use of letter writing in a BW class. He has the students write letters to people important to them, gives them an opportunity for peer review, but then also shares a letter of his own. The resulting discussion, which Shafer guides with a series of questions focused on feelings and clarity of ideas, shifts the students' focus away from spelling and other kinds of "correction" issues and toward content and substance. In the following class session after this collaborative work, students bring

> revisions [that . . .] were the result of a vigorous, recursive, unencumbered writing process—one that allowed students to see themselves as authors in a community or club of writers, rather than as patients in a clinic for the syntactically or mechanically impaired. [. . . T]hese students felt liberated to put expression first, treating their letters as serious drafts rather than objects for correction. (Shafer 66)

Shafer's approach demonstrates how effective collaboration builds writers' skills in revision and in addition, moves them toward the kind of metarhetorical awareness discussed above that is a key characteristic of successful professionals. It also reflects the "collaborative action" that Adler-Kassner and Harrington recommend.

A second skill of expert revisers is the ability to use a range of genres in writing and to exploit the requirements of a particular genre such as memos, research reports, or encyclopedia entries, whether chosen or assigned, to develop ideas. Whereas experts are fully familiar with a range of possible genres, using those appropriate to their discipline or profession as needed, BWs have limited knowledge of the possibilities of different genres and limited ability to use them. Partly, this weakness arises as a result of BWs' limited reading ability and experience. Partly, it arises from teaching that is not focused on demonstrating how different genres can be understood and exploited by writers. In any case, current findings show that BWs lack knowledge of and the ability to use various genres in writing.

Carroll's longitudinal study of writing development in the college years mentioned previously shows that learning about the genres appropriate to a particular area or discipline is a developmental process that BWs can begin to work on even in their first writing course (137). The students at Pepperdine University are clearly not BWs; those in Carroll's longitudinal study tend to be relatively well-prepared students who generally have high SAT or ACT scores (the lowest SAT verbal score among her subjects was 410) and are attending a private university). However, Carroll's goal of helping students write in the genres appropriate to their discipline and their growth in ability to do so shows how important a knowledge of genre is to overall writing development for well-prepared students like those at Pepperdine as well as for BWs (137–38).

The third skill that appears among professional writers, or even among more experienced writers in college classrooms, is the skilled use of text and context. This skill entails not only an understanding of the audience, topic and purpose for a text, but also the texts within it (outside sources in a research paper, for example) and the contexts from which they arise. Here again, reading experience or lack of it plays a key role in the challenges faced by BWs. The skill of text and context requires the ability to read and understand outside source material as well as the ability to present and discuss this material in ways that are appropriate for the audience to which the writing is addressed.

Nancy Sommers' work in two reports published in the early 1980s shows that BWs differ from experienced writers in that they lack the knowledge of text and context that might lead to successful, substantive revision. Sommers' two studies comparing and contrasting BWs and expert writers both show that the experts have a rich view of revising as a by-product of writers' ability to place a text in a context suited to a particular audience. The revisions that expert writers make to texts go far beyond changes in wording and sentence structure typically made by novice writers. This finding supports the notion that all BW courses might usefully incorporate extensive reading experience and audience analysis to help BWs develop some skills in the use of text and context.

The final skill described and discussed in *Revision Revisited* is skill in the use of a variety of tools that experts have in their "toolboxes" for writing. Professional writers know about an array of tools that help them write efficiently and effectively: computer-based word processing and all the online tools that come with it (online dictionaries, spelling and grammar checkers and so on), along with such tools as style or grammar handbooks, thesauruses, and pre-writing templates like webbing or cubing. These tools are available to BWs as well, though a lack of knowledge or experience limits their use.

Studies show that direct instruction in the use of the toolbox can be helpful. An early study supporting this claim was reported by Saur at the Basic Writing Conference in 1985. She found that using reading and collaborative rereading and rewriting of texts can be useful to BWs as can brainstorming to develop content. Such techniques are part of the essential toolbox for revision that can be useful to BWs. Similarly, Ann Berthoff's suggested use of dialogue journals offers yet another tool for BWs to see revision as a complex process that has a role in all parts of writing, not just at the end of the process.

Mary Moran's 1997 study published in the *Journal of Basic Writing* found that BWs who were stronger readers did a better job with revising if they worked on their texts by reading them aloud (Moran 86–88). This is consistent with the strategy of one of the various pieces of support for the importance of the toolbox in revising for BWs, just as it is for professional writers. The toolbox skill is the one place where a focus on error is appropriate, but the research with professionals shows that they use the toolbox with a focus on clarity and eliminating distractions for readers. BW teachers can help students become more skilled with the toolbox if they can keep this focus in their teaching as well.

A "Pivotal Moment:" Some Suggestions and Recommendations

There is much to be done to help BWs learn to revise their writing successfully. We hope it is clear from this brief discussion that not nearly enough research has focused on helping BWs develop the awarenesses and skills essential to effective revision. Indeed, BW scholarship is at what Gene Wise calls a "pivotal moment" (qtd. in Adler-Kassner, "Structure" 229) where pedagogies, strategies, and structures can begin to take into account the contextual changes in student populations and the significance that real life experiences have for learning and for student writing. But in doing so, it will be essential for this scholarship to look explicitly at every aspect of the writing process, including revising.

In response to her reading of this chapter, Catherine Haar, one of the other authors of this volume, shared a set of BW papers with us. These papers had been written, submitted to Ms. Haar, and revised. With their revisions, the students were asked to write "revision notes" in which they explained to their teacher how they had tried to change their papers. The teacher comments and student notes are quite instructive. Ms. Haar's initial comments address the students' relative success in conveying their ideas and feelings about topics they chose, related to their experiences as adolescents (dealing with such matters as personal experience with teen pregnancy, important teachers, positive work experiences, and so on). In response, the students' revision notes include commentary not only on their attempts to make their writing more correct by fixing their mistakes, but especially on their attempts to develop their ideas and convey their points by additions, rearrangements and other changes that constitute substantive revision. The point here is that careful, thoughtful teaching that encourages BW students to develop awarenesses as well as skills and that goes beyond correction can make a significant difference in BWs' ability to revise substantively and successfully.

In 2000, Lynn Quitman Troyka, a leader in Rhetoric and Composition Studies and especially in BW, wrote an open letter to George Otte and Trudy Smoke, then the editors of the *Journal of Basic Writing*, which they published in the journal. The piece was called "How We Have Failed the Basic Writing Enterprise." In her letter, Troyka notes that we have failed to help BWs in part through a lack of research on how best to teach them to write well. This claim certainly applies to the teaching of revising for BWs. In preparing this chapter, both of the authors have looked carefully through the literature and found little focused research on the teaching of revising for BWs. We have tried to show that like all other student writers, BWs need to develop the awarenesses and skills that are evident when professionals revise. The challenge now is to develop a broader array of proven, effective techniques, a few of which we have described in this chapter, for doing so.

5 Revision and ESL Students

Kasia Kietlinska

A few years ago, in one of my classes, when I returned students' papers and discussed revision as an option for students to improve their writing, an English as a Second Language (ESL) student stayed after class and asked me, "So you want me to write a new paper, because this one is wrong, right?" The question, while not necessarily reflective of how all of our students view revision, may indeed be symptomatic for how ESL students perceive it. And my student certainly found a sympathetic ear. I could still remember the times when I was an ESL student myself. The teacher's suggestion to "revise" simply meant a nicer way of saying my paper was bad and needed corrections.

Despite popularity of revision in classroom pedagogy, the concept still lacks a full theoretical elaboration. The picture gets even more complicated for ESL students, with their additional problems related to mechanisms of Second Language Acquisition (SLA) and a broad variety of cultural assumptions they bring into the classroom. Therefore, it is not surprising that much of the available research on ESL students' revision focuses on whether ESL, or Second Language (L2), writing is similar to or different from that of Native English Speaking (NES) students. In our approaches to revision in the ESL classrooms, and particularly in the actual practical applications, it is indeed necessary to understand to what extent L2 students' needs are like those of our NES students. Understanding this would allow us to transfer composition theory findings and applicable First Language (L1) classroom techniques to ESL classrooms. It would also help us modify these techniques to respond to needs that are essentially different from those of NES writers.

History of the Discipline

Originally, when the study of L2 writing began as an area of second language studies, it did not receive much attention since the focus was on spoken language, with writing seen mostly as an orthographic representation of speech. The assumption of English Language Institute (ELI), the first ESL program in the country established in 1941 at the University of Michigan, was that once students mastered the language, they would write. As a result of behaviorist influences, ESL writing was strictly controlled to discourage fossilization of students' interlanguage, or in other words, to prevent student errors, natural for intermediate stages of foreign language acquisition, from solidifying into a habit. Revision, therefore, focused entirely on sentence-level errors. The serious study of L2 writing did not really begin until the 1960s. After the creation of Teachers of English to Speakers of Other Languages (TESOL) in 1966, the discipline remained more closely affiliated with second language studies than with composition studies (Matsuda 15–19). Consequently, there was very little research on L2 writing as independent from TESOL until the 1980's (Krapels 37).

In the late 1970s and 1980s, this strong emphasis on L2 studies gave way to writing process research. Paul Kei Matsuda points to Vivian Zamel's seminal work (1976 and 1982), which started a trend of emphasizing similarities between L1 and L2 writing and, practically speaking, treated writing needs of ESL and NES students as identical (21). In this new trend, competence in the composing process and literacy skills in L1 were perceived as much more important for acquiring writing skills in English than the actual L2 language competence (Krapels 40).

However, even some traditional process-approach scholars, such as Illona Leki and Ann Raimes, who focused on similarities between L1 and L2 learners, also admitted the existence of differences. While insisting that practicing writing was more important than acquiring English language skills (*Understanding* 78), Leki also acknowledged that, "With the distinctive burden of learning to write and learning English at the same time, ESL students have needs which set them apart from mainstream English-speaking students" (*Understanding* 27). Similarly, Raimes, who generally tends to view ESL and basic L1 writers as very similar, still noted: "We need to know what characterizes them [ESL students] as writers grappling not only with a written code but with a linguistic code that is still being acquired" (40).

Therefore, it is not surprising the pendulum is shifting from the process approach. Newer research focuses on differences rather than similarities between L1 and L2 writing again, but this time with a much more pragmatic approach, acknowledging applicability of the process approach whenever it might help students. Matsuda clearly sees the future of the discipline in overcoming the still relatively rigid barrier between TESOL and composition studies (18). He postulates an interdisciplinary approach, which would integrate L2 writing into composition studies (25).

The history of the discipline seems instructive as it reveals the futility of one-sided ideological approaches. The newer ESL writing research departs from the process orthodoxy and very convincingly argues for unique needs of ESL students. In his 1993 article, Tony Silva discusses the ESL revision patterns as distinct from those of NES students:

It is clear that L2 composing is more constrained, more difficult, and less effective. L2 writers did less planning (global and local) and had more difficulty with setting goals and generating and organizing material. Their transcribing was more laborious, less fluent, and less productive—perhaps reflective of a lack of lexical resources. They reviewed, reread, and reflected on their written texts less, revised more— but with more difficulty and were less able to revise intuitively. (200)

These differences have led Silva to suggest that L2 writing theorists and teachers need to "look beyond L1 writing theories, to better describe the unique nature of L2 writing" (201).

Diversity of the ESL Student Population

The uniqueness of the ESL population is additionally heightened by an incredible diversity of ESL students, who all share the non-native status in the English language but vary in almost everything else. Leki discusses differences among the ESL population in age, education level, writing and literacy skills in L1, proficiency levels in L2, attitudes about the U.S., not to mention cultural differences resulting in highly diverse attitudes toward language, writing, teaching and teachers, classroom instruction methods, classroom communication styles, etc. (*Understanding* 39).

The most traditional distinction that may strongly affect classroom pedagogy, and more specifically the teaching of revision, is that between the international ESL students and the immigrant ESL students. While the former tend to have high L1 literacy and writing skills, their L2 proficiency is much higher in reading and writing than in speech and oral comprehension. Also, it is worth remembering that in order to qualify for study in the U.S., these students are required to successfully pass the Test of English as a Foreign Language (TOEFL) exam in their home countries, which guarantees a high degree of familiarity with English grammatical and syntactic structures. On the other hand, the immigrant ESL students, mostly graduates of American high schools, usually speak fluent English, with little or no foreign accent, but show problems in literacy skills, often in both L1 and L2 (Leki, *Understanding* 43). Typically, they also have very weak metalanguage skills (Ferris, "One Size" 145).

I can vividly remember a Polish student I had in an ESL individual tutorial section, mostly because his was a rare case where I had access to his literacy and metalanguage skills in both languages. Having come to the US at the end of middle school, the student was quickly mainstreamed and never received any extensive ESL training, so his English was very limited, particularly in writing. When I tried to use Polish to explain certain more complex ideas, and particularly raise issues of language rules and usage, I soon discovered that his L1 literacy development stagnated at the middle school level when he stopped having access to more sophisticated, school-oriented discourse in Polish. His case convincingly illustrates the problems of many immigrant ESL students for whom the language transfer has come at an inopportune time, so that their literacy in L1 has been stunted while it has not developed in L2.

Newer research, with its focus on unique needs of L2 students, takes a more nuanced approach to defining separate categories of ESL learners. Ann Johns divides L2 students into three rather than two groups. She discusses both international students, the smallest group but academically most proficient and most competent in metalanguage as a result of English as a Foreign Language (EFL) study in their home countries, and immigrant students, whom she calls Limited English Proficient (LEP) learners, who have no academic language proficiency and are often required to take ESL classes in addition to other college courses. However, she also distinguishes a separate category of Emergent English-Dominant Learners, mostly children of immigrants, at least to some extent educated in the U.S. schools. Members of this group tend to have oral and cultural competencies close to those of native speakers but lack expertise in academic writing in both languages. This particular category of ESL students has recently become a center of more research. This "Generation 1.5," as they have been labeled, following the title of the 1999 essay collection, *Generation 1.5 Meets College Composition: Issues in the Teaching of Writing to U.S. Educated ESL Learners,* edited by Linda Harklau, Kay M. Losey, and Meryl Siegal, has been recognized as posing the most serious challenge for teachers. These students often show fossilization of interlanguage forms but lack metalinguistic skills necessary to address the issue and are not usually recognized as having any ESL problems (Johns142–44). Consequently, it is not surprising that teaching methods that could be successful for international students would not necessarily work for LEP students or for "Generation 1.5" learners.

All of these differences between L1 and L2 students, as well as those within the L2 population itself, are going to have a strong impact on how these groups will approach revision. Before we proceed any further, however, it is worth realizing that the existing research on revision patterns of ESL students is rather limited and tends to focus on various forms of feedback, as a necessary step in revision, more than on revision itself. This is, of course, understandable when we take into account the strongly grounded writing-as-a-process template of drafting, feedback, by both teachers and peers, and finally revising. While the template is actually helpful in understanding and teaching revision, let us for a moment look at what is currently known about ESL students' revision attitudes, patterns and effectiveness.

Revision Attitudes of ESL Students

Contrary to what most American academics, teachers, and students may believe, the concept of writing as learning, where the formation of ideas occurs simultaneously with writing, and where multiple drafts, followed by continual revisions, are perceived as a natural production process, is far from universal. Therefore, ESL students, and particularly international students, are not accustomed to the concept of multiple drafts (Leki, *Understanding* 71), and they may naturally view revision in solely punitive terms as a means to correct surface mistakes, without even trying to develop and refine content. Also, ESL students do not fully understand the U.S. academic audiences and writing conventions, so it is harder for them to revise in a way that would conform to these expectations. Students who are still in the process of gaining proficiency in English use native language conventions, and this transfer is not necessarily individual and random but "involves recurring patterns of organization and rhetorical conventions reminiscent of writing in the students' native language and culture" (Connor 5). In many cultures, for example, it is not acceptable to discuss personal issues in the academic setting and to use personal experiences as evidence in the academic discourse (Leki, *Understanding* 67–68). Also, in more authoritarian cultures, it is a sign of respect for sources to cite extensive passages and paraphrase very closely to the original while the same strategy here carries the stigma of plagiarism (Leki, *Understanding* 71–72).

Besides, both international and immigrant students may have to grapple with individual resistance developed toward American culture. International students, whose stay in the U.S. is usually temporary, do not want to abandon their successful L1 writing patterns whereas immigrant students often suffer from confusion about their identity, torn between their home cultures and demands from the U.S. academic culture (Leki *Understanding* 42). When I started graduate school in the US, after working as an assistant English professor in Poland, I was not completely ready to assimilate into the landscape of the American academic culture. My main difficulty was to accept my professors' comments when they suggested departures from Polish academic writing conventions. It took me a while to abandon a very formal, digressive discourse, heavily overloaded with specialized terminology, and gradually move to include personal pronouns, simpler language, and more straightforward thought development. Many of my immigrant students, on the other hand, react with dismay when told that in order to appeal to American academic audiences, they need more sophisticated formulations and more nuanced, morally neutral approaches, often very different from their home language norms.

Revision Patterns of ESL Students

These complex and often ambivalent attitudes certainly affect revision patterns of ESL students. While in general L2 writers tend to revise more than their L1 counterparts, it is definitely harder for them (Silva

195). The reason for this difficulty in revision may be attributed to the fact that all international students as well as a significant number of immigrant students may be unable to revise "by ear," which is a typical revision strategy for L1 students (Silva 195).

Moreover, like L1 basic writers, ESL students tend to correct mostly surface-level errors, since they understand revising as mere editing and hardly ever substantially rework ideas (Raimes 38; Roca de Larios 23), but ESL students focus more on grammar and less on mechanics and spelling (Silva 195). What is a little surprising, however, is that ESL students do not follow the linear pattern of drafting first and revising later, typical for L1 basic writers, but revise "recursively" i.e. "create text—read—create text—read—edit—read—create text—read—read" (Raimes 53), a pattern typical for more skilled L1 writers (Randsell and Barbier 7). It is perhaps caused by the fact that they just cannot freely articulate their thoughts in a foreign language, so they construct writing as they go, constantly assembling and disassembling language structures, following grammatical, syntactic, and lexical rules of English they had studied but not necessarily mastered. So, ironically, what skilled L1 writers do as a sign of mastery of language, a sense of comfort and natural habit of revision, here could perhaps be caused by the opposite feelings of insecurity and self-consciousness.

REVISION EFFECTIVENESS OF ESL STUDENTS

When revision is such a struggle for ESL students, is it effective? Does revision improve the quality and accuracy of their writing? Unfortunately, research findings are not fully conclusive, and there is some degree of skepticism. On one hand, some studies indicate that revising does help ESL students to improve their writing abilities. Charlene Polio, Catherine Fleck and Nevin Leder, for example, found that whether or not the students received any editing feedback, they improved their writing accuracy in the revised essays (55); they improved their accuracy between the beginning and the end of the semester (53), but they did not improve revision skills over time (55). Consequently, Polio, Fleck and Leder contended "that learners can and do correct their own language without feedback" (61). While research by Polio, Fleck and Leder clearly focused on language accuracy rather than content, the study by Ann K. Fathman and Elizabeth Whalley found similar results on the impact of revision on content and demonstrated that again, irrespective of feedback, the prevailing majority of students improved the quality of their content (183).

On the other hand, Dana Ferris, while also a committed believer in revision, sounds a little more skeptical. In her book *Treatment of Error in Second Language Student Writing*, she lists studies that confirm the effectiveness of revision as well as those that cast doubt upon the ESL students' ability to improve their writing as a result of revision. She contends that there is no compelling evidence that revision makes a difference in the long run but it seems to moderately improve the quality of the revised papers and increases the students' awareness of themselves as writers. She basically identifies the issue as an area for future research (26).

In spite of this rather inconclusive tone of research findings, many ESL writing experts agree that the key factor in increasing the effectiveness of revision in L2 student writing is time (Leki *Understanding* 82; New 81; Roca de Larios 23). In her frequently quoted passage, Raimes says, "ESL writers need more of everything: more time, more opportunity to talk, listen, read, and write in order to marshal the vocabulary they need to make their own background knowledge accessible to them in their L2" (55). Polio, Fleck and Leder agree: "Additional time does lead to self-correction" (62). Consequently, rather than giving up on revision as a strategy of improving ESL students' writing, we should structure our classroom practices to give students more time to revise. It is logical that students who still have to wear two hats, struggle with language and tackle writing skills, would need more time to process both.

My personal experience confirms that time is an important factor. Even though I was a relatively proficient ESL writer when I entered graduate school in the U.S., I was much slower than my American fellow students. Taking in-class written exams, I recall, meant more than just arranging ideas to offer meaningful interpretations; it also meant a struggle with language, a constant review of correct grammatical forms and appropriate vocabulary. It is quite natural, then, that when given more time, ESL students get a chance to incorporate revision into their habitual writing practices and thus to adjust to the conventions of the American academic community, where revision is a standard practice.

Revision Feedback by Teachers

To learn how to revise their own work, however, students need more than just time. It has been an accepted part of the classroom pedagogy to facilitate feedback on drafts, either by peers or teachers, in order to assist students in their revision skills, and consequently help them improve their writing. This last contention, while commonly accepted by teachers, is far from obvious among researchers. A lot of theoreticians, particularly of the liberal process orientation, do not believe that teacher feedback is necessarily effective in improving student texts. Teacher comments are often criticized as inadequate, inconsistent, and often misinterpreted by student writers (Hyland 255). The most frequently cited study, conducted by Vivian Zamel in 1985, found that teachers often missed errors, corrected minor problems while ignoring serious global issues, and gave ambiguous comments. She generally concluded that teacher feedback was not helpful (Leki, "Coaching" 61). While such findings certainly indicate a need for caution in how teachers respond to their students' drafts, suggestions that teacher feedback should be abandoned altogether sound highly premature, particularly since research is not conclusive and often directly contradicts this skepticism (Leki, "Coaching" 65–66).

Fiona Hyland's study, for example, has suggested that student revisions have been positively influenced by teacher feedback (257 and 265). Also, numerous works by Dana Ferris exhibit a high degree of trust that teacher feedback is generally an indispensable part of the revision process. While admitting that "there is no 'one-size-fits-all' form of teacher commentary" (Ferris et al. 178), she notes that most revisions influenced by teacher feedback have led to improved writing ("Responding" 122). Teacher feedback, Ferris believes, "can have significant, positive effects on student revision" ("One Size" 148–49). According to her own collaborative study, 85 percent of errors were corrected in revision (*Treatment* 8). Even when she notes inconsistencies in student responses to feedback, she uses that as an argument for reform rather than abandonment of teacher feedback. Ferris admits, "The findings suggest two conflicting but coexisting truths: that students pay a great deal of attention to teacher feedback, which helps them make substantial, effective revisions, and that students sometimes ignore or avoid suggestions given in teacher commentary" ("One Size" 149). Ferris proceeds to offer numerous classroom strategies teachers should use to improve the quality of their feedback. And improvement rather than abandonment of teacher feedback is indeed a more reasonable and more realistic strategy in ESL classrooms.

One of the reasons why abandoning the teacher feedback would be a highly problematic step is the prevailingly favorable attitude of L2 students themselves. ESL students almost universally value teacher feedback (Ferris, "Responding" 122). Because L2 students perceive themselves as foreign language learners, they tend to be less intimidated and stigmatized by errors (Raimes 53; Leki, *Understanding* 81; Ferris, *Treatment* 32). Moreover, students strongly expect feedback and may react with disappointment if they don't get it (Raimes 53). We need to remember that many ESL students come from cultures which perceive teachers in highly authoritarian terms; therefore, teachers are expected to correct problems, and their refusal to do so may easily be interpreted as ignorance or laziness.

In my interview with Besma, the most successful ESL student I have ever taught, she strongly emphasized her need for thorough teacher feedback, harshly criticized former teachers who did not offer it, and related this preference to her Iraqi background. She did not seem to have a problem accepting criticism, and she wanted all her errors corrected and explained. "I do not want to make the same mistakes again," she said (Arabo). Her teacher from the tutorial support class confirmed this preference, speaking about the student's "heavy reliance on the teacher" and "an incredible ability to learn from the teacher's comments" (Wynn).

In this context, it seems rather ironic that radical process approach proponents, who generally argue for student empowerment, in this case easily dismiss students' own preferences. John Truscott, the most vocal critic of teacher feedback, and particularly of grammatical corrections, believes that students' demand for corrections does not mean "teachers have to give it to them" (qtd. in Ferris, *Treatment* 8). While not always necessarily decisive in themselves, students' attitudes certainly have to be taken into account in any pedagogy reforms, and dismissing them when it suits one's political agenda seems condescending, if not outright harmful to the students.

Recently, the debate has shifted from the question of whether teachers should give feedback on their students' papers to how such feedback should be construed to maximize its effectiveness. While the general consensus is that students benefit from comments about content, which encourage them to implement global revisions, there is far less agreement on whether grammatical feedback is equally effective. Once again, the main fault line of the debate seems to follow the general perception of ESL writers as either similar to or different from their NES counterparts. Because of the anti-grammar orthodoxy in the process theory, those who emphasize similarities between L2 and L1 writers tend to follow what Ferris calls "'benign neglect' of errors and grammar teaching" and discount the importance and validity of grammar feedback (*Treatment* 4). On the other hand, the researchers who focus on the distinct nature of ESL writing believe that correcting grammatical errors is necessary in order to prevent fossilization of the students' interlanguage (Johns 153).

The most vocal of the process camp is Truscott, whose debate with Dana Ferris best exemplifies the two antagonistic positions. Truscott maintains that grammar correction is ineffective at best and at times even potentially harmful to L2 writers (Truscott 118; Hyland 256). Excessive attention to student error, argue such process advocates as Truscott, Zamel, and Krashen, "may short-circuit students' writing and thinking process, making writing only an exercise in practical grammar and vocabulary rather than a way to discover and express meaning" (Ferris, *Treatment* 49).

On the other hand, while admitting that research on effectiveness of error correction and grammar instruction is incomplete and often inconclusive, Dana Ferris believes that teachers should not abdicate this, often very tedious duty (*Treatment* 9). L2 students need additional intervention, since they are still in the process of learning syntax, morphology and lexicon of English (Ferris, *Treatment* 4). To facilitate this learning process, Ferris goes beyond just feedback and proposes grammar minilessons. In radical disagreement with her process-advocating colleagues, Ferris says: "Well-construed error feedback, especially when combined with judiciously delivered strategy training and grammar minilessons is beneficial and highly appreciated by ESL students" (*Treatment* 49). In her own collaborative study, published in 2000, Ferris found that 85 percent of marked errors were corrected in revision (*Treatment* 8). Similarly, Fathman and Whalley noticed the effectiveness of grammatical feedback. Irrespective of the kind of received feedback (form, content, or both), all students improved content, but grammatical accuracy improved only when grammar feedback was given (Fathman and Whalley183).

The main difficulty in resolving the grammar controversy involves a virtual lack of longitudinal studies. For practical reasons, appropriate longitudinal studies are extremely difficult to design, particularly when we take into account that SLA processes, as well as the processes of acquiring writing literacy, often take many years. Ultimately, then, we do not understand exactly how the students' responses to teachers' grammatical feedback, followed by students' revising, get translated into the long-term improvement in grammatical accuracy. Ferris' frustration with this "catch 22" situation, then, is fully understandable. "If studies show improvement in short-term," she complains, "critics say that this doesn't help understand long-term effects. If long term improvement can be showed, critics say it may be a result of other factors" (*Treatment* 16). It is likely that the anti-grammar research by process advocates has been designed in an unrealistic way. It is simply impossible to see clear improvement over the course of one semester, or even a year. That doesn't mean, however, that teachers should stop correcting grammar and offering mini grammar lessons, because that might deprive our students of a chance to learn self-correction. Sherry Wynn, Besma's tutor, attributed the student's success mostly to her ability to acquire self-correction skills as a result of numerous and thorough corrections, often accompanied by metalinguistic explanations, received during two semesters of tutorial sessions. What we basically need, then, is a simpler, more common sense approach: to believe that a short-term improvement is a step toward long-term results.

My own path toward becoming an English speaker and writer, however intuitive and personal a memory of one's individual learning process may be, is a good illustration that students really need all the feedback they can get, both for content and form. Starting as a high school student in Poland, I learned English through hundreds, if not thousands, of grammatical exercises, all of them corrected and explained by my teachers. When I began composing, which was a while after the beginning of my ESL study, I also received numerous comments, including those about my language accuracy and correctness, together with appropriate grammatical terminology and rules. This was a very intense and often frustrating process, and it lasted a few years, but at some point more and more rules did become automatic, and I learned how to correct myself if I slipped.

If we were able to assume that our ESL students had taken intensive ESL courses, emphasizing grammar and syntax, prior to our writing course, or that they were taking them simultaneously, we could perhaps abandon grammar corrections and focus exclusively on global content issues. Since this is not a realistic assumption, however, we have to include the elements of grammar and syntax both in our corrections and in minilessons, hoping that students will eventually internalize them. We are, after all, the only source our students have to learn these, and if we abdicate, there is nobody else to fill the vacuum.

Moreover, the standard process advocates' arguments that corrections stifle students' creativity and willingness to take risks are culturally misguided. This very American assumption that our students' self-esteem is fragile and can easily be damaged by criticism is simply wrong. In reality, ESL students from most cultures are very resilient; they accept the teacher's authority with much less hesitation than their American counterparts, and they are culturally conditioned to expect criticism and error correction from teachers. Besma spoke very clearly that it was natural for her Iraqi teachers to point out mistakes and equally natural for her to accept these corrections (Arabo).

Admittedly, there is a danger of overemphasizing grammar, which in certain circumstances may negatively influence fluency and creativity in writing. For most ESL students, however, the greater danger is to neglect grammar, which might simply misguide our students and result in fossilization of erroneous language forms (Johns 153). And these errors are not necessarily as benign as many process advocates would have us believe. Any teacher who has spent time in the ESL classroom will attest to how difficult it is to find a workable compromise between correcting every single error, an often futile endeavor, and focusing exclusively on content, an impossible feat when errors make content hardly accessible.

Timing of Revision Feedback

Another important issue regarding revision in ESL is when teachers should give feedback. Most researchers agree that in order to do any meaningful revision, students need to receive feedback earlier than in final drafts (Ferris, *Treatment* 62; Leki, "Coaching" 64). Also, it is a typical recommendation that content and form revision should be strictly separated, and global content feedback should precede any comments on more local language issues, which should occur very late in the process, at the editing stage. According to Elizabeth New, starting with Zamel's research, this pattern has become part of the process approach orthodoxy (93).

Such a strict separation of content from form, however, seems to create a false dichotomy (Ferris, *Treatment* 79). The standard process template when students produce a draft and then revise, focusing on content first and leaving editing for the very final phase of writing, is simply not realistic for ESL students, who have to build content out of bricks of form currently available to them, even in composing first drafts. As I have already observed, ESL writers tend to go back and forth: write, revise, write, revise. They have to focus more on surface because they are not yet able to access the layer of deep revision. To use Alice S. Horning's terminology, ESL students typically lack metarhetorical (knowledge of themselves as writers), metastrategic (knowledge of their own personality type and its influence on their writing behaviors, including revision) and metalinguistic (terminology to discuss language issues), awareness in a foreign language (8–9). These kinds of awareness are usually proportional to the level of proficiency in English. The more comfortable the students become in English, the more able they are to reach beyond the surface editing and tap into their L1 literacy skills to develop an awareness of themselves as writers in English.

Moreover, some recent empirical studies also seem to support this reasoning and undermine the content-first template for feedback and revision. Tim Ashwell, for example, tested the hypotheses of whether the content and form feedback should be provided separately, and whether content feedback followed by form feedback is superior to other patterns (231). His research confirms that students generally perform better when given feedback, but questions the strict separation between the two kinds of feedback as well as their content-before-form template. "It would appear from the evidence here," Aswell says, "that the recommended pattern of content feedback followed by form feedback is not superior to a reverse pattern or to a pattern of mixed form and content feedback. [. . .] The mixed pattern exhibited an advantage over the two other patterns" (243). Finally, then, the feedback that fits unique needs and revision patterns of ESL students involves mixing form and content comments rather than adhering to the content-first template.

Most Effective Techniques of Revision Feedback

Apart from the grammar debate and the controversy surrounding the timing of content and form feedback, Ferris offers many practical and specific recommendations about what kind of feedback is the most effective. She identifies most typical ESL error areas as related to deeper language structures and lists errors in verb tense and aspect, articles and other determiners, noun endings (plural and possessive inflectional endings), errors in word form (nouns instead of adjectives) and word order as the most prevalent (*Treatment* 41–42). She also believes that recent research in corpus linguistics, the computer analysis of large samples of texts in English, designed to examine frequencies of various kinds of lexical, morphological and syntactic usage, will inform scholars and teachers about what students need to revise the most (*Treatment* 42–43).

For now, Ferris carefully examines various techniques of teacher feedback, and her very thorough and practical approach offers a lot of useful information about how teachers can structure their responses on student papers. In her view, teachers should offer indirect rather than direct feedback (marking the error but not correcting it), because it increases students' own investment in the process, except for low-proficiency students, for whom direct corrections might be more beneficial (*Treatment* 19). Moreover, she believes that for long-term success, coded feedback works better than simple circling of errors (uncoded feedback), particularly in conjunction with grammar minilessons in class (*Treatment* 20). She also contends that comprehensive rather than just selective feedback may be more appropriate for ESL students.

Naturally, specific styles of offering feedback and teaching revision skills will vary, depending on teachers' skills and preferences as well as students' needs. As Ferris so aptly suggests in one of her article titles, "One size does not fit all." However, that does not necessarily mean that all feedback is equally effective. Seriously concerned about effectiveness of teacher feedback, Ferris offers a few suggestions about appropriate comments. In her own experience, she tends to solicit good revision results to feedback by asking for specific information from students' own lives, for their responses to assigned readings, and for some grammatical error correction. Comments about higher order issues related to argumentative logic and structure do not usually achieve similarly positive results ("One Size" 149). Therefore, she recommends that teachers should always evaluate their students' competence in grammatical terminology and ability to self-correct by ear but also their ability to comprehend such composition theory terms as thesis, topic sentence, transition, etc. ("One Size" 152). Also, to empower their students, teachers need to take into account students' feedback preferences, discuss these preferences with the students, and assess effectiveness of their own feedback on the basis of students' reactions and their abilities to improve their writing (Ferris, "One Size" 153).

Finally, teachers should develop useful classroom practices to actively help students develop effective revision strategies. Ferris offers some practical advice such as pairing higher order issues with specific illustrations of what exactly could be done; discussing revision strategies in class; showing marked essays and asking what individual comments mean and how to improve writing based on these comments; offering individual assistance in oral conferences in order to help students process feedback and revise effectively ("One Size" 154).

While our knowledge of the impact teacher feedback has on revision by ESL students has certainly increased in recent years, there are still a lot of missing links, and the exact nature of the relationship between the teacher feedback and the revision process and its effectiveness remains largely unexplored. We clearly need more research on what teachers say about their students' writing and what students do as a result. In her work on responding to ESL writers, Lynn Goldstein defines her goal as "understanding of how student writing, teacher commentary and student revision mutually shape each other" (86). She criticizes the overly simplistic conceptualization of the process "as a linear one in which students write, teachers respond with commentary, and then students revise" for ignoring other factors interacting in complex ways (87). Trying to incorporate these other factors, Goldstein proposes a list of questions as possible guideposts for further research (78). I am sure that designing empirical studies targeting these specific questions will increase our understanding of this complex issue of how teacher feedback shapes revision practices of ESL writers.

Peer Revision Feedback

Another part of the classroom pedagogy related to revision that becomes more complicated for ESL students is peer feedback. A standard practice in process approaches to writing instruction, peer editing seems far less accepted by ESL students. Gayle L. Nelson and Joan G. Carson observe that ESL students tend to mistrust their peers as critics and often fear being embarrassed in front of peers by their low skills in English (116). In their study of Chinese and Spanish speaking students, Nelson and Carson noticed the participants' strong preference for the teacher's comments to those offered by their peers. Students also seemed to treat the teacher's suggestions more seriously by implementing them more often in their revisions (124).

Similar findings emerge from Zhang's study of mostly Asian students who overwhelmingly chose teacher over peer feedback. Offered a stark choice of either feedback by the teacher or by peers, 94 percent of Zhang's study participants selected the former (Jacobs et al. 309). These results are not surprising when we realize that most ESL students come from countries where teacher-student relationships are strongly hierarchical. "In countries with a large power distance," Nelson and Carson contend, "teachers are viewed as the holders of truths, wisdom, and knowledge, and they pass this knowledge on to their students" (129). Fellow students, on the other hand, do not have this status. My Iraqi student Besma echoed this sentiment when she called peer review sessions "a waste of time." The one positive aspect of the experience she found was: "I could see writing of others, and it made me feel mine was not so bad" (Arabo).

Such differences in cultural norms are also the most convincing explanation for other findings by Nelson and Carson, and particularly for students' strong preference for negative comments and their very different communication styles, which had a strong impact on the effectiveness of the peer response session. Both Chinese and Spanish students understood the purpose of the session as a search for mistakes in each other's essays, so they soon began playing down positive comments as simple sweetening pills for problems and mistakes (121). "Well, for me I hope they give me negative things because I need to revise my paper," said one of the Chinese participants in the transcript from the videotaped discussions (qtd. in Nelson and Carson 122). While both groups shared this inclination for negative comments, the Chinese and the Spanish students viewed their participation in peer review groups very differently. Coming from a more collectivist culture, the Chinese students focused on maintaining positive group relations, often by toning down or avoiding any direct commentary on other students' papers. Their Spanish peers, on the other hand, viewed their group interactions as task-oriented and focused on cooperation in order to improve their works (Nelson and Carson 126–27).

Nelson and Carson's examples help us realize the complexity of the standard peer review routine when it is implemented in the ESL classrooms, where varying cultural norms of interpersonal communication and often varying levels of our students' language proficiency make effectiveness of peer responses less guaranteed than in regular L1 composition classrooms (Ferris, "Responding" 130). Therefore, it is hardly surprising that in the final conclusions from their study, citing language and cultural difficulties, Nelson and Carson recommend, "It may be time to reconsider the use of peer response in ESL composition classes" (128). To back up this conclusion they refer to "a growing body of ESL research [which] indicates that peer response may not be as effective with nonnative speakers of English as with native speakers" (129).

However, this general skepticism regarding the role of peer feedback in the ESL writing pedagogy, while understandable, does not perhaps have to be so radical. Ferris, for example, admits that peer responses in ESL classes are a little like "the blind leading the blind," but also values editing skills students acquire by working on their peers' papers (*Treatment* 102). Other researchers note the following benefits of peer collaboration: receiving social support from peers, learning through collaboration, receiving a broader audience for their writing, and receiving alternatives to teacher feedback, to name just a few (Jacobs et al. 308). Also, including a peer review stage in the students' work on the paper tends to increase the number of drafts and, consequently, lengthens the writing process. Thus, it becomes a very handy practical application of Ann Raimes' contention about ESL students' need for "more time" (55).

While ESL students do indeed prefer feedback by teachers to that by students, that does not mean that they do not value both, even if it is to a different extent. Such a high percentage of teacher preference in Zhang's research may be a direct result of his question formulated in stark either/or terms. In the study by George M. Jacobs et al., the question was formulated differently and it did, in fact, yield very different results. In this study, participants were to choose a positive or a negative response to the following statement: "I prefer to have feedback from other students as one type of feedback on my writing," and

93 percent expressed a desire to have peer feedback included in their writing process (311).

Explaining the reasons for their preference, the participants mentioned new ideas provided by peers and the peers' ability to spot problems they had not noticed themselves. Students also noticed the benefit of working on papers by others and saw their peers as more understanding, more encouraging, less threatening, and less busy than teachers (Jacobs et al. 312). Summing up the results of their study, Jacobs et al. say, "Although the students ranked teacher-centered feedback higher than feedback from their peers, the results show clearly that they did value both" (313). The researchers very convincingly present their findings as "middle path on the issue of types of feedback, in which teacher, peer, and self-directed feedback are judiciously combined" (Jacobs et al. 314).

This "middle path" approach allows for more revision opportunities and provides our ESL students with a more varied audience input, but we cannot simply ignore the skeptical voices. Therefore, we need to examine possible modifications to the standard peer response routine in order to find out how to make it appropriate for the ESL students and help them revise their papers most effectively.

One such modification is peer response training, which ESL students seem to need much more than their L1 counterparts. Assuming that a peer-review session is a rather self-explanatory exercise, teachers often introduce it briefly and then just think their students will catch on as they do it. While this assumption may work with L1 students, who most likely did peer reviews in high school and who work in their native language and culture, ESL students are not familiar with the concept and do not have the skills to review works of others. Recognizing this difficulty, and generally a bit skeptical about the practice, Ferris emphasizes that students should be "trained" and sessions should be "structured and supervised by teachers" (*Treatment* 103). Also Jacobs et al. stress the importance of a "well-planned implementation process" (314), necessary if peer feedback is to be successful. Their article offers a few practical suggestions of what teachers could do: sharing their own experiences of giving and receiving feedback from peers, providing sample peer review forms, critiquing student feedback, sharing models of successful peer comments in class, emphasizing the need for a balance between positive and negative responses, and facilitating positive attitudes to avoid hostility among students (Jacobs et al. 314).

Similarly, in her article "Preparing ESL Students for Peer Response," E. Catherine Berg offers an elaborate set of guidelines for training students to become more successful peer reviewers. The goals of her training, designed to last several days, are to convince students of the value of the practice, socialize them to each other, teach them to focus on the selected issues in their writing, and help them acquire appropriate terminology for their responses (20). To achieve these goals, Berg, like Jacobs et al. , emphasizes specific examples and modeling exercises in the classroom. In her set of eleven guidelines, the following seem the most specific and useful in the classroom pedagogy:

- "Demonstrate and personalize the peer response experience by displaying several drafts of a text written by someone who the students know that demonstrate how peer comments helped improve the writing."

- "Conduct a collaborative, whole-class response activity using a text written by someone unknown to students and stress the importance of revising the clarity and rhetorical-level aspects rather than sentence-level errors."

- "Familiarize students with the response sheet by showing samples and explaining its purpose as a tool designed to help them focus on important areas of the writing assignment."

- "Involve students in a response to a collaborative writing project by having them use the peer response sheet to respond in pairs or groups to a paragraph written by another group of students. Based on the responses, have the pairs or groups then revise their original collaborative paragraph."

- "Provide revision guidelines by highlighting good revision strategies and explaining that peer response helps authors understand the difference between intended and perceived meaning."

- "Study examples of successful and unsuccessful peer responses using videotapes or printed samples to examine level of student engagement, language used, and topics discussed." (Berg, "Preparing" 21)

While all these guidelines and practical classroom applications of the concept that ESL students have to be trained to become successful peer respondents certainly sound very convincing, we need to know if training students actually results in visible improvements in their revised essays. In another article, "The Effects of Trained Peer Response on ESL Students' Revision Types and Writing Quality," Berg verifies the success of peer response training. Comparing revision outcomes after peer feedback by trained and untrained students, Berg found that trained students' responses generated more content changes ("Effects" 226). She also discovered that trained students generally scored higher on improving the overall quality of their own drafts as a result of peer feedback followed by revision (Berg, "Effects" 228).

In general, then, even though research findings regarding the peer review routine in ESL classrooms may seem confusing, its closer examination points out to complexity rather than contradiction. Clearly, in L2 classes, peer review should not be used reflexively, as simply a natural stage in revising, the way it is treated by the process orthodoxy. However, when introduced carefully, with well-designed student training, and without unrealistic expectations, peer review should remain a viable part of the ESL classroom pedagogy.

Alternative Strategies to Support Revision

Another technique of assisting ESL students in developing their revision skills is self-monitoring. One of the least popular, least studied and, perhaps, least practical ways of facilitating revision for ESL writers, self-monitoring promises a high degree of autonomy. Andy Cresswell, one proponent of the method, explains self-monitoring as an interactive technique, where students write annotations about language and composition issues they confront as their drafts evolve, to which the teachers respond in writing. He believes that, like peer evaluation, self-monitoring encourages "reader-based prose," because it pushes students to become aware of writing as a form of communication with the audience and aware of themselves as personally vested in the revision process. Ultimately, students are expected to become their own readers and "to develop heuristics to solve composing problems independently" (Cresswell 235). This explains why self-monitoring does not appear a very practical option. As we know, the ability to self-monitor and revise without any external feedback characterizes the most proficient writers, and expecting ESL students to be able to easily acquire this very advanced skill does not sound very realistic.

Apart from carefully designed teacher feedback and peer review practice with prior training, there are other classroom revision strategies that appear more helpful to ESL students than self-monitoring. One such strategy is contrastive rhetoric, a branch of linguistics and SLA theory, which explains problems of ESL writers by referring to the rhetorical strategies typical for their first languages (Connor 5). Developing Robert Kaplan's seminal ideas, contrastive rhetoric emphasizes different cultural norms internalized as different discourse modes in various languages. In his famous "doodles" article (1966), Kaplan analyzed paragraph development in ESL student's essays and related it to students' L1 backgrounds. Using drawings to illustrate lines of reasoning typical for different cultures, he suggested that Semitic languages favor developing ideas in a series of parallel coordinate clauses, Asian languages prefer an indirect approach with the main point presented at the end, and Romance languages as well as Russian lean toward digressiveness. Naturally, all of these rhetorical conventions are very different from the typical linear organization of Anglo-European expository prose (Connor 15). In teaching ESL students, these cultural preferences constitute possible obstacles, but if approached with full awareness, they may actually become useful points of reference in guiding students toward new rhetorical conventions. Also, this approach may be socially helpful to students as it celebrates their own language and cultural heritage (Connor 26).

When carefully examined, however, contrastive rhetoric has serious practical limitations. Expecting teachers, whose students come from multiple backgrounds, to study individual contrasts between English and these various languages, and then formulate appropriate revision strategies, seems hardly realistic. Besides, topical structure analysis, the recommended tool of contrastive rhetoric, appears arcane. As Ulla Connor and Mary Farmer say, the method expects students to "assess both the global coherence (what the essay is about) and local coherence (how sentences build meaning in relation to each other and the overall discourse topic)" and to chart the progress of sentence topics (128). While conceptually interesting, it requires teachers and students to have a strong background in linguistics and, ultimately, does not seem practical.

Other means of facilitating revision, while also potentially promising, would require further research to check whether there really is a sufficient gain in revision skills and writing improvement to validate their use. Computer technology certainly has that potential but it also requires training in peer feedback and explicit instruction on revision and computer strategies (New 80). Also, collaborative writing assignments may have a positive influence on student revision practices. Alan Hirvela's experimental, fully collaborative communities of readers and writers offer ESL students an opportunity to negotiate choices throughout the entire creative process, from drafting, peer reviewing, to revising. This group production offers ESL students "greater opportunities for meaningful review of what they are learning and practicing in a writing course." As Hirvela adds, "From a general language teaching perspective, students are able to practice the target language in authentic and meaningful communicative contexts as they interact with each other," (12). Since the ESL population is so diverse in cultural backgrounds as well as in L2 proficiency levels however, it is easy to imagine many problems in creating a collaborative setting.

The strategy that seems more effective than many others in helping ESL students improve their revision skills is individual tutoring. Whether done by faculty members in separate tutorial courses, or in writing centers by teachers or trained student tutors, the procedure can be very effective, particularly when there is close collaboration between the writing teacher and the tutor. Besma, my successful Iraqi student, was placed in a tutorial support section, taught by another faculty member from my department, with whom I frequently communicated about the student's progress. The results were astounding: she learned such high-level revision skills and improved her writing so dramatically that she received the second highest grade in the mainstreamed course. My own experiences as an ESL student were very similar to Besma's. In order to pass a highly competitive entrance exam to the English Department at the Gdansk University, I had to be highly proficient in English, including writing. Because Polish public schools provided rather ineffective foreign language training, my parents hired a tutor. Even though I started at the beginners' level, after a year of two-hour sessions, twice a week, I passed the writing exam. Of course, again, the method would have to be checked in a more disciplined context of a formal research involving more than one or two subjects.

Above all else, our ESL students need more time and more individual attention than their L1 counterparts. Therefore, reducing the number of assignments, extending time limits, providing more exercises explicitly focusing on revision, preceded by some form of carefully designed feedback (Leki, *Understanding* 87), and, whenever possible, offering individual tutorial support seem the most practical solutions for ESL classrooms. Achieving the environment in which teachers will be able to respond effectively to specific needs of their L2 students will only be possible in small writing classes. The current financial predicament of many public colleges and universities creates a push for increasing class sizes and mainstreaming ESL students, but they will not benefit from integration. Since their needs are significantly different from those of their L1 peers, ESL students should be taught in separate classes, which will enable them to focus on their revision skills and consequently to improve their writing (Silva 202).

Also, it would be extremely helpful if L2 students enrolled in writing classes were offered support in regular ESL courses, either prior to enrollment or simultaneously, or at least were required to receive a certain TOEFL score as a prerequisite for the course. The most holistic of all language skills, writing involves higher order thinking, reading, and comprehension skills, which our ESL students often transfer from their L1, as well as proficiency in English. Both elements, literacy skills and language proficiency, are equally important. That is why the frequently perceived dichotomy between our students' writing abilities and their language proficiency is highly problematic. When Leki says, "L2 writers don't need more work with language but rather with writing" (*Understanding* 78), I am provoked to ask: What language will they write in? How can they write in English if often they do not know English? Of course, I am not trying to play down the importance of general literacy skills Leki refers to in the quote, but the transfer of these literacy skills from our students' first language cannot occur if their proficiency in English is not high enough. The main question should be how to successfully tap into our students' L1 literacy skills and enable them to transfer these skills into acceptable English, following the language, genre, and audience conventions appropriate for the academic context.

Therefore, there is an urgent need for a separate theory of L2 writing, and the newest research supports such a reconfiguration of the discipline. To argue for this, William Grabe, for example, presents a long list of differences between L1 and L2 writers, including such specific items as epistemological differences in values, beliefs and cultural socialization, perceptions of functions of writing and writing topics, audience awareness, textual conventions, and cultural attitudes towards plagiarism, to name just a few (46). Such significant differences make it impossible to teach ESL writers the same way we teach their L1 counterparts. This theory of L2 writing needs to bridge the gap between the TESOL approach, focusing entirely on English language skills and often perceiving students' native language as an impediment to English proficiency, and the process approach in the composition studies, focusing on native language literacy but ignoring the need for English grammar, syntax and other sentence-level features. Finally, then, the field needs to be defined more precisely as a separate area between TESOL and composition studies, studying the unique needs of the ESL student population.

6 What's in a Textbook?

Robert Lamphear

One of the most useful tools an instructor possesses is the textbook. While this chapter focuses on handbooks, the gamut of tools at an instructor's disposal—handbooks, focused texts and readers—can augment the classroom experience for both students and instructors. Consequently, one aspect that all handbooks must address is the need for revision. The scope of this study included current texts associated with the major publishers who often frequent local conferences and professional development activities (listed in the Appendix to this chapter). Although these texts represent the majority of relevant offerings on this topic by these publishers, by next year these will be supplemented, replaced, revised or eliminated by others, so that this output becomes reduced to a snapshot capturing a moment-in-time view of collegiate handbooks.

All of the handbooks focus on the concept of the writing process as a method to present the concept of revision, as will those of the foreseeable future. Still, most textbooks, even handbooks, relegate a disproportionately few pages to revision for the value it offers to first year college composition students. Usually embedded at the end of a discussion of the writing process, these fragments generally focus on three major phases of revision: revising, editing and proofreading. When students move into the paragraphs looking closely at sentences, diction and mechanics, they edit. Proofreading "means reading to correct any typographical errors or other slips such as inconsistencies in spelling and punctuation" (Lunsford 105). Students often confuse the latter two activities with revision, believing correcting surface errors creates a perfect essay. Although these phases remain crucial for the success of the final product, they occur as mere steps in a process, the final steps.

However, the main function of revision should not be limited to a sequential process, but rather an evolution of an essay through re-visioning a work, allowing the students to see their initial effort differently. Revision touches all aspects of writing—a pre-writing outline or thesis tends to be revised repeatedly. Yet these activities do not replace the need for students to dedicate a portion of time to this final writing process phase. Most first year college composition students fail to realize that the expectation for quality writing, achieved through revision, will extend beyond the composition course to other academic and professional pursuits, including resumes, cover letters, proposals, reports, memos and e-mails.

All major publishers offer unique approaches within the handbook section(s) devoted to revision, aiding students in the quest for an effective paper and providing instructors ideas to move their students closer to achieving this goal. Once students view their work objectively, the possibility for meaningful revision exists. The techniques included in this chapter offer examples from a variety of publishers in an attempt to acknowledge that whatever text instructors choose will supply a reasonable approach to revision. An attempt has been made to demonstrate some of the uniqueness found in selected textbooks after establishing common points found in most of the reviewed works.

Handbooks

The 2004 *Hodges' Harbrace Handbook (HHH)* typifies the handbook approaches to the process of revision. After introducing the three major phases of revision, the text makes an effort to establish the importance of revision by suggesting that throughout all portions of the writing process, the writer continually revises in a recursive fashion, yet a period of the process must be focused on specific revision activities. The section on the revision process focuses on the need for the writer to "recall your purpose, restate your thesis, and reconsider your audience" (Glenn, Miller and Webb 446). Here the technical insert also suggests many writers save each draft to map the work's progress (446). The section heading "Anything and everything on the page can be revised" captures another valuable, self-explanatory suggestion. This section reinforces the other common areas that effective writers achieve: well developed, unified, coherent, cohesive and complete ideas. The remainder of the chapter guides the students through typical problem areas—tone, introductions and conclusions—before continuing with the other phases of the revision process.

At this point, *HHH* introduces the concept of peer editing with an emphasis on ensuring standards are established for both writers and reviewers. This process, if not well handled, can create extreme frustration for students and discourage them from the revision process altogether. Students fail to perceive how someone struggling in the same situation they are experiencing can help them. Students must be guided to understand their weaknesses and strengths. Clarifying those areas to others where assistance is sought or where the most assistance may be provided allows students success in the peer review process. This section continues to indicate that a draft must be ready for review, but often students submit work that hasn't been edited, or even proofread. These surface errors then become the focus of the critique, which provides little assistance to the writer and perpetuates the notion that editing is revision.

These peer review sessions must be structured so both parties understand the expectations. *HHH* offers a sample checklist for this activity where the embedded parenthetical references refer to the earlier sections in the chapter where the topics of the question were discussed:

- What is your purpose in the essay (32a(1))? Does this essay fulfill the assignment?

- Does the essay address a specific audience (32a(2))? Is that audience appropriate for the assignment?

- What is the tone of the essay (33a(3))? How does the tone align with the overall purpose, the intended audience, and the context for the writing (32a)?

- Is your topic sufficiently focused (32b)? What is the thesis statement (32c)?

- What assertions do you make to support the thesis statement? How do you support these assertions? What specific evidence do you provide?

- Are paragraphs arranged into effective sentences (32d)? What order do you use? Is each paragraph thoroughly developed (31c)?

- Is the introduction effective (33b(1))? How do you engage the reader's attention?

- Is the conclusion appropriate for the essay's purpose (33b(2))? Does it draw the essay together or does it seem disconnected and abrupt? (457–58)

Ultimately, this method of inquiry helps the student writers and peer editors develop a more holistic approach than mere editing. With minor modifications like the elimination of the second person references, these questions can be an effective guide for the reviewer. The final question regarding the use of abruptness in context of the conclusion prompts further inquiry into the flow of the entire piece through well-crafted transitions. This checklist supplies students with a basis that can evolve into their individual heuristic.

Following this checklist, *HHH* suggests the writer submit a cover letter, with the draft for review, indicating the topic and purpose, strengths and areas of concerns. This enables those involved in the peer review process to establish a bit of dialog by allowing the writer to explain what is desired and to provide more specific, directed guidance for the reviewer's response. The final peer review sections warn about the varying quality of the feedback and explain the value of providing feedback, since peer collaboration helps both the writer and reviewer. The handbook then includes an edited, student essay with revisions and peer feedback included. As an example of this and the editing process, focusing on sentence level and word choice corrections, the handbook offers students a view of the various stages this essay traversed to evolve into a finished piece included at the end of the chapter. Additional editing and proofreading checklists refer to the other pertinent sections in the handbook.

These, then, seem to be the common revision points included in most handbooks: 1) showing revision as an integral part of the writing process; 2) stressing the need for a clear set up of purpose, audience and voice; 3) venturing beyond surface errors during peer editing sessions; 4) using checklists to guide the reader through various revision processes, important concepts and the related sections for review in the text; and 5) illustrating basic concepts through example student drafts. While these are all prevalent in the majority of handbooks, each offers non-mainstream variations to provide options for writers to master their skill.

While most texts follow similar patterns, some attempt various methods to allow students to take a fresh view of their work. Most indicate that students should distance themselves from their writing for a specified time span, which is rarely possible when the composing effort begins on the due date's eve. More practical approaches to this problem include a method of inquiry from the essence of critical thinking.

In the 2003 edition, *The St. Martin's Handbook* (*SMH*), for example, suggests students reread to ensure conveyance of their meaning, which may be difficult if students feel they have conveyed the point, just as the best of proofreaders subconsciously insert missing words. Another suggestion this textbook offers encourages the reconsideration of the students' rhetorical stance primarily focusing on how an audience perceives them—a good focus for peer editing sessions discussed at this point in conjunction with audience, purpose, thesis, support and organization. In addition to reviewing the introduction and conclusion, *SMH* addresses reconsideration of the work's title.

The text directs students to examine paragraphs closely to ensure compliance with the guidelines for clear relation to the paragraph's topic; sentences for varying length, structure and openings; and wording, tone and format. Even though some consider the inspection within a paragraph to belong to the editing phase in the process, all of these operations precede the ideas about editing and proofreading confined to the next two pages. Yet within these pages can be found good editing suggestions for using the find function within most edit menus of word processing software to locate keywords that highlight errors, such as searching for "however" or "for example" to ensure proper comma usage. This technique may also be helpful in locating redundancies, excessive unintentional passive constructions and use of non-active verbs. Students are encouraged to keep track of the mistakes they find to add to their individual heuristic. Within the editing section emerges a significant insight from *SMH* directing students to create an editing list by reviewing comments from previously graded papers, which adds value to instructors' comments. Some editing list examples are provided in a table format. Using some type of an error log, where students discover, identify and correct their previous work in a list, ultimately they begin to the create an individual editing inventory, which in turn contributes to their heuristic repertoire. This strategy may help eliminate surface errors and reinforce grammar rules that apply to proofreading, but must not stop there. The section concludes with a student's final draft that has gone through several revisions in earlier portions of the textbook with an activity challenging students to find modifications from the editing and proofreading phases.

A distinctive feature of the *HHH* revision chapter is that one of the technical hints addressed is the use of grammar checking software. Students are cautioned to evaluate the suggestions made by various software programs, much as they are warned to questions peer feedback (449). Grammar checking software, however, cannot revise the students' essays. With the assistance of basic artificial intelligence techniques, the software may provide some grammatical assistance and corrective suggestions, which focus on the elimination of passive constructions rather than on the myriad of potential sentence level errors that only a human mind can discover. Unfortunately, too often students feel that because they used a grammar and/or spell checker, they have revised, or fixed, their essays only to provide homonym errors and misspellings like Martian Luther King.

Many handbooks include diagnostic tests, such as Ann Raimes's 2003 version of *Keys for Writers,* as part of their ancillary instructor materials. This type of test, which also appears in most of John Langan's texts like *Sentence Skills with Readings* of 2001, breaks major grammar issues into specific sets of exercises. When students review the exercises answered incorrectly, those grammar rules should be given extra attention. Reviewing the test provides the instructor with a method of doing a relatively quick grammar review, so it does not have to become the focus of the freshman composition course. If common problems persist in students' writing, some further grammar discussion may prove necessary by referring to the appropriate area of the handbook, so the students realize the value of this as a reference tool. Basic grammar skills that some students find difficult to grasp can be better conveyed using more simplified explanations, which can be found in texts like *Basic Grammar and Usage* by Penelope Choy and Dorothy Goldbart Clark; *New Handbook for Basic Writing Skills* by Cora L. Robey, Cheryl K. Jackson, Carolyn M. Melchor and Helen M. Maloney; and *The Least You Should Know about English Writing Skills* by Paige Wilson and Teresa Ferster Glazer.

Keys for Writers provides other useful ancillary materials for both the instructor and the students available through a companion website (college.hmco.com/keys.html), as offered by many handbooks. In addition to the diagnostic and other sample tests, this site provides over sixty transparency masters, several focusing on revision, and PowerPoint slides for classroom presentation of pertinent topics. Both the instructor and student portions of the website allow access to Digital Keys 3.1 Online, a complete online handbook. The student accessible portion of the site also contains several PDF format documents, including another version of a peer-editing sheet, to aid with writing activities. The site encourages student involvement with interactive Web activities. Flashcards are provided to offer "a quick review of important terms and concepts" and some specific vocabulary "flashcards derived from *The American Heritage College Dictionary*" list "100 words you should know." The increase in students' vocabularies from these tools will prove invaluable when searching for the proper wording during the revision process.

In another valuable section of the website, Raimes introduces the handbook through a guided tour of the text. Students must purchase required books for a course. They rely on the instructor to tell them what to do with these tomes, but in the case of handbooks, familiarizing them with the textbook helps them understand its value as a reference tool. Another good example of combining an online source with the handbook can be found in Lynn Troyka's *Quick Access* from 2001. In both of these cases, as well as several others, the entire text being available in a CD or online version provides students a familiar method to search for the information they need. The tools and techniques from these various sources can be extremely effective in editing and proofreading, important phases in the process, but students must be reminded of the revision's larger concerns beyond syntactical efforts.

The Blair Handbook provides didactic inquiry for the students to develop their writing heuristic. After the common process approach to revision, *The Blair Handbook* prompts students to ask a series of questions that focus on rhetorical strategies:

- Why am I writing this paper? (Review the assignment.)

- Do all parts of the paper advance this purpose? (Outline by paragraph and make sure they do.)

- What is my rhetorical strategy: to narrate, explain, interpret, argue, reflect or something else? (Review Chapter 6 ["Assuming Stance"] to fine-tune strategy.)

- Have I stated the paper's theme or thesis clearly? (If not, do so, or have a good reason for not doing so.) . . .

- What does my audience know about this subject? (Avoid repeating elementary information.)

- What does my audience need to know to understand the point of my paper? (Provide full context and background for information your audience is not likely to know.)

- What questions or objections do I anticipate my audience raising? (Try to answer them before they are asked.)

- Which passages sound like me speaking and which don't? (Enjoy those that do; fix those that don't.). (Fulwiler and Hayakawa 276–77)

The questions are followed by parenthetical suggested actions for students to take. Caution should be used, as in the case of the last of these questions, since often one's voice changes when adapting to a formal writing voice rather than a speaking voice. Such contradictions may only serve to confuse writers, rather than instilling the required skill to reflect on their writing. This confusion can be mitigated somewhat if students review the Listen for your voice heading in the next section.

This section suggests using revision strategies under the following headings from the section. After each heading from the text here is a brief summary of what each section contains:

- Establish distance: contains similar suggestions about setting the work aside for a while, but includes distancing by reading aloud.

- Reconsider everything: where the writer is reminded to review even those areas not commented on by others.

- Belief and doubt: introduces a system of check marks and questions marks with two distinct personas, a supportive friend and one "suspicious and skeptical."

- Test your theme and thesis: discusses adapting to a changing thesis.

- Evaluate your evidence: provides specific questions for the evaluation and references to the related chapters.

- Make a paragraph outline: utilizes a pre-writing tool to map the essay.

- Rewrite introductions and conclusions: offers ideas similar to adapting the thesis and insuring these paragraphs function after the essay's modifications.

- Listen for your voice: emphasizes retaining the writer's personality, while in formal papers sounding less conversational and more like a presentation.

- Let go: prompting students not to become enraptured with their words and phrases, thereby remaining open to change.

- Start over: provides some good suggestions for re-visioning a piece like abandoning the first draft, even suggesting an inadvertent loss, such as a lost computer file, may prompt a greater discovery, hence a stronger essay. (Fulwiler and Hayakawa 277–79)

Complimenting these inquires, the text introduces focused revising, which uses the ideas of limiting, adding, switching and transforming. Limiting entails suggestions that students focus their work to short time spans and create a narrowly scoped topic. Although adding appears to conflict with the limiting section, the recommended additions include adding expert voices and details. Students strengthen and clarify with authority and support the focused thesis of the essay. After some typical recommendations are presented for revision, the ideas of switching and transforming are introduced, both of which enable students to view the work from alternate perspectives. With switching, the emphasis moves to altering point of view, tense and sides. Switching sides on an issue truly probes pro versus con arguments. With transforming the initial essay draft is shifted to a different genre—a journal entry, a letter, a documentary, a book with chapters, a magazine article, talk show debate, or any other medium of expression.

Understanding the value of addressing students' increased familiarity with technology, Lester Faigley designs *The Brief Penguin Handbook* in a format that parallels Internet Web pages. Faigley's inclusion of the writing process appears within his first section titled "Composing in the Digital Era," where he incorporates an abundance of visual images, which not only enhance students' involvement and engagement with the handbook's ideas, but also anticipate the use of visual images within students' writing projects. Throughout this handbook Faigley applies his design technique, creating a unique approach that appeals to students who are already comfortable with Web design formats. In fact, significant additions in *The Brief Penguin Handbook* provide instruction for the creation and use of graphics in text, culminating in their value in oral presentations.

Faigley also demonstrates in "Writing for the Web" how the writing process exists not as a chronological linear progression, but one in which the activities of planning, composing and revising meld into an evolution of a Web page. This insight guides instructors to ensure adjustments to instruction corresponding to the students' world, while providing the basics of the writing process. It may no longer be as effective for the instructor to enforce a process which students cannot imagine since it fails to apply to their electronic environment. By showing students how various steps interrelate to achieve the desired purpose, such as utilizing an outline in the revision process, the instructor enters the students' realm.

Revision Focused Textbooks

Several texts focus on the revision process providing instructors and students with insights into how to manage the process. All of the publishers listed in the appendix offer a variety of texts that help instructors and students understand more about how to revise and the importance of revision to achieve a finished piece. Examples included here expand on a text used in another chapter, a book focusing on the student in its approach and an anthology that combines ideas from multiple perspectives.

As Carol Trupiano elucidates in the "Best Practices" chapter, Donald M. Murray's 2004 edition of *The Craft of Revision* approaches the entire writing process, the initial phases well covered by the first two chapters, as a continual effort to revise until reaching his final chapter "The Craft of Letting Go." Following "Reading for Revising," which clarifies the concept and purpose of peer review, Murray's chapters focus on specific areas to revise: with focus, with genre, with structure, with documentation. Students also must concentrate on essay development, including sensitivity to how it sounds and maintaining clarity for the audience. While several of these areas appear obvious, Murray's presentation makes the ideas very accessible to the students.

As an example of demonstrating value in the world after college, Murray includes a section in his chapter "Rewrite with Focus" concentrating on the writer's voice within a business context entitled "How do I Make the Boss's Idea My Own?" (57–58). Murray's chapter "Rewrite with Genre" directs students to establish the correct format for their writing based on their purpose and audience, not restricting the options to standard rhetorical modes, but including forms the students will encounter like grant proposals and memos (85). The chapter "Rewrite by Ear" further emphasizes the importance of voice to help students distinguish and use different voices. To supplement Murray's efforts to make these concepts clear in his own terminology, he includes interviews and case studies of professional and student writers at the end of most chapters to emphasize his points.

Richard A. Lanham's approach in *Revising Prose* captures his readers' attention by acknowledging that evaluation criteria are rarely explained or emphasized in previous instruction. He comprehends the problems that plague first year college writers. Initially Lanham provides practical exercises to first understand revision, then the differing rhetorical situations, and finally the reason revision is important to the emerging writer, bringing relevance to what many instructors preach with an application students can grasp.

Lanham's first chapter focuses on one of the most important ideas enhancing the active nature of writing. Techniques like eliminating excessive prepositional phrases and the conjugations of to be, or in essence, not to be, combine structure with style, a major concern of revision. He ensures in the next few chapters that students have a clear understanding of revision. Lanham clarifies the different writing situations they'll experience with the chapters "The Official Style" and "The School Style." Perhaps the most important, his final chapter "Why Bother?" guides students through the significance this skill has for their lives. With such an approachable format that engages his audience, Lanham offers not only a guide, but also a model that can only be surpassed by several minds collaborating.

Wendy Bishop edited the anthology *Acts of Revision* offering several unique perspectives on revision techniques too, from Brock Dethier's "Revising Attitudes," involving how writers often approach revision with resistance revision, to Jay Szczepanski's "Why Not Hypertext? Converting the Old, Interpreting the New, Revising the Rest," regarding composing and revising multimedia. The articles are presented, of course, not in a linear progression, since revision is far from a linear process. The premise Bishop uses to unify the work presents authors with a strong understanding of revision's value. Bishop envisions an audience that has accepted this process as writers and in her compilation provides a variety of approaches to re-visioning their work. In her introduction, she encourages writers to review these ideas, accept those with others they encounter that work well for their writing style and reject those that cannot be applied.

READERS

Bishop also offers a unique reader, *On Writing: a process reader.* While some readers still attempt to pigeonhole essays into the nine rhetorical modes (narration, description, definition, exemplification, division/classification, comparison/contrast, process analysis, causal analysis, and argumentation), Bishop has associated various steps that writers encounter with readings that exemplify the issues she presents, such as "Writers and Ways of Writing" and "Language Matters." Stephen Reid in *Purpose and Process: A Reader for Writers* takes a similar approach including a thematic table of contents. This idea of a thematic approach to readers offers instructors the ability to deal with issues students encounter. Lisa Ede's *Work in Progress,* which has evolved considerably from preceding editions in the 2004 version, offers another excellent example of combining a reader, primarily of student examples, and the ideas needed to understand academic requirements.

While revision tends to be presented as a phase in a consecutive process, revision remains a recursive process that evolves over not only several drafts of an essay, but from all the writing students produce. Instructors need to aid students in the creation of an individual heuristic to perform their own holistic evaluation of what is written. While textbooks, especially handbooks, aid in this effort, the stock questions provided may not be applicable to all students. Instructors need to balance the general suggestions that all students need with the individualized areas of improvement that students require. With the range of textbooks available, instructors may need to break away from the required text to find what works for individual students. Since instructors encourage distinct voices rather than a formulaic approach, students need heuristics based on what works for them.

The approach of revision as a mere phase in a process limits the potential of revision and reduces it to editing and proofreading. Students need more. Instructors provide this by selecting effective textbooks and using the information available in these resources to adapt to the specific needs of their students. Focused texts can help achieve and hone first year college writers' skills, while good texts with readings can aid in establishing connections to pertinent issues or presenting valuable knowledge and tools. Students must be able to take a multifaceted approach to their writing by moving from a checklist to a broader view of re-vision. Limitations created by confining revision to one phase of a process could cause students to miss the concept that revision occurs from the initial idea to the final product and must be performed regardless of the rhetorical situation, whether in an academic or career situation. All of the publishers listed in the appendix provide excellent options allowing instructors to exercise academic freedom to adapt the course focus to what works well with the student population; however, readers rarely function well without a handbook as at least a reference tool, which instructors need to incorporate in the students' revision activities.

Appendix: A Listing of Books from Major Composition Publishers

Allyn & Bacon: *The Little, Brown Handbook*, 9th Edition by H. Ramsey Fowler and Jane Aaron; *The Scribner Handbook for Writers*, 4th Edition by Robert DiYanni and Pat C. Hoy; *The Allyn & Bacon Handbook*, 5th Edition by Leonard J. Rosen and Laurence Behrens; *The Longman Handbook for Writers and Readers*, 3rd Edition by Chris M. Anson and Robert A. Schwegler; *The Penguin Handbook* by Lester Faigley; *The New Century Handbook*, 2nd Edition by Christine Hult and Thomas Huckin.

Bedford/St. Martin's: *A Writer's Reference*, 5th Edition by Diana Hacker; *The St. Martin's Handbook*, 5th Edition by Andrea A. Lunsford; *A Writer's Guidebook* by Rise B. Axelrod and Charles Cooper; *The Bedford Handbook*, 6th Edition by Diana Hacker; *The Everyday Writer*, 2nd Edition by Andrea A. Lunsford.

Houghton Mifflin: *Keys for Writers: A Brief Handbook*, 4th Edition by Ann Raimes; *Writing Skills Handbook*, 5th Edition by Charles Bazerman and Harvey S. Wiener; *The Beacon Handbook and Desk Reference*, 6th Edition by Robert Perrin; *Practical English Handbook*, 11th Edition by Floyd Watkins, William Dillingham and John Hiers; *Writers INC* by Patrick

Sebranek, Verne Meyer and Dave Kemper; *Essential English Handbook* by James Kirkland and Collett B. Dilworth.

McGraw-Hill: *The Pocket Reference for Writers* by Michael Keene and Katherine H. Adams; *Writing From A to Z*, 4th Edition by Sally Barr Ebest, Louis Gerald Alred, Charles T. Brusaw and Walter E. Oliu; *Sentence Skills with Readings*, 2nd Edition by John Langan; *A Writer's Resource* by Elaine Maimon and Janice Peritz; *Rules of Thumb*, 5th Edition by Jay Silverman, Elaine Hughes and Diana Roberts Wienbroer; *Easy Access*, 3rd Edition by Michael Keene and Katherine H. Adams; *The Short Handbook for Writers*, 2nd Edition by Gerald J. Schiffhorst and Donald Pharr; *The McGraw-Hill College Handbook*, 4th Edition by Richard Marius and Harvey S. Wiener; *The Borzoi Handbook for Writers*, 3rd Edition by Frederick Crews, Sandra Schor and Michael Hennessey; *The Random House Handbook*, 6th Edition by Frederick Crews; *The Writer's Handbook*, 2nd Edition by Elizabeth McMahon and Susan Day.

Prentice Hall: *Prentice Hall Guide for College Writers*, 6th Edition by Stephen P. Reid; *Blair Handbook*, 4th Edition by Toby Fulwiler and Alan Hayakawa; *The Scott, Foresman Handbook*, 6th Edition by Maxine Hairston, John Ruszkiewicz and Christy Friend; *Simon & Schuster Handbook*, 6th Edition by Lynn Quitman Troyka; *The Contemporary Writer*, by Edna M. Troiano and Julia Draus Scott; *Prentice Hall Handbook for Writers*, 12th Edition by Melinda Kramer, Glen Leggett and C. David Mead; *Brief Handbook for Writers*, 3rd Edition by James F. Howell and Dean Memering; *Quick Access*, 4th Edition by Lynn Quitman Troyka.

Thomson: *Hodges' Harbrace Handbook*, 15th Edition by Cheryl Glenn, Robert K. Miller, Suzanne Strobeck Webb and Loretta Gray; *The Writer's Harbrace Handbook*, 2nd Edition by Cheryl Glenn, Robert K. Miller, Suzanne Strobeck Webb and Loretta Gray; *The Brief Handbook*, 4th Edition by Laurie G. Kirszner and Stephen R. Mandell; *The Holt Handbook*, 6th Edition by Laurie G. Kirszner and Stephen R. Mandell.

7 Revising with Word Processing/ Technology/Document Design

Douglas Eyman and Colleen Reilly

Innovations in technology have historically provoked profound changes in literacy acquisition and expression. From the development of the written alphabet to the printing press, changes in technology affect the way we think, write, and communicate and, by extension, the way we teach written communication. The personal computer as writing tool is now as ubiquitous as the printed page, and like advances in writing technology before it, the computer has affected the process of writing at every stage, from invention, through revision, to delivery. This chapter begins with a brief history of computers and revision and then examines the potential impact on revision practices and strategies of both computer technologies and the recent expansion of composition to include multimodal processes and productions. Throughout the chapter, we provide concrete suggestions for using available computer technologies to encourage substantive revision, while demonstrating the need for informed and critical instruction in concert with the use of technologies to affect changes in students' perspectives on and employment of revision in their writing processes.

SCHOLARSHIP ABOUT COMPUTER APPLICATIONS AND REVISION

Since the introduction of computers into writing classrooms, scholars have questioned whether computer applications positively affect students' writing and writing processes. Some of the issues raised include the degree to which computer applications prompt students to write more and engage in substantive revision given that these applications, such as word processing software, seem to make revision easier. One of the first major studies of word processing and revision was Colette Diaute's 1983 "The Computer as Stylus and Audience," which argued that student writers would revise more easily and more quickly than they would with traditional pen and paper writing technologies; similar studies stressed the inherent freedom and flexibility of composing on-screen as important factors in revision practices (Bean; Marcus; Sudol). However, subsequent work suggested that student writers (as opposed to experienced writers) performed fewer revision activities on-screen than they would have on paper (Collier; Harris,1985; Hawisher; Lutz). It has been suggested that the differences are a function of access and experience with composing on the computer (Tone and Winston; Owston, Murphy, and Wideman)—thus studies done in the 1980s and 90s may not be as reliable as similar studies that have been published more recently, which reflect the current situation regarding student access and experience. A 2003 meta-analysis of research about the effects of word processing on student writing indicated that all of the studies that were published between 1992 and 2002 found that students using computers did make more changes to their writing than did students using pencil or pen and paper (Cook, Goldberg and Russell 4).

One strain of recent research indicates that revising on the computer screen with word processing applications can impede revision. Several studies (Crafton; Hill, Wallace and Haas; Klonoski; Tone and Winchester; Yagelski) have noted that students' reliance on spell check and grammar check applications often lead to a focus on surface error correction at the expense of substantive revision. Additionally, Crafton notes that the user-friendly and transparent appearance of the interface blocks critical analysis of how it determines/controls the writing process: "User-friendly point-and-click software may actually disguise the ways the medium acts as a metaphor. We cannot see how technology conditions the expression or how it operates as a model, a cognitive structure, that organizes our thinking" (319). Furthermore, Crafton argues that for basic writers in particular, using computer technologies for writing adds an additional layer of complexity to the already complicated process of composition. Hill, Wallace and Haas agree that revising on the screen encourages localized, sentence level rather than global revision, but attribute this as much to inadequate task definition of revision as to the tools used to accomplish it (105; see also Yagelski).

Another potential barrier to revision is the small window provided by the space on the screen: Daniel Kies suggests to his students that the "screen is just too small a canvas for us to get a sense of our draft as a whole. So printing a draft, often and regularly, is the only way to truly see the work holistically. A printout will allow us to better see the connections between the major parts of our work and to judge the work's unity and coherence."

While the aforementioned research certainly has merit and requires our attention, we agree most strongly with the perspective that emphasizes the importance of thoughtful, conscious, and critical instruction in assisting students to use computers and computer applications to foster global and substantive revision. For example, in a study of 12th grade writers that found students focusing on surface error, Yagelski noted that "the students' revision choices were strongly influenced by the teacher's retaining all authority for determining what constitutes 'good' writing and by her emphasizing correctness as its most important criterion" (216). Other studies have shown that instructor feedback and writing prompts have a greater effect on the depth of revision than the technology employed (Reynolds and Bonk; Tuzi). In the remainder of this piece, we demonstrate how in combination with thoughtful and critical instruction that encourages reflection, writing teachers can use a range of computer applications from word processors to Web design applications to help students develop more substantive revision processes and improve their writing.

Basic Computer Applications and Revision Strategies

In a study of the effects of oral and online discussion and its impact on revision, Beth Hewett notes that "revision changes revealed different qualities when developed in different environments, suggesting that medium shapes revision" (217). We would further suggest that the tools available in a given medium offer particular affordances for revision practices; in this section, we address the different practices facilitated by the tools that are available in word processing programs that are widely available in most computer classrooms and campus computer labs. We demonstrate how thoughtful instruction in the use of these basic tools can facilitate the types of revision we would like to encourage. Some of the examples specifically reference features of Microsoft Word ™; however, most of the tools discussed below are available in most of the text processing programs that students are currently using, including Corel WordPerfect™ and open-source applications such as OpenOffice.

Cut and Paste

One of the key features of word-processing applications is the ability to select text of any length (word, sentence, paragraph, page), remove it from its current location in a document, and place it in another location. Many early adopters of word-processing applications in writing classes pointed to this feature as an indicator of the possibilities for deep revision as opposed to surface revision because the actual work of moving text had become both simple and immediate. Simple revision exercises can be accomplished using only this basic feature. For instance, Nick Carbone suggests the following exercise for emphasizing the possibilities of deep revision using cut-and-paste: students can cut the concluding paragraph from a draft, copy it, put it in a new window, and then write a new draft with that final paragraph serving as the first. If the student's final paragraph merely repeats what is their current first paragraph, (an instance that highlights the need for revision of the introduction or conclusion or both), the same exercise can be performed using a paragraph from the middle of the draft. This exercise encourages students to think in terms of global revision practices and helps them to see the possibilities of large-scale revision—in this case, cut-and-paste is a practice not simply for moving smaller elements within a text, but is a vehicle for radical revision involving the composition of a new but related text. Furthermore, this exercise, particularly if they draw on text from the first draft to compose the second, can demonstrate to students how the process of writing can advance their thinking on a topic by showing them that if they begin the new paper at their conclusion, which represents the culmination of their thought process, they may produce a text with more depth and complexity, having worked out some of the issues through the initial writing process.

Font Formatting

Font formatting is another basic component of all word-processing applications, but it can be used to encourage students to see the elements of their writing style via visual markers (a practice that has been shown to work particularly well with basic and ESL writers). An instructor can ask students to change active verbs to boldface, highlight passive constructions in italics, use larger fonts for descriptive words, underline the thesis statement, or select particular font colors for topic sentences in each paragraph. This kind of visual marking presents a striking image of the text and can show the writer elements that may be overused or missing. Obviously, this sort of exercise requires instruction in identifying these constructions within a text, which may also help students gain control of their prose by providing them with the tools needed to analyze and discuss it.

Textual Analysis Tools

Most word-processing programs offer automated tools that attempt to analyze and provide data about a text's organization, style, grammar and spelling. While these tools can be used to support revision strategies, they require a great deal of instruction and scaffolding in order to be used effectively. Heilker notes that students often interpret suggestions from these automated tools, such as the grammar checker, as having a degree of authority equal to that of a human instructor, resulting in a displacement of the writer-audience relationship to a writer-computer relationship in the rhetorical situation (65). Although most of these automated analysis tools emphasize sentence-level constructions, Microsoft Word also provides an AutoSummarize tool that can be helpful when considering revisions of a text's organization: the application examines the document, selects topic and thesis statements, and may either highlight those elements within the document, place the summary in a new document, or place an "executive summary" at the beginning of the current document. The summaries and outlines produced by this tool can help students to visualize the organization of their text and show them how it may potentially be viewed by an outside observer.

Many word-processing applications will also produce simple statistics about the current document (often incorporated into the grammar-checking feature). The statistics include counts of the numbers of words, sentences, and paragraphs, as well as the average number of words in sentences and sentences in paragraphs. Microsoft Word also provides the percentage of sentences that are in the passive voice. Checking these statistics can be a useful revision tool if employed critically: if students tend to write short, choppy sentences (or long, wordy sentences) the tool helps them to note the average number of words per sentence in their documents. Similarly, a student can check the percentage of passive sentences in the document in order to assess whether or not they unknowingly and unconsciously tend to use passive constructions. Like grammar and spell checking components (which tend to emphasize surface-error correction), this and other automated analysis tools should be used along with instruction and reflection concerning the writing practices and values that they support. For example, the passive voice can be used very effectively and strategically to downplay agency and avoid placing blame. Students should be asked to discuss why the passive voice is flagged as an error by the software, examine the types of writing that the absence of the passive voice encourages, note rhetorical situations in which it is or is not the most appropriate choice.

Track Changes

The Track Changes feature in Microsoft Word is accessible from the Reviewing toolbar (View > Toolbars > Reviewing). Accessible from the Reviewing toolbar are several options: users can turn Track Changes on or off, choose which changes to show, move through changes to reject or accept them, and add balloon comments. With the Track Changes feature enabled, the writer or reviewer can insert recommendations directly into a text (which is more intrusive than using the commenting feature, but which allows an instructor to make suggestions for revision so that the student can see a model of how that instructor expects him or her to approach the process of revision). Accept or Reject Changes allows the writer to accept a correction (thus making it part of the revised document) or to reject a suggestion. This is particularly useful when using the Track Changes feature as part of a peer-review or collaboration process. From the Tools menu, user can Compare and Merge Documents, which allows the student and/or instructor to quickly see the changes that have been made between revisions while keeping discrete copies of the work performed thus far intact; this could be useful for developing and grading portfolios in which success is measured to some degree in terms of the types and depth of revisions completed. Such comparisons provide a striking visual representation of the alterations made to a text.

The Track Changes feature in Microsoft Word can be used to help students to see and reflect upon their revision process and prompt them to move from less to more substantive, global revision. In order for the results of this feature to be useful, however, students need to be taught to use it consistently and correctly, otherwise the results will be meaningless and inaccurate. Implementation of the Track Changes feature in the writing process requires a strong schedule of due dates during the drafting and then revision process, clear instructions for students to follow (see Appendix A), and instructor oversight. As with all technologies, for this feature to encourage students to reflect on and alter their revision processes, its use must become a natural part of the writing process, be consistently required, and be commented upon constructively for it to make a difference.

In composition classes, students can be asked to use the Track Changes feature at various points in the writing process, from invention to the revision of drafts. During the revision process, it may be best to designate a specific date for the end of drafting and the start of revision, although this point may be largely artificial. Students can turn on the Track Changes feature as of this date and the alterations that they make to their texts in each subsequent composing session, however brief, will be recorded. The highlighted changes can then be used to help students become aware of the types of revisions they make, use that awareness to alter their processes and explore revision on more than one level, and help them to receive comments from their instructors regarding the types of revision in which they engage. The first time students track their changes, they may be surprised to learn that most of their revisions are sentence level and localized. This recognition—again resulting from visual cues—can prompt some students to attempt to engage in more global and perhaps significant revisions, such as adding and deleting content and restructuring across sections. The use of this feature is even more significant if students are asked to reflect on their experiences and brainstorm changes that they might make to their revision practices in light of what they observe. Additionally, instructor feedback on the drafts showing the revisions helps to reinforce the importance of focusing on revision and making the process as productive and substantive as possible.

Moreover, students can be taught to use the Track Changes feature to assist in the development and revision of collaborative projects. When working on a text collaboratively, each student can add their changes in a particular color using the Track Changes feature, thus highlighting the contributions of each group member. This can be helpful in encouraging equal participation and differentiating various versions of the text from one another. Such use of this feature requires the instructor to help students coordinate the addition of changes and the acceptance or rejection of the additions made by their peers. Students need to be taught to both add and then negotiate the changes made by others when composing and revising texts. Without establishing a clear and systematic process for incorporating this feature into their writing process, its use can cause more confusion and simply introduce more work into the collaborative writing process.

Highlighting and Commenting

Both highlighting and commenting can also be helpful in the revision of collaborative projects and in the process of peer review. Word's highlighting tool allows a student or peer-editor to accent text in a range of colors, creating a system in which different colors indicate various types of content, grammar, and spelling errors. Because revision is a recursive process that occurs within all of the stages of drafting (particularly when that drafting is completed via a word-processing application), highlighting can also be very useful for marking places in a text that may need to be revisited or reassessed during the composing process. For instance, in the initial draft of this chapter, this section contained a sentence fragment that might have been left incomplete had it not been highlighted during the drafting process. Highlighting can be very useful in the peer-review process, as the writer can visually mark the passages or elements that he or she would most like feedback on. Additionally, in creating a collaborative text, peers can highlight the sections of a draft that are unclear or need attention, and these sections can receive more attention during group writing sessions.

The commenting feature can also be useful in peer review, collaborative writing, and receiving comments from an instructor. There are two kinds of commenting tools available in most word-processing applications: in-text commenting (using a different font color for each commentator), and annotations that appear in the margins or as pop-ups and are indicated by highlighting that appears on a word or phrase. The annotations feature is less intrusive and using that type of comment mitigates the feeling of violence done to a student text, particularly since the annotations—even if they appear in the margins—can be hidden with the click of a mouse on the appropriate menu selection. If the student and instructor have access to sound capabilities it is possible to also add audio commentary to a draft, but the file size expands very rapidly with the addition of audio comments.

When working collaboratively, rather than making changes directly in the text, students can make suggestions for changes or ask for clarifications by adding annotations using the comment feature. Additionally, commenting can be used in conjunction with the Track Changes feature to explain why particular changes were made or to request that peers examine a particular section of the revised text carefully and approve it. In revising this chapter, we used both Track Changes and commenting to communicate about the alterations that each of us made to the initial draft; these features proved indispensable to our long-distance writing process.

OTHER APPLICATIONS FOR PEER REVIEW

Besides using the features of word processors discussed above, peer review, an important part of the revision process in many writing classes, can also be facilitated by the use any number of online peer review applications (Hewett; Tuzi). Online peer review allows students to continue working with peers and mentors outside of the classroom and the comments of peers can be easily recorded and accessed by instructors and by the class as a whole so that the peer review process can be examined, assessed, and improved.

In the traditional classroom, peer review typically involves exchanging papers, commenting on drafts, and meeting to exchange direct feedback and engage in talk-aloud protocols. Using network technologies allows us to teach students new modes of collaboration that not only streamline the peer-review process, but also offer private partnerships (using email), semi-public group work (using course management systems or discussion boards available only to the group or class), or a completely public process (using Web sites).

Electronic peer-review can be used both inside and outside the classroom: students can work together in person on a document on one terminal and revise collaboratively or switch seats in a computer classroom, thus allowing peers to work directly with each other's drafts. Nick Carbone advocates collaborative revision as a form of electronic review:

> Have students copy just the first and last paragraphs from an essay into a new file. Have them swap files and fill in a classmate's essay—in other words, based on the first and last paragraph, what do they think the argument is and what will the essay say? Or, have them post their first and last paragraphs in a discussion area, and then they can talk online with one another about what they expect to see and why (n.p.).

Online peer-response may take the form of comments on drafts, responses to drafts, or discussions about the writing process or about specific texts. Students can exchange documents in class for a close reading, have readers email comments to writers, and then continue the discussion or talk-aloud reviews begun in class on a group discussion list, where students can post work and receive feedback from multiple peers. Commenting on sentence level issues proves to be more difficult if the text is posted online and cannot be written on. Thus, Web-based discussion lists privilege a different kind of peer critique and students can be prompted answer questions about the organization and the validity of the ideas expressed in their peers' texts rather than the surface errors that they may see.

Online, Web-based peer review applications also provide a space where each student in the class can upload their text and review detailed comments from one or more members of the class. Generally, such applications allow instructors to develop a list of questions for students to answer about the drafts of their peers; the answers to these questions are posted on the webspace as well and can be viewed by all students in the course. Additionally, most applications also allow for students to make specific comments about the content, style, or conventions of particular paragraphs in the posted drafts and these comments are attached to those places in the text. While posting drafts and peer comments on the Web poses privacy issues that should be discussed, the practice facilitates class discussion of peer review as a practice and allows instructors to easily review and comment on the process and intervene as needed. Additionally, the comments of multiple peers can be accessed by students both in class and wherever they have access to the Web. Of course, the use of such applications proves to be most beneficial if accompanied by class discussions on how to write constructive comments and maximize the features of the online application and how to respond to and distill the comments of multiple peers and translate their suggestions into revisions.

Remediation, Redesign, and Revision

Teaching new media composition provides other opportunities to use computer technologies in ways that help students view and apply revision strategies that result in substantive changes in both the form and content of their texts. In the most basic sense of the word, remediation (as defined by Bolter and Grusin, 28) of print texts, such as essays and research papers, into other media has the potential to encourage deep revision by prompting students to rethink the purposes, audiences, and structures of their original texts. When composing a traditional course paper, students may be told to imagine specific audiences and/or purposes for their writing, but those imagined audiences are largely superficial; the instructor is often perceived as the final, primary audience. Additionally, as noted above, students have difficulty separating revision and editing and often make only superficial changes even after being taught how to revise. However, introducing students to new communication media accompanied by new environments and contexts for their writing may alter the situation sufficiently to require students to rethink their content and formatting choices and make significant changes or risk composing texts that are inappropriate for new contexts.

One way to use technologies to prompt revision is to have students remediate print texts by asking them to create a presentation supported by PowerPoint slides based on a paper they have written; in order to complete this activity, their audiences, purposes, and substance of their material must change based on the new context for their work. A change in media from largely textual to visual/textual/oral requires altering and adding to the information. Writing a presentation of material for a classroom audience, for example, requires students to consider the aspects of their information that would be most understandable and interesting to their peers. Additionally, they may have to define terms and concepts that they did not feel they had to define for their instructor. PowerPoint is also an interesting technology to use when revising the structure and organization of a text. PowerPoint encourages a linear, hierarchical structure that may help students see the ways that their own texts do not fit this pattern and also may reveal to them the limitations of such an organizational pattern, demonstrating that organization as well as content and other aspects of the text should be consciously chosen and are open to revision. Finally, because PowerPoint is a visual medium, students can be prompted to do more research to find visual elements, including a layout and design as well as graphics, to supplement their textual information. This act of extending research into the revision process is commonly overlooked when revising academic print texts. While looking for supplementary visuals to create presentations, students may find other information that may add a new dimension or element to their previous texts, prompting them to view the subject or issue in a new light. This fresh look at their subject matter resulting from the additional research and refocusing of the print text for a presentation format can help students to see the usefulness of other types of revising activities. Remediation, if done thoughtfully, requires students to dismantle and reassemble texts with a new focus and for a new audience, creating a space where substantive revision may occur.

Other media such as MOOs, websites, and digital video can also be employed to prompt a reconsideration of revision and help students to see the limitations of their typical print-based composing processes. Thus remediation can promote revisioning not only the texts but the process by which composition is done. When developing a website, for instance, students may focus on the layout and visual design features separately from the content, acknowledging the rhetorical aspects of design and the importance of considering the effects of design elements on textual arguments. In contrast, in a print piece, content is all and format is often not considered or only thought of minimally in order to conform with instructor-imposed standards of layout or style largely because such linear academic texts are presented "as though there is nothing visually rhetorical in them" (Wysocki 182). Furthermore, the content included on a website needs to be shaped in order to be suitable for online reading, easy navigation, and visual appeal. Because websites have links to other related sites, in order to create an effective site, students need to do research online to find other texts to which theirs can be connected. Such research and linking helps students to become more aware of the context, at least online, in which their texts are located, which may help them to better situate their arguments and position them vis-à-vis those of others.

In order for students to benefit from remediating print texts in other media and prompt a long term intervention in their composition processes, they need to be asked to reflect on their remediated texts and their development processes and locate points of departure from their typical workflow when writing with new media. As with other technologies employed in writing, simply using them is insufficient; the students have to become conscious and critical users through group discussion and individual reflection. Asking students to reshape texts for other media can highlight the contextual nature of the essay and other unquestioned hegemonic modes of writing ubiquitous in the academy. Analyzing what must be added, deleted, and reshaped to make the academic essay appropriate for other media dominant in other contexts, such as workplaces, shows the situational aspects of the essay while revealing its limitations as a genre as well as the values it reflects, which are often unexamined (Wysocki 182). In a reflective piece, which could be structured as an essay, website, video or even audio text, students can be asked to discuss the changes that they needed to make to their print piece for the new medium and examine the success or failure of those changes and of the new environment to convey their ideas, information, and arguments. Students can be asked to discuss in detail the changes that they made to the content and format of the piece, other changes that they now see they should have made, and the degree to which their remediation is successful in terms of offering a more complete, interesting, or effective representation of their ideas.

Conclusion

Our discussion highlights many ways that computer technologies can be used to help students to rethink their revision practices and develop more substantive strategies for future revisions. As we demonstrate above, many computer technologies exist that can prove useful for revision. Even simple applications, such as word processing programs, contain features with the potential to improve and facilitate individual and collaborative revisions. Throughout our discussion, however, we have highlighted the idea that the use of technologies is insufficient for helping students see and alter their composition practices. Instruction and conscious reflection on the part of teachers and students are needed to make any technology—whether it is paper and scissors or the latest peer review application—a productive means for helping students to revise their work more globally and substantively.

Appendix: Directions for Using the Track Changes Tool in Microsoft Word

When you revise your papers/work for our class, please track the changes that you make for the following reasons:

- To allow you to reflect on your revision process
- To help you to make changes to and improve your revision process
- To allow me to view and make suggestions concerning your revision process

After you complete a draft of a paper, you should turn the Track Changes feature on so that all the changes that you make to the paper are visible. When you submit the paper, submit it with the changes still visible. Do not erase or alter them.

Using the Track Changes Tool

1. Open your draft in Word
2. From under the Tools menu, select Track changes
3. Start making changes to your document. The changes you make will be recorded in the text on the screen.
4. When you are done making changes, save the document and close it as usual. Repeat this process each time you make revisions to the initial draft of your text. Each time that you open your document, the changes from the previous work session will still be visible.

When you turn in your document, submit the version with all the changes in it. I can then view the document with and without the changes.

Customizing the Look of Your Changes

If you want your changes to appear in a different color or format, follow these instructions for customizing them.

1. Open your document in Word

2. From under the Tools menu, select Options and then Track Changes

4. Change the mark and color for each type of change that you want to alter.

5. Click OK. All subsequent changes will conform to your selections.

8 Professional Writers and Revision

Alice Horning

A key feature of professional writers' working strategies for writing that distinguishes them from student or novice writers is their approach to revision. No professional writer would ever consider submitting for publication or professional review a piece of writing that had not been thoroughly revised. The professional writers studied in *Revision Revisited,* none of whom had "writer" in their job titles, had no difficulty with the idea of someone wanting to study their revision practices. Student writers often do little if any revision, and will resist revision even if they may improve their writing and their grades by revising successfully, especially since it is clear that revising touches on every part of the writing process (Sudol ix). Students' attitudes toward revision arise from the general approach to teaching followed in many writing classes in college, a view of revising that focuses too much on the skills needed to revise and too little on the underlying awarenesses which inform effective revision. Students' and teachers' views of revising need significant updating as current research is revealing more and more about how writers execute successful revisions of texts. The distinction between awareness and skill in revision will be reviewed here first, summarizing the findings from my research for *Revision Revisited*. Then, two case studies with writers whose work appears in other parts of the book will be presented. The data reflect the importance of awarenesses in effective revising and suggest specific pedagogical strategies for the teaching of writing.

Awarenesses and Skills: A Summary

The research findings in *Revision Revisited* draw on the nine case studies done for that report. The subjects were all practicing professionals in a variety of fields; none had "writer" as a job title, but all were in professions that entail extensive writing: two academics, four workplace writers including a public relations person, an editor, and two attorneys, and three members of the clergy. Each subject answered questions about writing and revising strategies generally and about the goals of the revision under study, and then revised a document drafted previously. During the revision, each subject completed a think-aloud protocol (Smagorinsky 3–19), explaining the changes being made. After the observation, I received the subjects' drafts produced in the session along with the draft they had created prior to the session. I produced a written account of the session which each subject also read. If additional drafts of the document were produced later, the subject also gave me those. The cases are presented in full detail in the book.

Professionals' Awareness

The findings show, first, that professional writers have three particular kinds of awareness of themselves as writers: metarhetorical awareness, metastrategic awareness and metalinguistic awareness. Metarhetorical awareness refers to writers' knowledge of themselves as writers. One of my first subjects described her process by saying "I always do this and change it later," indicating that she was aware of a certain way of beginning. Professional writers know the strategies they use and how they work. Even those strategies that are ultimately unproductive in terms of generating a final document are ones they know they have available for use. By contrast, novice writers may or may not be aware of their strategies or may not have any particular strategies other than to simply start writing, or perhaps do some outlining or brain storming if required by a teacher.

For professionals, metastrategic awareness arises from their knowledge of themselves as people, especially in terms of personality type, and the implications of this self-awareness for their approaches to writing. In one of my mini-case studies, the subject was a strong introvert who would not normally consult with others for help with writing. However, when she was in difficulty with a writing task, she sought out counsel from others as she worked on the document she was producing. Metastrategic awareness is helpful in just this way: writers know when they are in trouble and know how to shift to a different, typically non-preferred approach, to solve a writing problem or create a stronger draft. Novice writers seldom have sufficient strategies available to make such a shift possible.

A third awareness that professional writers have is specific knowledge about language, metalinguistic awareness. The professionals I studied were all fully familiar with and aware of the features of their written language that needed attention in their drafts. They would comment on the phonological features of a sentence ("too many puhs" said one, referring to a string of words starting with "p"), structural issues ("here's a sentence that needs help" said another), or issues of tone or formality or use of a particular word (leading one to stop work to consult a thesaurus). Professional writers' revision is distinctive in this way. They know about language, know what they know and what they don't, and pay attention to language *per se* as they revise. Novice writers do not have enough metalinguistic awareness to attend to language issues in revision unless teachers point out errors or problems in word choice or usage, sentence structure and related matters.

Professionals' Skills

In addition to their level of awareness, professional writers also have four skills useful to revising: skills in the use of collaboration, in genre, in audience and context, and in using tools effectively to rework a text. These skills are ones that do get some attention in the teaching of writing in college classrooms, though not all get as much attention as they could and should. With respect to collaboration, for example, professional writers use collaboration in a way different from the kind of work students are asked to do in a writing course. Professional writers generally ask other content-area experts for substantive commentary on their writing.

In my work on *Revision Revisited,* for instance, the full manuscript was read by another expert in Rhetoric and Composition Studies and came back to me with detailed comments on nearly every page of the manuscript as well as four pages of more global discussion of the overall organization and development of my argument. I will be eternally grateful to this very thorough and careful reader, since his comments surely helped me write a much better book. My subjects often revised in response to comments from experts; the medical writer was constantly reworking his texts in response to expert readings from doctors and university medical researchers. Hardly any professional writer asks for or gets feedback on thesis, comma usage or the level of detail in the summary. And while teachers will correctly say that learning to write is different than being a professional writer, the more we can move student/novice writers in the direction of professionals, the stronger their writing and revising will be.

A second skill professional writers have lies in their ability to use the particular genres of their writing to good effect. A knowledge of genre led one writer I studied to rethink the document she was writing, changing its modality from email to letter to formal memo. Other professionals I studied were preparing encyclopedia or reference book materials for non-specialist audiences, requiring a particular approach to both content and form. The matter of genre is one that gets some attention in teaching writing, particularly beyond the level of first-year composition. Students may be asked to compose letters or editorials, case studies or arguments that will be sent to real audiences. One of the most engaging lessons I have seen in a classroom entailed the use of Lewis Carroll's poem "Jabberwocky," asking students to rewrite the poem as a news report. This kind of work helps students develop skill with the use of different genres in ways similar to those professional writers exploit productively in writing.

Another skill of professional writers that most writing teachers address successfully in class involves the understanding and use of texts and their contexts. This skill is central, certainly, to research writing, where teachers do a lot of work with college writers. To use a source to support an argument, student writers must understand the source and where it came from, i.e. its context. Students get plenty of opportunities to develop this skill and plenty of practice using it in research papers and reports of various kinds that are a standard feature of many college classes from first-year composition to upper-level courses in all disciplines.

A different manifestation of the skill of text and context is the issue of audience, another area typically addressed carefully in college writing courses. Professional writers work in the context in which they write and so are keenly aware of its impact on their writing and revising. Their sensitivity is important to their revision: one of my academics noted in her revision some changes based on the fact that her text was a paper to be presented at an academic meeting, likely to be attended by both graduate students and other professionals in her field. The Episcopal priest juxtaposed an Old Testament and a New Testament passage in a revealing way, but noted in her revision that this juxtaposition required full explication in her sermon. There are many such examples for both novice and professional writers.

The last of the skills professional writers have is the ability to use a toolbox for writing, both on the computer and off of it. Here again, teachers spend plenty of time in class, in workshops, in conferences with students talking about the toolbox skills. Using spell check, grammar check and other computer functions to produce stronger writing is fundamental among professional writers, even those who, like one of my attorneys, sometimes disagree with a program's feedback on sentence structure. Professional writers make skilled use of the dictionary, grammar handbooks, and pre-writing tools like outlines or webbing to help them produce clean, well-structured sentences and paragraphs that are error-free and clear. The medical writer I studied was able to revise and reformulate the text he was working on by using an outline/template for the document. In college writing programs, teachers show students a variety of paper and electronic tools and give them many opportunities to practice using them to improve their writing.

Methodology for the Case Studies

In creating the case studies presented below, I have followed the format I used in *Revision Revisited*. The two subjects agreed to provide results of (in the case of Subject A) or to complete (Subject B) the Myers-Briggs Type Indicator, a personality instrument, and to be interviewed about their general approaches to writing and revising. They also agreed to answer questions about their work on their chapters that appear elsewhere in this book. These writers, unlike those studied in *Revision Revisited,* are writing teachers and scholars who probably have an even higher level of awareness about their personal strategies for writing than the writers I studied previously. The methodology, then, includes the following parts: first, completion of the Myers-Briggs if necessary, administered, scored and after the observation, interpreted by me (I am a licensed user of this instrument). Then, the subjects completed an extensive interview with me exploring their general approaches to writing and strategies for revising text. The list of questions used appears in Appendix A at the end of this chapter.

Once these preliminary steps were completed, the subjects could move on to the remaining steps in the study. The third step entailed a more detailed set of questions concerning the project at hand (see Appendix B at the end of this chapter). This third step generally occurred shortly before the observation portion of the study. In the fourth phase, the writers took a draft prepared prior to the observation, and spent an hour revising it while I watched. While they were revising, I asked the writers to talk out loud about the processes, strategies, changes and thinking that they were using, and audio taped their comments. This procedure is called a "think-aloud protocol" in research. I received copies of their first drafts and the revisions that resulted from this revising session, as well as copies of further drafts produced at a later time. Finally, I prepared a written account of what happened in the revising session and asked the subjects to read and comment on my account to produce convergent data, adding validity to my case study approach. One further point that warrants mention is that my role in this work was as a participant-observer, since I am a contributor to this book and its editor as well as an observer of the work of these writers.

Case studies: Writing Teachers Revising

For each of the case studies presented here, I will provide a description of the subject's responses to the background questionnaire and then a discussion of their description of the project at hand. Following this, several samples of the changes made during the revision process will be presented with analysis in terms of the awarenesses and skills demonstrated by these writers.

Background Questionnaire for Subject A

Subject A is a full-time faculty member at a medium-sized public university in the Midwest. She holds a permanent non-tenure track teaching position which entails the expectation that she will not do research or publish her scholarly work, but will devote her time to a full load of classes and to service on committees and other responsibilities at the university. Before moving to this full-time position, Subject A worked at the university as a part-time faculty member in the writing program for about fifteen years. She completed her PhD in English in 1994, focusing on Old English poetry. Her language background includes reading knowledge of German as well as Old English.

Subject A had completed the Myers-Briggs four years prior to this project and had received a detailed interpretation of her results. Her reported type was ENFP (extraversion, intuition, feeling and perceiving), with a very clear preference for intuition and moderate preferences for extraversion and feeling. Her preference for perceiving was only slight. She thought, on reflection, that she might be more of an introvert than the Indicator results suggest, but has adopted extraversion due to her work as a teacher. In addition, she also thought that she preferred judging, at least in some ways. Given the slight preference for perceiving in her reported type, her self-identification of a different preference is not surprising.

Turning to Subject A's typical approach to writing, when asked if she uses collaboration, Subject A reports that she rarely collaborates on documents for most purposes. Typically, Subject A does all of her writing on a word processor, without use of a Dictaphone or outside editor. She will use paper for flow charts of her ideas or brainstorming, and likes to print her drafts so she can edit on paper, but the bulk of her writing work is done on the computer.

When asked to describe her writing process and typical strategies, Subject A reports that she does a fair amount of thinking about a writing project before and after beginning it. She often thinks about a project when she is stuck somewhere that she needs to be physically present but can be mentally absent. She will also rehearse or plan writing mentally while doing other things like walking her dog. At some point in this process, she will sit down at the word processor and dump out her thoughts into a file. The resulting beginning generally has "no architecture" but offers a global start on the task. If working collaboratively, she can sometimes see the architecture or structure in another's writing more easily than she can see it in her own. If she has notes or will make use of secondary sources, she uses those to provide some discipline and organization to this first draft.

The background interview with Subject A suggests that she does not plan much before writing. She begins a project and sees what emerges as her first few attempts take shape on the computer screen, a more global and exploratory approach to beginning to write. Her overall strategy is fairly consistent with her type preferences for intuition and perceiving (Jensen and DiTiberio 53–57, 69–71). Her process suggests a high level of metarhetorical awareness, but relatively little metastrategic and metalinguistic awareness. This finding may help to explain why drafting is such a laborious and complex process for her. As an experienced writer, she surely has the four skills of writing readily available for use (collaboration, genre, text and context and the toolbox).

Task Questionnaire for Subject A

Subject A and I met a second time for the observation portion of the research. In this portion, there are three steps: first, an additional set of questions (see Appendix B of this chapter) on the task at hand, then an opportunity to practice "thinking aloud" on a simple paragraph I wrote for this purpose, and finally, the audio taping, with the subject's permission, of about an hour of revising work with the accompanying think-aloud protocol. The task questionnaire begins with a question about any further thoughts the subject has had about his or her writing strategies since the background interview was completed. Subject A did have some additional ideas.

She described the beginning of her process in much greater detail. In preparing the draft that she planned to revise, she noticed that she tends to begin work with her own ideas and waits to integrate source materials by "sneaking up" on them after the text has already begun to take shape and a plan is apparent. She often begins with a set of categories or some pre-existing scheme. She also noted that she tends to think in either-or, binary terms and then in revising, reworks her text to reflect what she described as "more mature thinking."

Moving on to discuss the passage she planned to work on in the session, the working title of this portion is "Definitions and Distinctions." There are plenty of sources, but they will be added at a later time. She thinks of the audience as teachers of writing with relatively little experience in teaching and little contact with trained rhetoricians. She thinks some of the readers of her chapter will have some background information on revision theory and practice, but more of them will think of revision as editing. Most readers won't have a more global view of revision as working on the larger issues in texts. She has spent a few hours a week for a few weeks creating the first draft.

Responding to the questionnaire issues, she notes that she doesn't have a specific thesis at the moment; the draft she has is filled with many more questions than answers. Her goal in this revision session is to work on both text content and design. To create a readable text, any text must have a clear point and set up of the sequence of ideas at the outset, an "engine paragraph" that provides a précis and sets out the overall plan of the text. This opening paragraph must tell what she wants to say and what order she will say it in, but she is not sure she can prepare this paragraph at this point. She feels the current draft has many either-or ideas in it. She wants to expand these with the use of metaphors and to show that students and teachers see revision from very different vantage points. The preliminary work concluded with a short practice passage (see Appendix C) which the subject worked on briefly, talking about the changes she made to it to understand the think-aloud procedure.

Observation of Subject A

Subject A begins her work by reading through her entire text of a page and a half, making some notes on the paper copy, indicating a place where she will take a paragraph out and move it to the end of the text for the time being. She uses journalism's heuristic (who, what, when, where, why, how) to organize her ideas. The paragraph that is out of order is about teachers of writing and will need discussion later in the chapter.

She focuses her attention on the "who" paragraph, expanding it by adding several sentences. Here's the original draft that she brought to the session:

> Continuing to ask the journalist's basic questions, we should consider the "who" of revising. Is the act "revising" if a student makes corrections marked by the teacher and that's it? On one hand, we might consider that the student is doing clerical work. Often the student will say, "I did what you said. I hope the grade is better." Teachers need to inquire what else happens when a student just makes corrections. Does the student reread his or her work with greater pleasure? With a better understanding of sentence rules, word choices, integration of quotations into a text, or whatever the teacher marked? If so, there may be more going on than just clerical work. What if a student responds to questions about a passage or an idea not by considering the passage and explaining it better or further but by dropping the offending section? Sometimes there's not a lot of power-sharing; a student feels obligated just to respond to the teacher's objection. It may be that when a student drops something instead of working on it, her or she is feeling silenced or disregarded. Or the student may be making a power move of another sort: if this displeases you (teacher) then I'll withhold it altogether. Between these two extremes of agency, we find multitudes of ways to share power.

In the margin, she had written a note that said "Teacher's comments as disruption of audience and purpose." In revising, she changed this paragraph into two paragraphs as follows:

Continuing to ask the journalist's basic questions, we should consider the "who" of revising. Normally in a writing class, peer editors and the teacher comment on a draft and the writer works with the suggestions. Peer suggestions can run the gamut from unusable to useful, from small-scale editing to large issues of structure, and student writers normally understand the need to evaluate the advice and decide what to use. Suggestions from a teacher, however, often carry more force, considering the teacher's experience and power to give a grade. Thus, students may think of revising as complying with a teacher's explicit feedback, particularly editing marks. Often we wonder, is the act "revising" if a student makes corrections marked by the teacher and that's it? On one hand, we might consider that the student is doing clerical work. Often the student will say, "I did what you said. I hope the grade is better." Teachers need to inquire what else happens when a student just makes corrections. Does the student reread his or her work with greater pleasure? With a better understanding of sentence rules, word choices, integration of quotations into a text, or whatever the teacher marked? If so, there may be more going on than just clerical work. At the same time, this is revising of a very limited sort, the student having minimal agency and thinking of the activity as mainly following a specific set of directions.

What if a student responds to questions about a passage or an idea not by considering the passage and explaining it better or further but by dropping the offending section? Sometimes there's not a lot of power-sharing; a student feels obligated just to respond to the teacher's objection. It may be that when a student drops something instead of working on it, he or she is feeling silenced or disregarded. Or the student may be making a power move of another sort: if this displeases you (teacher) then I'll withhold it altogether. Between these two extremes of agency, we find multitudes of ways to share power.

She says that she wants to add to the description of an ordinary college writing class. Students can and do help one another through processes of peer review, but they don't always pay as much attention to this feedback as they do to responses from an instructor.

At this point, Subject A pauses in her work to reread what she had written, asking herself if it worked. She has drawn on her personal experiences with students, noting that the interaction of students and teachers over a text is often full of misunderstandings. Peer editing has the status of suggestions, but teacher comments are somehow something more than this. Still, students have some level of "agency" and may choose to refuse or ignore the feedback given by other readers. She notes that she has a couple of competing ideas to present and struggles to clarify her point, which is about students' level of agency in the writing and revising process. She's not satisfied with how she is thinking about the issues, but decides to put in what she can and see what will happen.

She then moved on to later sections of the text, making changes after rereading what she had changed so far on the screen. At this point, fatigue set in. The think-aloud process is very demanding for both writer and observer, so we called a halt to the session, which ran for about fifty minutes.

Analysis of Revising: Subject A

Subject A's discussion of her writing process at the second session I had with her reveals a much more complete and complex picture of her revising strategies. This picture is consistent with those of the other professional writers I studied in *Revision Revisited* in that Subject A has a very high level of metarhetorical awareness, though limited metastrategic and metalinguistic awareness. Her skills are, like all professional writers, very strong.

In both the first and second descriptions of her process, Subject A indicates that she knows how she works at writing. It is very clear that for this writer, the general notion of revision touches all parts of her process. Her typical beginning strategy takes the form of an exploratory draft that is almost a kind of free writing on the topic at hand without a pre-set plan. Source materials will be added later through a process of "sneaking up" on them, not clearly a matter of conscious choice and decisions. She is aware of how the computer supports her writing, but sees it clearly as a tool or means to an end; this point will be discussed below in the skills section. Her approach is to begin by sketching out her ideas without drawing on source materials, with full knowledge that revisions will lead to the addition of these at a later time along with other changes.

These points are reflected in Subject A's comments at the beginning of her think aloud. She was looking through her draft and planning her work as she talked aloud. One observation she makes is that the computer has changed her writing and revising processes substantially. In part, this change is a result of the fact that, as she says, the word processor allows the writer to "park" ideas in various places while dealing with other parts of the text she refers to as "things you don't understand." This comment was made after she planned to move a paragraph from one part of her prepared draft to the end while she focused on other sections of the text. Once she forms up a plan for how to revise, she moves to sit at the computer screen and begins to work.

A further point raised by her pre-revising discussion reflects her metarhetorical awareness. She notes that students often revise by correcting surface errors noted by their teachers, behavior she describes with the phrase "clerical work." In describing this observation as a metaphor, Subject A captures the key feature of her metarhetorical awareness, her conscious use of metaphors to describe the writing and revising processes, whether her own or those of others. Besides the examples noted above. at one point in the think-aloud, she says she may be "writing herself into a canyon." At another point, she refers to part of her text as a "riff," a term used to describe musical improvisation that moves away from the main themes of a composition. Finally, she says in the think-aloud that she knows the chapter will need an "engine paragraph" to drive the whole piece.

In general, Subject A's think-aloud reveals little metastrategic or metalinguistic awareness. Although she was aware of her personality preferences based on administration of the MBTI in another group, she showed no awareness of how her type might impact her writing processes. Other writers I have studied who have metastrategic awareness refer to their type preferences and see how they affect their writing behavior. With respect to metalinguistic awareness, she does note at one point that the spell check has flagged the word "syntactical" and that it does not sound right to her either, and there are other points in the tape where she says "the computer doesn't like that" but they appear to be reactions to the word processor as a tool and not a by-product of particular sensitivity to language.

In terms of the four skill areas that professional writers have, Subject A seems to have considerable skill in all of these areas. On the matter of collaboration, the background questionnaire shows that she has the skill to collaborate successfully with colleagues as illustrated by the project done for the local community college and one for her church as well. Again in the background questionnaire, she comments on her knowledge of genre, saying that her chapter is modeled on a scholarly monograph or research report. She knows that she will need to bring in outside source materials and she has a plan or strategy for doing so that she refers to as "sneaking up" on the sources. Her skill in this genre of research writing reminds me of one of my academic writers whose revising is presented in *Revision Revisited*. This academic said that she used sources "strategically" to support her points in the text and planned specifically to do so.

In the area of text and context, Subject A's skill is reflected in her sense of her audience, also noted in the interviews prior to the actual revision session. She has thought about the audience for this book and what the readers might already know or think about revising. Subject A clearly has solid skills in text and context and will make use of these in her text. When she draws on her own classroom experience for examples to illustrate her points, she demonstrates her skillful use of text and context, choosing appropriate texts in the educational context of the book.

Finally, the toolbox is very much in evidence as Subject A interacts with the computer all through her think-aloud work. At the beginning of the think-aloud, she comments on using the word processor's ability to move text around and uses it to move paragraphs to the end of the file. These are paragraphs she will use later in the text or elsewhere. In ways typical of a person with a feeling preference, she notes that "the computer doesn't like that" when a red (for spelling) or a green (for a grammatical problem) line appears on the screen. This reaction from the computer would be a concern to someone whose main goal in life is the preservation of harmony with all things, animate and inanimate.

I want to make one further comment about this writer's work. While her verified personality type preferences are ENFP, she says that to some extent this is a type she has adopted as a result of her choice of teaching as a career. Jensen and DiTiberio suggest that a sign of mature writers (such as the professionals I have studied including this one) may be able to use both sides of each dimension of personality and I think this may be the case for this writer (75–104). As an extravert in terms of her energy sources, as a writer, I think Subject A may draw on this preference, based on her claim that she works on writing while doing other things. However, her need to think carefully about her text in ways not possible while the think-aloud was in progress is a more likely comment from an introvert. In knowing Subject A as a colleague, I tend to think of her as an introvert, chiefly because she often will mention very thoughtful insights that do not appear in her ordinary conversations and interactions, clearly the by-product of introverted processing. Thus, she may have a somewhat different set of preferences in working on writing than those reflected in her scores on the MBTI. Finally, this use of the Myers-Briggs is one illustration of the type of current research that is revealing more about writing and especially revising processes used by professional writers.

Background Questionnaire for Subject B

Subject B is also a teacher at the same state university in the Midwest as Subject A, but he is a member of the part-time faculty, teaching 3 or 4 sections of first-year writing each term. He holds a PhD in English, completed in 1982, and has studied the work of William Saroyan extensively, publishing a book and other scholarly work on Saroyan over the years. He has been teaching on a part-time basis at the university for three years, working previously at other institutions in the area and as a lecturer during his PhD work in another state. His language background includes a good reading knowledge of French with some speaking ability, fair skill in German and experience with Greek and Latin in his undergraduate education. He also knows a little Armenian.

On the MBTI, Subject B's reported type is INTJ (preferences for introversion, intuition, thinking and judging). In an interpretation session I did for him, he generally confirmed his reported type, though he said he has been making some effort to change his approach to life, particularly on the thinking/feeling dimension as well as on the last dimension, judging vs. perceiving. His scores on the instrument reflect clear preferences on all four dimensions. With introverts, though, and especially for someone who is trying to change, shifts in behavior may not be easy to see or capture. His introversion and intuition are certainly reflected in the fact that, at the end of our Myers-Briggs discussion, he said he was surprised by feedback he had gotten from another contributor to the book who read his chapter. He wasn't aware of the length of his draft (about sixty manuscript pages) until this reader pointed out that he had created his text originally as a single-spaced text and was proud to have kept it to thirty pages.

In terms of his writing behavior, Subject B reports that he probably spends around ten hours a week working on writing or document preparation. His prior training in writing included being a student himself in first-year composition in his undergraduate work, and having a course on teaching writing in graduate school. He says that he likes to be very thorough when working on a topic, reading as much on the topic as he can, including complete collections of materials with the goal of "knowing the field" of the topic by time he is through. Once he has done some brain storming on his topic, he starts work on a new project by looking through his own book collection for sources, and then will make notes on these as well as lists from the bibliographies of sources at hand of additional materials that appear relevant to his work. Thus, unlike Subject A, Subject B begins with his source materials and references and builds his text directly from these.

When he begins drafting, Subject B begins writing and as the draft develops, he sees the direction it is going to take. When this vision for the whole project becomes clear, he will add headings to the document so he can see the categories of new material. He adds new material then, category by category in each of the headings. He generates new text on the word processor, but then prints out his writing so he can edit and add notes in longhand, repeating this process as necessary. The main goal is to get his ideas down on paper in one form or the other. The end comes when he runs out of time, and at that point, he says he will perform surgery on his draft, choosing parts that appear relevant to the topic and goals of the written piece. Conference presentations and feedback may lead to additional changes. The overall picture reveals that for Subject B, revision is deeply woven into every aspect of his writing process.

Task Questionnaire for Subject B

Subject B completed the task questionnaire with me just before he worked on his draft chapter for this book, following the same procedure used with Subject A. We discussed his answers to the questions listed in Appendix B; then, he worked briefly on the practice passage to understand what is required for a "think-aloud" protocol, and finally, he spent about 45 minutes working on his draft, reading it aloud and commenting on his plans for revision.

In response to the question about whether he had any additional thoughts after the background interview, Subject B indicated that he realized that using a computer-based word processor has had a major impact on his writing and revision. The impact of computers on revision is discussed elsewhere in this text (see chapter by Eyman). His usual working procedure for revision of drafts is to print out his text, read it carefully in its paper version, planning changes, and then go back to the computer to make the planned changes to the text on the screen. This strategy, again, shows how revision is thoroughly integrated into the way he works. His topic is creativity and revision and because it is a new area, he has read extensively before beginning to draft the chapter, spending about two hours a week for the past six to eight months on this project.

With respect to audience, Subject B understands the readers of the book to include graduate students as well as professionals in the field of Rhetoric and Composition Studies. His thinking about the audience's needs or his assumptions about the readers is a bit fuzzy, he says. He thinks they are probably intelligent people who just don't know very much about literary theory or creative writers. Thus, the readers of this essay are not very knowledgeable about his topic, but they are more informed than average people one might find in the street.

On the question of topic/thesis or main idea, Subject B said his topic is creative writers and revision. When he thinks about imaginative writers, he asks the question, what areas does this touch on or what questions does it raise? The chapter is about the nature of creativity and whether there is creativity in the act of revision. Is the creative moment in drafting of a text or in revising? Subject B seeks to review the theoretical/psychological literature on creativity and to compare these sources to the actual revision practices of imaginative writers. The research he examined for his chapter also reflects the general claim of this book that many new findings are shedding light on how writers work at revision. Prior to beginning work on his own material, Subject B practiced the think-aloud procedure using the weather passage (see Appendix C of this chapter).

Observation Report for Subject B

Because he had brought a printed version of his chapter and did not have his computer disk to use, Subject B's revision observation consisted of him reading a big chunk of his text aloud and commenting on it. He said that his normal work strategy would be like this: having a draft, printing it on paper and planning for changes that need to be made when he goes back to the word processor. He noted that the observation is a little different than his normal work strategy, and that the work of reading through the manuscript and marking sections to change on the paper copy is one that he would normally follow much later in the overall process of writing and revising.

After making a few changes to the first four paragraphs, he comes to the fifth paragraph. Here, he observes features in his own writing that he does not like: the use of the phrase "chicken and egg" in the opening sentence of the paragraph, which reads as follows: "This is a 'chicken and egg' scenario which strikes one in engaging this area of research." He judges this phrase to be "a little homely" and circles it for later rethinking.

He is reasonably well satisfied with his paragraph and moves on to read the next part. Here, he finds his own writing variously unfocused and too long. He is also not sure that the issues he discusses here need to be included. In this part, Subject B noted that this project has taken on a life of its own and he is not sure but thinks it might develop into a book-length study of creativity and revision. He says he generally does not have trouble producing a manuscript of the requisite length, so he is looking to limit his discussion in this draft. In the rest of his think-aloud, he comments at a number of points on sections he might omit from this chapter, perhaps for use in his own book project at a later time, partly a by-product of our discussion of the length of his chapter. Subject B's thinking about a second writing project points yet again to the fact that revision bears on every part of the writing process, from creative beginnings to conceptualizing a major project to content and organization to choice of words and phrases.

He moves on to read the beginning of the next section. The first paragraph seems okay to him, but when he gets to the second paragraph in "The Psychology of Creativity" section, he is clearly rethinking his writing. Here's the paragraph:

> Most of these psychological studies have considered artists as a general category—composers, painters, sculptors—as well as writers. And scholars such as Jacob Bronowksi emphasized the similarities between the greatest scientists and poets—he wrote about William Blake as well as Albert Einstein and saw their creative activity as being essentially similar. Yet there have been virtually no studies dealing specifically with the creative process of writers. Usually writers form a subset of the larger category of artists to be considered. Empirically, then, it would make most sense to begin with the

testimony of writers themselves when attempting to construct a theory of literary creativity and revision however few scholars have actually done so.

He changes the phrase "essentially similar" by deleting "essentially" and then alters "virtually no" to "few," handwriting both of these changes on the page. These changes may reflect a need to add some hedging to his phrasing. It is typical for writers who prefer INTJ in their personality according to the MBTI to make very definitive statements, but a professional writer, even without explicit metastrategic awareness would revise to soften unqualified claims in just this way, according to Jensen and DiTiberio (174–75).

He puts a horizontal line in the right margin next to this paragraph, adding one of his question marks, and also draws a line under "however few scholars have actually done so" at the end of the paragraph and puts a question mark next to these words as well. In his comments, he says that there are a few problems here. First, he is concerned about the accuracy of his claims. It isn't that there are "no" studies, but that they are not sufficiently detailed for his purposes. There is new research, in a book he just got, that he will add on creativity and brain studies, based on the work of Alice Flaherty, whose name he writes in the margin. However, he is also concerned about the overall length of the chapter and says he will have to decide whether this paragraph includes "too much information." In contrast to Subject A, Subject B was very focused on his source materials as the focus of his discussion. Subject A was much more concerned with exploring her own ideas as the starting point of her draft process.

In this section, as part of his commentary, Subject B observed that he was struggling to understand his own ideas, and that he saw that he was trying to pull together two ideas: first, that creative writing comes easily to writers and second that writing is a kind of play. Revision, he notes in the text, counters this idea, since it is "hard work!" However, this subject's choice to focus on the role of revision in creative writing opens up yet another relatively new area of investigation in revision studies. His observation about the workload of revision, at the top of page 8 of his draft, came at the end of the audio tape I used to record this revising think-aloud protocol, and is the end of the observation session for Subject B.

Analysis of Revising: Subject B

This think-aloud and the interviews prior to it reveal that Subject B has a great deal of metarhetorical awareness, typical of professional writers like those I studied in *Revision Revisited*. In the interview, he describes his writing processes in great detail, acknowledging his use of the computer for word processing. He also notes the fact that the chapter he is preparing for the book is somewhat more structured and schematic than his usual writing. In the think-aloud portion, he comments at several points about the organizational structure, about where he might add, delete or rearrange elements, reflecting an awareness of his processes as a writer and the impact of revision on every part of his work. Finally, his observation during the think-aloud that his reading and planning for changes is a strategy he does use, but ordinarily at a somewhat later point in his overall writing process, reflects a writer who knows his own strategies for successful writing.

Subject B's responses to the questionnaires and his think-aloud do not show any metastrategic awareness, the second kind of awareness professional writers have. Like some of the other professionals I have studied, Subject B had not taken the Myers-Briggs Type Indicator. He was unaware of his type preferences and did not use them in his comments on his writing strategies or in his revising. However, it may be useful to note that Subject B's work on his chapter is consistent with his type preference for intuition, the preferred type for writers. Many of his comments, such as when he says he is "like a squirrel gathering nuts" as he accumulates paragraphs, quotes, source materials and so on, suggest a "big picture" view that is typical of writers with a preference for intuition. Like Subject A, the lack of metastrategic awareness may account for some of this subject's difficulty with drafting, since his concern was to present the large landscape of creative writing and the role of revising in it. The result was a very long draft with many references that he had to edit several times to be somewhat more focused and less complete.

In terms of the third awareness found in expert writers, metalinguistic awareness, Subject B's work in planning his revisions shows only a little of this type of awareness. He does say at one point that a sentence is "a little homely" and he makes some changes to individual words and sentence structures as he goes through the text. However, little of what he says suggests a direct or specific sensitivity to language of the kind seen in some other professional writers. In his reading of this chapter, Subject B pointed out that this was a very brief observation of his revising, which normally includes much more attention to language issues (i.e. metalinguistic awareness) at a later point in his process. This comment raises the critical point that inevitably, brief observations of writers' processes provide only snapshots of the whole.

Turning to the four skills found among the expert writers I studied, Subject B does not show particular skills in collaboration. He reports in response to the background questionnaire that he rarely collaborates when he writes other than in the sense of making use of editorial comments provided by the editors of professional journals as he prepares work for publication. And in terms of genre, as noted previously, he is aware that the chapter he is preparing is somewhat different than other kinds of writing he typically does, such as academic conference papers. However, neither collaboration nor genre is a particular skill revealed here.

With respect to text and context, Subject B's responses to the background questionnaire and task questionnaire do not show marked audience awareness or concern. However, in introducing his many and varied source materials, he does make sure to provide the context for his sources to make clear their relevance to the ideas he is trying to present. His use of sources is highly polished and flexible as he uses both direct quotation and paraphrase/summary to integrate the ideas of psychologists, literary critics, creative writers and others in support of his own ideas.

Finally, in terms of tools, Subject B does not show much use of tools since he was mostly reading and reflecting on his overall presentation. He did say at one point that he thought he probably used and relied on the word processor to a greater extent than he had previously thought. Other than this comment, and perhaps because he was not working on the text on the screen, this think-aloud does not show any particular use of tools.

Cross-Case Analysis

Taken together, the work of these two professional writers shows chiefly that they have a very high level of awareness of their preferred techniques and strategies for writing, which I have called metarhetorical awareness. These writers know how they work. They may not have the formal terminology to describe or account for their techniques, such as Flower's term "satisficing" (46, 48) but they clearly do know how they work. Their approaches are consistent with their shared preference for intuition in terms of the four dimensions of personality. Both writers focus on overall organizational structure to a great degree in these writing sessions. Their metarhetorical awareness is also suggested by their similar uses of metaphors to describe or explain their processes. Both writers have a clear preference for intuition, so they characteristically can see the broad issues and connections in their ideas and are likely to notice patterns that the metaphors reflect.

These writers started from very different points with their drafting and revising activities, with Subject A concentrating much more on trying to shape her own ideas without reference to source materials. Subject B began with his sources and developed his draft by presenting them, not so much to the exclusion of his own ideas but with much more of a focus on marshalling the sources to support his points. A reader of this chapter in an earlier draft noted that expert writers may not have a plan at the outset because they see a draft as a starting point for a piece of writing. If they don't do much or any pre-writing planning, this approach is less problematic than it might be for novice writers who are less likely to revise effectively. This observation suggests that in teaching, revision strategies must play a much greater role in the writing classroom and require more focused and direct teaching. In particular, as I argued in *Revision Revisited,* the teaching of revision should be more concentrated on helping novice writers build the three kinds of awareness I have described.

Finally, the work of these two writers reflects the truth of the observation found by Subject A in Sudol's book on revising, that revising touches every part of the writing process. If writing can be divided into prewriting, drafting and revising, these writers show that much revising can go on in the prewriting stage, as is true for Subject A. Her approach entails a "discovery draft" (Murray) that is not truly the beginning of a piece but that may get revised into a beginning. There may be several such discovery pieces before she begins the real work of writing. For Subject A as well as for Subject B, prewriting and drafting both entail revising as the text unfolds. Thus, it is clear here and everywhere in this book that revising is thoroughly integrated into every part of the writing process. In addition, particularly in the case of Subject B, the studies he reviewed for his chapter are part of the new findings about writing processes and strategies that shed light on how writers revise successfully. Because he has looked at highly respected creative writers, Subject B's work brings new insights about revision to bear on the teaching and learning processes.

Pedagogical Suggestions: A Summary

This chapter has reviewed the findings on the revision strategies of professional writers, showing that they have awarenesses and skills usually lacking among novice writers. The professional writers whose revising has been presented here show particularly strong metarhetorical awareness. Other professional writers I have studied and reported on in *Revision Revisited* show very high levels of metarhetorical, metastrategic and metalinguistic awareness. In addition, professional writers have strong skills of all four kinds I have described. Naturally, in teaching, the focus tends to be on developing novice writers' skills rather than on their awarenesses, partly because it is easier to focus on skills and partly because there is only so much teachers can do in a semester or even a year of writing instruction, in, for example, first year composition courses.

Teachers of writing, at least at the college level, typically focus their work on developing writers' skills—collaboration, genre, text and context and tools. Instead, it should be clear that the skilled writers whose work has been discussed here are skilled in part because of their fairly strong levels of metarhetorical awareness. To develop metarhetorical awareness, the many kinds of reflective writing tasks are most useful. Teachers might also have students read the work of writers who have reflected extensively on their own processes, such as Annie Dillard and Anne Lamott. When students create portfolios of their writing and reflect on their development and progress as writers over a semester or year, the resulting insights can serve to help students' developing metarhetorical awareness.

To encourage metastrategic awareness, teachers might incorporate the concepts of personality preference into their work, with or without the direct use of the Myers-Briggs Type Indicator. In most educational institutions, particularly colleges and universities, it is easy to find someone on campus who is licensed to administer, score and interpret the MBTI for students. Understanding personality preferences and their impact on writing behavior can give student writers useful approaches to writing and revising. Use of the work of Jensen and DiTiberio and the more popular and accessible version of their research by DiTiberio and Jensen can be useful for teachers and directly or indirectly for students. The educational implications of personality type are thoroughly explored by Gordon Lawrence in *Teacher Types and Tiger Stripes,* another useful resource.

Finally, teachers can help build language sensitivity by discussing particular aspects of language formally in class and tapping into computer tools to help with word choice, sentence structure and organizational issues. To help student/novice writers become more like professional writers, teachers should help them build all three kinds of awareness that those writers possess. Doing so will help novice writers become skilled and expert at writing. If revising touches every part of the writing process, developing students' skills in revision will make them better in every part of writing. The new research discussed in this chapter and the others in this book suggests that we are moving toward a deeper understanding of writing processes that expands the concept of revision. These new insights can and should be shared with students learning to write.

Appendix A: Background Questionnaire on Writing and Revising Strategies

1. Taping: ok? Y n
2. Subject name and today's date:

    Mbti Type Preferences And Scores:

    Self-Id Preferences If Different:
3. Languages spoken or known and level of ability:
4. Position/official job title:
5. Length of time in job:
6. Highest degree and year of award:
7. Approximate amount of time spent preparing documents:

    Per Day? Per Week?
8. Specific training in writing in or before present job/when?:

    courses

    seminars

workshops

other

9. How much collaborative work do you do in document preparation?

10. Describe your writing strategies or habits. . . .

   paper vs. wp

   use of dictaphone

   do you have an editor or typist or other person who looks at your writing?

11. Describe your approach or process for writing generally. . . .

   prewriting

   drafting

   final copy preparation

   use of spell check/machine-based editor

Appendix B: Questionnaire for Revising Session

1. Name and date:
2. Any thoughts about process since first interview or observations, comments, etc.?
3. Title of chapter?
4. Is there research involved in this document, and if so how much and what kind?
5. Is there a model for this document or a pattern followed?
(If so, ask for copy of model or pattern document.)
6. Length parameter (# of words, pages or time):
7. Time spent on this document to date:
8. Audience for document:

9. Audience needs/writer's assumptions about audience:
10. Topic of document/thesis/point/main idea:
11. Purpose/use of document:
12. Focus of revision (rhetorical, technical, design/mechanics):
13. Definition of readability?
14. What will make this a readable document?

Appendix C: Practice Passage for Think Aloud.

If this were your draft, how would you change it?

> The repeated blasts of Arctic air are hard on the hands and face. The weather has been pretty lousy lately. It has been cold, windy and the typical gray of Michigan in the winter. The days have been getting longer, so there are more hours of daylight, but the solid gray of the sky has been depressing. Mornings are still very dark and cold. At this point in the winter it always seems like spring may never come. There are few visible buds on the trees but few birds are around. On the plus side, the absence of birds means no loud chirping in the mornings, but there is also little sense of spring coming on.

9 Creative Writers and Revision

David Stephen Calonne

In this chapter I shall explore several related questions concerning the ways "creative" or "imaginative" writers shape and revise their work. Following a brief survey of creativity and revision, I consider the testimony of writers of poems, plays, short stories and novels regarding revision, inspiration and their own professional practices, both with conventional writing technologies and the computer. A discussion ensues of authorial changes to proofs and galleys, the role of collaboration and editors and revision after publication. I then turn to process criticism—one of the techniques literary scholars have developed to study revision—and conclude with an overview of the implications for the study of literary revision of parallel texts, poststructuralism and hypertext.

The very categories or "types" of writing need to be questioned since all writers face the same fundamental issues. Are essays, for example, to be considered "creative writing"? If not, why not? One might invoke here the writer's originality, style, or force of personality in distinguishing a "creative" essay from a more pedestrian effort. And when we consider the question of "genre" and the purposes of various forms of writing, it is obvious that the author of a scientific paper or a newspaper article and a poet are after rather different things. The scientist and the journalist presumably seek to convey "objective" facts about the world as concisely and accurately as possible. On the other hand, the poet, novelist, playwright are after lovely, terrible, intangible, interior, "subjective" truths about the human mind and heart: truth is beauty, beauty truth, as John Keats sang.

CREATIVITY AND REVISION

It is precisely this valorizing of the artistic, aesthetic aim that has led to the "romantic" view of literary composition. The activity of the creative writer in antiquity as well as in the Romantic period became linked to a kind of sacred divine mission to reveal resplendent spiritual realities: in Latin, *vates* means both poet and prophet. And *The Gospel According to Saint John* begins: "In the beginning was the Word, and the Word was with God, and the Word was God." Ancient Greek "logos" is word, the divine word (*Oxford Companion to the Bible* 463). Because of this sacralizing connection of the word and writing to the divine afflatus, discussions of creativity have often been reverential. If the poet is an inspired being who makes contact with a transcendental realm in the act of composing then it follows that literature springs—like Athena—directly and perfectly from the head of Zeus. No revision is necessary because the work, like the creation of the cosmos, has in a sense a divine origin.

The Romantic conception of inspiration thus tended to ignore or minimize revision as the central locus of creative activity because composition presumably comes effortlessly to geniuses. However, the documentary evidence suggests otherwise. While inspiration undoubtedly exists, revision is just as much a part of the practice of creative writers as of journalists, scientists, diarists, letter writers and mundane composers of e-mail messages. But exactly how do writers make a work of art? What words, ideas, images, paragraphs, chapters do they add, delete, revise, move around and in what sequence? The actual behavior of writers suggests that the dividing lines between initial idea, drafting, letting the material "incubate" and revision towards a final published work are often blurred. Each step of the process leads forwards and backwards. Perhaps by understanding the revision process we can begin to fathom the mystery of literary creation.

Indeed, when we study revision, are we studying a discrete activity, or are we confronting the actual genesis of the work of art? One might well argue that the initial "bolt from the blue," the moment of inspiration is the easy, given part and the hard work of revision is the real creative act. Anyone who doubts that revision is creative should examine the drafts of *Finnegans Wake* by James Joyce. Joyce's astonishing manuscript is a maze of crossed-out words, bold scrawls, huge Xs splayed across the page, squiggly lines, scratches, a labyrinth, a massive, splendid, messy, outlandish display of genius. Indeed, examining Joyce's mad pages one might well ask the frequent question about the dividing line between genius and insanity: these outpourings appear to be the ravings of a psychotic. Yet out of that chaos, Joyce made his own unique order. It is rather like Michelangelo shaping his *David* out of a huge block of marble, chipping away by hand slowly at his gargantuan marble slab to reveal the lovely precise shape conceived by his imagination's eye hidden in the stone.

Furthermore, in writing a draft, writers often speak of finding what they have to say in the process of trying to say it. They find their way to their true thoughts about a subject only through wrestling through the fierce struggle of putting words down on paper. The Romanian essayist and aphorist E.M. Cioran remarked wittily: "Perhaps we should publish only our first drafts, before we ourselves know what we are trying to say" (65). In the search for expression, one finds out that to which one is really committed. And there is often great surprise for the writer as he/she discovers in the act of writing what lies dormant within the self. The starkness of black typed words on the white page—and as we shall see, subsequent page proofs and galleys—compels a new encounter with the complexities of self-expression. It is significant that W.H. Auden, when rejecting some of his poems for inclusion in his *Collected Poems,* declared they were not "authentic." Since writing them, he had moved on, or was able with time to see in them a falsity which he had not previously apprehended. One revises until one achieves the most stylish presentation of the self, or—as Vladimir Nabokov thought—until the words have yielded the writer as much pleasure as they can.

The question of revision did not arise in preliterate, oral cultures in which myths, ritual activities and epic poetry were improvised/memorized and passed on from generation to generation. There was of necessity variation in the multiple versions of each performance of the work. Creativity was demonstrated in the process of continual "revision" of a primal version of a myth or poem. However, slowly and gradually, humans shifted from oral to written culture. One of the immediate practical problems in attempting to understand the history of revision is the fact that the classics of antiquity are mute. How was the Sumerian epic *Gilgamesh* composed? That is, how did the version we have inscribed on clay tablets in cuneiform script happen? And Homer, if he/she existed, left no blotted pages of the *Iliad* and *Odys-*

sey for us to study. These are oral compositions, recited by *rhapsodes,* but at some point a single or several human beings (I say "human beings" advisedly—Robert Graves argued in his novel *Homer's Daughter* (1955) that the "author" of *The Odyssey* was a woman) wrote down an actual text. We possess no manuscript drafts of poems in process by Sappho, Catullus, Horace or Virgil. And we are in the same ignorant situation with respect to the great dramatists Aeschylus, Sophocles, and Euripides. It was not until several versions of the same text on clay or papyrus proliferated that the question of an "authentic" text arose. And it was not until Gutenberg's movable type and the conception of an "authoritative" version of a literary work that the multiple issues and problems of revision have preoccupied scholars.

As we move toward our own times, the complexity brought into the question of revision with the advent of the printing press led to the rise of textual criticism in which the scholar in a sense "revises" the work of another author. The ancient *palimpsest*—a piece of parchment or a tablet on which one or more earlier erased texts can be discerned—is an apt symbol for the problems confronting the student of revision: what is the relationship between all the various drafts of a literary work? Which one may lay claim to greatest "authenticity"? During the development of Classical and Biblical studies, scholars attempted to discover the most accurate form of texts through a study of the manuscript tradition. Modern researchers then continued this tradition of "textual criticism" with reference to literary works.

The textual critic attempts to establish a "definitive" version through minutely checking what the author "originally" wrote, searching for typographical errors and possible mistakes by earlier editors. The subsequent printed editions must then also be studied and checked against what are believed to be the author's original "intentions." They may make "emendations" to the text (from Latin *emendere:* "to remove lies") and often provide an *apparatus criticus* at the bottom of the page which contains variant readings. One can immediately see the problems which arise during this process, since a great deal of second-guessing and intuition is required of the scholar in establishing a putative authentic text. Indeed, as we shall see at the conclusion of this essay, the whole procedure raises the question of whether such a thing as a "true, original, authentic, original" text even exists. Fredson Bowers at the University of Virginia (a great deal of textual criticism has been published by the University of Virginia Press) defined the four functions of the textual critic in the following ways: "(1) To analyze the characteristics of an extant manuscript, (2) to recover the characteristics of the lost manuscript that served as copy for a printed text, (3) to study the transmission of the printed text, and (4) to present an established and edited text to the public" (Holman 475). The activity of the textual critic may thus be said to be the study of revision in all of its possible permutations.

During the rise of Romanticism and the beginnings of the twentieth century the psychology of creativity began to preoccupy philosophers and psychologists. Friedrich Nietzsche, Sigmund Freud, Otto Rank, C.G. Jung, Jacques Maritain, Ernst Kris, Johan Huizinga, Albert Rothenberg and Howard Gardner have all explored the creative process. How do writers, musicians, artists, scientists get their ideas and what happens to these ideas once they appear? One can see immediately the connection of revision to this question, since it is rare that the initial inspiration does not require some—or considerable—reworking and elaboration. In some cases, vague ideas lie fallow in the subconscious for a time and then seem rather suddenly and mysteriously to take tangible shape. This corresponds to what Isaac Asimov termed the "Eureka Phenomenon." What has *seemed* to be a sudden burst of "inspiration" ("eureka"—"I have found it!"—is what Archimedes exclaimed when he discovered in his bathtub the law of the displacement of bodies) in this view is actually a long, submerged process of silent shaping by the powers of the unconscious which only *appears* to be a sudden implosion of energetic creative force. Yet great artists seem to get their ideas from nowhere, and the belief in inspired, spontaneous, untutored genius has become a familiar commonplace in the popular imagination.

A frequently cited paradigm of the creative process introduced by G. Wallas in *The Art of Thought* (1926) also informs the work of later theorists such as Catherine Patrick's *What is Creative Thinking?* (1955) and Silvano Arieti in *Creativity: The Magic Synthesis* (1976). Arieti summarizes Wallas's conception of creativity as involving four stages: preparation, incubation, illumination, and verification (15). This paradigm mirrors the testimony of writers who prepare through thinking about their project and gathering materials; the second stage of unconscious silent activity; the third "eureka" or inspirational moment and finally verification or revision. Yet as we shall see, many writers experience revision itself as an essential aspect of creating a work of art and "inspiration" is only one stage which they encounter during a long, involved process.

WRITERS ON REVISION

In the next five sections, I shall discuss several major aspects of revision: writers' own reports of their revision practices; revision and computers; the role of collaborators and editors; revision of proofs and galleys and revision after publication. When we turn to the testimony of authors themselves, we find a number of individual revision practices. Our sources for this information are writers' manuscripts, printed computer sheets, proofs, galleys, published texts, letters, notebooks, diaries, journals as well biographical studies. A good deal of documentary evidence and scholarship on literary revision has appeared in the past twenty years. David Madden and Richard Powers's *Writers' Revisions* is an excellent bibliography of articles and books about literary revision. Interviews are another important source and the series begun by George Plimpton—*Writers at Work: The Paris Review Interviews*—provides valuable insights regarding the composing process. The University of Mississippi Press has also brought out more than thirty interview volumes in their *Literary Conversations* series, while William Packard, the editor of the *New York Quarterly,* has edited two volumes of interviews with poets, *The Craft of Poetry* and *The Poet's Craft* . Thirty-one profiles from *Writer's Digest* containing additional insights concerning revision have been published under the title *On Being a Writer.*

John Kuehl's *Creative Writing and Rewriting: Contemporary American Novelists at Work* includes drafts and published versions of work by Eudora Welty, Kay Boyle, James Jones, Bernard Malamud, Wright Morris, F. Scott Fitzgerald, Philip Roth, Robert Penn Warren, John Hawkes and William Styron. *Writers on Writing,* edited by Robert Pack and Jay Parini contains essays by contemporary American writers on their working habits. *A Piece of Work, Five Writers Discuss Their Revisions: Tobias Wolff, Joyce Carol Oates, Tess Gallagher, Robert Coles, Donald Hall* includes manuscript pages along with the commentary by the writers themselves concerning their revisions. Kenneth Koch's *The Modern Library Writer's Workshop: A Guide to the Craft of Fiction* includes a chapter on literary revision while Mike Sharples's *How We Write: Writing as Creative Design* has a section on revision which explores Wordsworth's working methods during the composition of *The Prelude*. The most frequent question posed in these studies may be summed up: "How does the writer do it?" That is, what is the process, the alchemy that allows him/her to make a poem, story, novel or play *ex nihilo*?

In particular, the writers are asked repeatedly about revision, as if this information might provide the clue to their creativity. When we hear a symphony, contemplate a painting or sculpture, see a play or read a literary work, we are experiencing the finished product, and thus we do not have access to the messy changes and jagged evolution of the ideas which have laboriously been shaped into harmonious form. Thus we must look "behind the curtain" to observe the metamorphosis of the ungainly draft/caterpillar into the glorious artistic butterfly.

Fortunately, most writers are eager to describe their revisions, however an exception is Vladimir Nabokov (a distinguished lepidopterist as well as novelist of genius) who did not relish the idea of sharing his literary larvae with the public. When asked by an interviewer if he would allow him to see his revisions, Nabokov replied haughtily: "I'm afraid I must refuse. Only ambitious nonentities and hearty mediocrities exhibit their rough drafts. It is like passing around samples of one's sputum" (*Strong Opinions* 4). Expensive sputum however: famous writers' manuscripts sell are expensive items on the collectors' market. One need only consult the catalogues of antiquarian dealers or visit eBay on the Internet to see the exorbitant prices fetched by literary manuscripts. Generally, the more revisions the writer has made, the more costly the manuscript: additional testimony to the abiding curiosity of the general public as well as literati regarding creative genius.

Invariably the *Paris Review* also reproduced manuscript pages of the writers interviewed indicating numerous deletions, additions, substitutions and crossed out passages. Good writers are as concerned about the mundane aspects of revision or "editing"—punctuation, semicolon or colon, is this paragraph too long?—as they are about whether the Muse will visit them that morning or not. Rhythm, phrasing, tone, word choice, euphony: manuscripts are frequently a labyrinth of ideas accepted and then rejected, proof of the intense pursuit of the ideal, the seemingly endless trial-and-error process at work. These pages perhaps are included as the evidence we seek as readers of the joys, agonies and mystery of the creative process. One of the most famous comments on revision is contained in the *Paris Review* interview with Ernest Hemingway concerning the ending of his novel *Farewell to Arms* (1926): "I rewrote the ending to *Farewell to Arms,* the last page of it, thirty-nine times before I was satisfied." The interviewer then asked: "Was there some technical problem there? What was it that had stumped you?" Hemingway: "Getting the words right" (*Writers at Work,* Second Series 222).

There is a wide range of revision practices recounted by writers: there are as many kinds of revisers as there are writers. Each has a personal set of habits, rituals and techniques which include a variety of individual, idiosyncratic approaches. Many report that the practical "nuts and bolts" aspects of composition—what type of pencil or pen to use, buying paper and expensive cartridges for the printer, getting situated happily and comfortably at one's desk, having hot coffee nearby and J.S. Bach on the radio—are equally important parts of the process. Many writers speak of the role of the "technology" of writing in the writing/revision process. Some write in longhand with a pencil, some with pen, some with typewriters, many with computers. Others have secretaries who transcribe their work or ask family members for help—Jim Harrison relies on his daughter as editor. Eudora Welty cut up her texts with scissors and pinned them together, allowing her to move sections of her stories around to see how they would best fit together. Vladimir Nabokov composed and revised his novels in pencil on index cards and was fastidious about his tools: "I am rather particular about my instruments: lined Bristol cards and well sharpened, not too hard, pencils capped with erasers" (*Writers at Work,* Fourth Series 101). And as we shall see, the computer has further influenced how writers revise. Yet all authors have two things in common: they experience writing and rewriting as organic, "natural" parts of an ongoing process which involves mysterious cognitive, emotional and spiritual areas of the self and they all revised their work before publication. Some, such as W.B. Yeats, W.H. Auden and Robert Lowell, revised it extensively even after publication.

We are dependent upon the narratives writers themselves supply concerning their craft, but in many cases we also have manuscripts and drafts which allow us to compare what writers say they do against what they do in reality. My sense is that virtually all of the accounts I have read are fairly reliable concerning the writers' actual practices, but the only way to verify this would be to make a case by case study of each author, comparing his/her accounts of the revision process with accounts of colleagues, friends and fellow professionals and comparing these accounts with the actual manuscripts and corrected galleys or typescripts. And although as we leave antiquity and the Middle Ages and come closer to our own times we know much more about compositional practices, we must however often rely on the testimony of the writers themselves and sometimes this information is suspect. John Livingston Lowes in *The Road to Xanadu: A Study of the Ways of the Imagination* suggested that Samuel Taylor Coleridge's famous account of the genesis of "Kubla Khan" in an opium dream is doubtful and that Coleridge had in fact developed his great poem from a number of books he had read which supplied his unconscious with the materials for inspiration (Perkins 11). Thus we must proceed with caution when we attempt to make generalizations regarding how "creative writers" go about their work

In terms of psychological types, writers fall into basically one of two categories: Dionysian or Apollonian. I take my terms from Friedrich Nietzsche's *The Birth of Tragedy* in which he characterizes ancient Greek culture as being dominated by two powerful gods in dialectical opposition: Dionysus the god of wine, ecstasy and unconscious instinctive power and Apollo, the god of reason, light, wisdom and consciousness. The Dionysian writers generally place their faith in the dark forces of the instinctive side of the mind, while Apollonian writers are devoted to reason and logic. When we turn to the authors' descriptions of their own behaviors, it can be clearly seen that they tend to fall broadly into one of these two categories. However, the fact that they are artists in the first place may suggest that they have a more direct relation to their unconscious, to the materials of dream, imagination, invention and fantasy. I do not mean to suggest that these are in any way hard and fast structures of creative activity. Of course writers constantly move back and forth between the two poles of expressive abandon and rational control, between romantic and realist, between flow and restriction, between Dionysus and Apollo—as we all do in our daily lives. Yet general personality types or structure do dominate the development of the creative self and we should not ignore this when we attempt to study revision.

The creative process many of the writers discuss follows the general outlines of the stages of creativity formulated by G. Wallas in 1926 in his seminal book *The Art of Thought:* preparation, incubation, illumination and verification. Malcolm Cowley, who edited the first volume of the *Paris Review* series, remarks in his "Introduction":

> There would seem to be fours stages in the composition of a story. First comes the germ of the story, then a period of more or less conscious meditation, then the first draft, and finally the revision, which may be simply 'pencil work,' as John O'Hara calls it—that is minor changes in wording—or may lead to writing several drafts and what amounts to a new work. (7)

Here we observe Wallas's four categories of creative activity, but Cowley omits Wallas's third stage—"illumination"—or what authors throughout history have called "inspiration." Cowley tells us "first comes the germ of the story" but he does not explain where this seed or kernel or "germ" idea originates.

In the following, I will survey the testimony of writers themselves regarding their revision practices. In general, they may be divided into three large categories: writers who claim "inspiration" (and thus compose some passages which require little revision), heavy revisers and writers with idiosyncratic or atypical techniques. No writers I have studied claim that they do not revise at all. However these categories obviously often overlap: many of the writers who are "inspired by the Muse," such as Henry Miller and William Faulkner also revised extensively. Faulkner once described the hard work of revision: "A great book is always accompanied by a painful birth. Myself, I work every day. I write entirely by hand. I know what the 'flash' of inspiration is, but I also try to put some discipline into my life and my work" (*Lion in the Garden* 72). For every comment of a writer describing his/her methods, we may find other comments which do not contradict the statement, but rather demonstrate that the writing and revision process can not be described in neat categories. Writers may also revise differently depending on the literary genre they are composing: a play may come more easily than a novel, or a poem more readily than a short story.

Poets, novelists, playwrights and short story writers all have insisted that some of their ideas come from inspiration by the Muse. These passages (which according to my research occur relatively rarely) are sometimes later published with little or no revision. Henry Miller spoke frequently of writing the exalted passages in his books as if taking "dictation." An interviewer asked him: "You speak in one of your books of 'the dictation' of being almost possessed, of having this stuff spilling out of you. How does this process work?" Miller responded: "Well, it happens only at rare intervals, this dictation. Someone takes over and you just copy out what is being said. It occurred most strongly with the work on D.H. Lawrence" (*Writers at Work*, Second Series 171–72). Miller says that he was obsessed and could not sleep during this "dictation" process.

His experience recalls Plato's dialogue *Ion:* "The poet is a light creature, winged and holy, and is unable to compose unless he is possessed and out of his mind, and his reason is no longer in him" (Murray 18). Plato's ideas on creativity greatly influenced subsequent literary theory regarding how writers get their ideas and would also shape the ways revision was considered. Miller's account also suggests C.G. Jung's idea of "possession" by a transcendent force or the "Muse" who speaks to the artist: the writer simply takes down the "dictation" (as Miller says). Homer ("Sing in me, Muse, and through me tell the story of that man skilled in all ways of contending"), Virgil ("I sing of warfare and a man at war. [. . .] Tell me the causes now, O Muse [. . .]") and Milton ("Of man's first disobedience [. . .] Sing Heav'nly Muse [. . .] I thence invoke thy aid to my advent'rous song") all begin their great epic poems by asking the Muse to help them compose poetry.

Miller also compares this experience of inspiration to Zen Buddhist practice:

> If, say, a Zen artist is going to do something, he's had a long preparation of discipline and meditation, deep quiet thought about it, and then no thought, silence, emptiness, and so on—it might be for months, it might be for years. Then, when he begins, it's like lightning, just what he wants—it's perfect. Well, this is the way I think all art should be done. But who does it? We lead lives that our contrary to our profession. (*Writers at Work* 172)

Miller's description here corresponds exactly to the stages of creative thinking—preparation, incubation, illumination—which we have outlined above. Furthermore, the artist prepares himself/herself in a manner reminiscent of religious apprentices to the holy life: only when the writer—like the Zen devotee—is ready will he/she be vouchsafed a vision. Igor Stravinsky memorably said of the way he composed music: "I can wait as an insect waits." The artist must learn patience, silence and emptiness in order to allow the work to find its own direction.

Miller declares that he frequently revises only after allowing his draft to "rest" for a while before he returns to work on it. When asked "Do you edit or change much?," he responded: "That too varies a great deal. I never do any correcting or revising while in the process of writing. Let's say I write a thing out any old way, and then, after it's cooled off—I let it rest for a while, a month or two maybe—I see it with a fresh eye" (*Writers at Work* 170). Miller revised his typescript by pen, then retyped the draft which possessed at this point a kind of maze-like, complex, lovely messiness like a manuscript by Balzac. Thus the revision process often includes shifting from one type of writing technology to another. "Writer's block" may be relieved by the fresh approach afforded by a different means of actually getting the words down on paper. Miller also comments on his physical, visceral relationship to his typewriter which he says acts as a "stimulus" to his writing: he enters into a "cooperative" connection to his machine (170). Just the act of touching the typewriter keys appears to "sharpen" his thinking. Like William Saroyan and Charles Bukowski, Miller's volcanic connection to the typewriter and the physical act of typing also had a significant impact on his revision techniques.

In his autobiographical text *My Life and Times* Miller speaks of his enjoyment of revision as an intense, engaging, creative activity:

> Some men write line by line, stop, erase, take the sheet out and tear it up, and so on. I don't proceed that way. I just go on and on. Later, when I finish my stint, I put it, so to speak, in the refrigerator. I don't want to look at it for a month or two, the longer the better. Then I experience another pleasure. It's just as great as the pleasure of writing. This is what I call 'taking the ax to your work.' I mean chopping it to pieces. You see it now from a wholly new vantage point. You have a new perspective on it. And you take a delight in killing even some of the most exciting passages, because they don't fit, they don't sound right to your critical ear. I truly enjoy this slaughter-

> house aspect of the game. You may not believe it, but it's true. (54)

It is interesting to note the aggressive nature of the metaphors Miller uses here to describe the act of revision: "taking the ax to your work," "killing some of the most exciting passages," and finally "this slaughterhouse aspect of the game." Yet this revision takes place only after he has put his work away for one or two months and returned to it with a fresh eye. Due to the intense familiarity the writer has with his/her work, they literally seem not to "see" their errors, repetitions, infelicities of expression, or structural, organizational or developmental problems. Time and distance allow re-vision. And there is pleasure in now being able to see more clearly. For Miller, revision is a reengagement with his earlier self which in a sense he attempts to clarify or "purify" by cutting away any material which does not express his new vision. Again, like Michelangelo with his sculpture, there is delight in carving away excess words, polishing the style, making the phrasing and rhythm of sentences gleam beautifully. What was potential becomes actualized as the ideas emerge into their proper form.

The Beat writers Jack Kerouac, Allen Ginsberg and William Burroughs often wrote in rushes of drug-aided euphoria (Benzedrine, ether, marijuana, LSD, alcohol, etc.). Kerouac typed his manuscripts in machine-gun-like rapidity nonstop through the night on huge continuous teletype rolls. Ginsberg was influenced by Kerouac's doctrine of "no revision" which for Ginsberg became "first thought, best thought." Ginsberg remarked that his poem "'Sunflower Sutra' is almost completely untouched from the original. It took me a long time to get on to Kerouac's idea of writing without revision. I did it by going to his house where he sat me down with typewriter and said, 'Just write a poem!'" (Mahoney 54). However, Ginsberg's most famous poem "Howl" clearly underwent extensive revision, as evidenced by the publication in 1986 of *Howl: Original Draft Facsimile, Transcript and Variant Versions*. "Howl" of course is a much longer poem and this again suggests that usually it is only brief lyric poems or passages in longer prose works which are written relatively effortlessly.

The Argentinean short story writer, poet and essayist Jorge Luis Borges also experienced writing as a form of "revelation." In a 1968 interview he remarked:

> When I feel I'm going to write something, then I just am quiet and I try to listen. Then something comes through. And I do what I can in order not to tamper with it. And then, when I begin to hear what's coming through, I write it down [. . .] So, I try to interfere as little as possible with the revelation, I believe, no? I believe the author is actually one who receives. The idea of the muse [. . .] Of course, I'm not saying anything new. (77)

As we noted at the beginning of this essay, the experience of religious "revelation" has been from antiquity conflated with the experience of artistic inspiration. The Muse speaks through the poet and the "secular" act of writing a short story becomes assimilated to sacred experience. Borges conceives of himself as *receiving* something from above or beyond: he strives not to get in the way of the messages which come to him. Yet Borges insists "there's nothing mystical about all this. I suppose all writers do the same" (77). And composition for him was not a easy thing: Borges remarked that when writing a story, the beginning and end were revealed to him, but he had to then go on to invent the middle of the story, discovering his way as he went along in the composition process (235).

In addition to novelists and short story writers, some playwrights report rapid writing. Eugene Ionesco, for example, says he composed his plays in three weeks or a month and did not do several drafts: "They came out very quickly. A few tiny details I changed, but I wrote them like that. Then I read them over. And when I had a secretary, I dictated to her at the typewriter. I hardly ever change it" (Weiss 96). Ionesco remarked that his plays take shape as he writes:

> I have no preliminary idea when I write, but as I write my imagination completes it. So the second half or more of the play takes shape in my head. Then I know how I'm going to end it. Though I must say that spontaneous creation does not exclude the pursuit and consciousness of style. (96)

Here we see again that inspiration also includes perspiration, or what Ionesco calls "the pursuit and consciousness of style."

The American poet and novelist Charles Bukowski speaks of the act of writing as an act of seizure, in which he is almost involuntarily led to write. At first he will

> play footsy with the goddamn chair and typewriter and table. Finally I sit down, drawn to the machine as if by a magnet, against my will. There's absolutely no plan to it. It's just me, the typewriter, and the chair. And I always throw the first draft away, saying 'that's no good!' Then I enter into the act with a kind of fury, writing madly for four, five, even eight hours. (85)

Descriptions of "inspiration" by writers are fairly consistent. The writing seems to take place almost "against the writer's will"—it is "automatic" in a sense, or autonomous. Notice Bukowski's analogy above: "Drawn to the machine as if by a magnet." There is a sense in which the will becomes passive, and some seemingly alien force seizes hold of the writer.

D.H. Lawrence writes in his "Preface" to his *Collected Poems* about the difference between the first poems he wrote at age nineteen, and his poems written the following year: " Any young lady might have written them and been pleased with them; as I was pleased with them. But it was after that, when I was twenty, that my real demon would now and then get hold of me and shake more real poems out of me, making me uneasy" (27). Lawrence's "Foreword" to his *Collected Poems* speaks instead of a "demon" of a "ghost" which possessed or "haunted" him as a young man and inspired "incoherent" poems (849). For Lawrence, the inspired poems (as opposed to the competent but unoriginal earlier poems which "any young lady might have written") he wrote seemed "incoherent": he himself did not fully understand them or where they came from. One recalls here Arthur Rimbaud's "Je est un autre" (I is another) and Jorge Luis Borges, "Borges Y Yo": "Borges and I." The writer is the caretaker of an indwelling genius, an inner daimon/demon which speaks in riddles like an oracle—speaks sometimes seemingly unintelligibly but in the pure language of the poetic unconscious. However in all writers' subsequent work these "messages from the gods," these transcendent words later undergo the revision process, although some of the "inspired" passages may remain virtually unchanged in the final publication.

Lawrence's friend Aldous Huxley corroborates Lawrence as "possessed":

> And then he would get the urge to write: and then write for eighteen hours a day. It was very extraordinary to see him work, it was a sort of *possession;* he would rush on with it, his hand moving at a tremendous rate. And he never corrected anything; because if he was dissatisfied with anything he would start again at the beginning. (Bedford 212)

Huxley also commented on the "cleanliness" of Lawrence's manuscripts: "The script runs on, page after page, with hardly a blot or an erasure" (Powell x).

When Lawrence did revise, he often started from scratch and wrote a whole new version of the text. His final novel *Lady Chatterley's Lover* (original title, *Tenderness*) was rewritten three times, from start to finish. Lawrence was an amazingly prolific writer, producing novels, poems, stories, letters, plays with seemingly effortless ease. He wrote in longhand, and the words seem to come quickly, flowing from his subconscious depths in a way unequalled by the other writers studied in this essay. One need only examine E.W. Tedlock's edition of *The Frieda Lawrence Collection of D.H. Lawrence Manuscripts* to be moved by the quick, lively, spontaneous outpouring of ideas which characterize Lawrence's genius. Here we find the passages described by Huxley above: long, pristine, seamless paragraphs which appear to have been written effortlessly. Lawrence's quest for a mystical communion with the world is evident in his prose and poetry: it courses on inexorably as if coming from an unquenchable and integral primal source, from a submerged fountain of creativity. But there is also, as Tedlock remarks, the "intense revision, the untiring rewriting" as evidenced by the reproduced corrected manuscripts in Lawrence's neat cursive hand of the stories "Odour of Chrysanthemums" and "The Blue Moccasins" (xxxvi, 34, 68).

Robert Graves claimed that only when the poet is possessed by the "White Goddess," by the Muse, does he write authentic poetry. However for Graves as for Lawrence, inspiration does not preclude revision. He writes that he will "revise the manuscript till I can't read it any longer, then get somebody to type it. Then I revise the typing. Then it's retyped again. Then there's a third typing, which is the final one. Nothing should then remain that offends the eye" (102). Graves's manuscripts—some of which are located at Southern Illinois University—began as "rough holograph drafts" and after heavy revision would be transformed into "a maze of lines, blots, and inserts" (Robert Graves Papers). Graves's amazing productivity—he published more than one hundred books (novels, poetry, plays, essays, translations, children's books) during his career—was clearly not impeded by his meticulous revision methods.

Some writers write rapidly in one genre and more slowly in another. For example, Samuel Beckett composed his play *Waiting for Godot* in only four months, while he labored much more intensively on his novels. Enoch Brater notes that

> Beckett began the *Godot* project methodically, writing only on his school book's right hand pages; when he ran out of space, he backed up to the verso sides he had skipped before. [. . .] Unlike most of his manuscripts, the text for this play was written clearly, almost, it seems, without hesitation. 'It wrote itself,' he [Beckett] told Peter Lennon, 'with very few corrections, in four months.' (Brater 10)

However, Beckett's manuscript of his novel *Malone Meurt* is replete with revisions, deletions, and doodles (49). Again, we notice the passive aspect of creativity: Beckett says the play "wrote itself." Like several other writers, Beckett's relation to writing in longhand and typewriting were complementary aspects of the revision process: "First he wrote in longhand, then he typed them, using the hunt and peck system, which he demonstrated by fingering the air. Things change between longhand and typing; the typewriter was his 'friend.' I suggest, 'collaborator'" (Gussow 41). This is a model we see repeated in many writers, the shift between writing by hand or by typewriter (and now computer). The writer perceives his/her work differently during the shift from pen or pencil, to typewriter/computer, to proofs and galleys and ultimately the finished publication in book form.

Sometimes a writer's approach to revision differs depending on the work they are creating. For example, Leslie Marmon Silko produced three or four versions of her novel *Almanac of the Dead* which required a great deal of revising. She could not begin the revision process until she had completed two-thirds to three-quarters of the novel. However, her novel *Ceremony* was created in a very different way: "I wrote *Ceremony* just like you'd write a short story. Each sentence was perfect before I went on to the next one. So there was no re-writing; there was very little editing" (Silko 116–17).

Other writers such as Sinclair Lewis, Aldous Huxley, and Vladimir Nabokov have emphasized the hard work of revision. For example, Sinclair Lewis declared that "Writing is just work—there's no secret. If you dictate or use a pen or type or write with your toes—it is still just work" (Lindemann 11). And Aldous Huxley wrote: "Generally, I write everything many times over. All my thoughts are second thoughts. And I correct each page a great deal, or rewrite it several times as I go along." Huxley would begin with a vague idea of where a project was going and develop his ideas as he wrote. He sometimes would produce a large manuscript, find out it was not working, and throw it away. Huxley found writing and revision "a very absorbing occupation and sometimes exhausting" (*Writers at Work,* Second Series 197).

Vladimir Nabokov concurs: he once revealed that he rewrote every word he had ever published several times and wore out his erasers before his pencils (Boyd 374). Nabokov did not compose to communicate a "message" about life but rather to refine and polish his words until they brought him aesthetic joy: "I have no purpose at all when composing my stuff itself except to compose it. I work hard, I work long, on a body of words until it grants me complete possession and pleasure" (*Strong Opinions* 115). Thus he finds pleasure—like Henry Miller—in revision, in working intensively to extract from writing its ultimate pleasures. In his essay "Inspiration," he wrote: "The words which on various occasions, during some fifty years of composing prose, I have put together and then canceled may have formed by now in the Realm of Rejection (a foggy but not quite unlikely land north of nowhere) a huge library of scrapped phrases, characterized and concorded only by their wanting the benison of inspiration" (*Strong Opinions* 311). Again like Henry Miller, Nabokov does not consider inspiration and the rigors of revision to be mutually exclusive: he is unashamed to delight in the ecstasy of inspiration, or to confess that he works hard at his writing.

Writers such as Eudora Welty and John Berryman revised in peculiar or idiosyncratic ways. Welty is perhaps the most "physical" reviser, using "scissors and pins" as she readies a manuscript for publication. When asked whether she used the typewriter, she responded:

> Yes, and that's useful—it helps give me the feeling of making my work objective. I can correct better if I see it in typescript. After that, I revise with scissors and pins. Pasting is too slow, and you can't undo it, but with pins you can move things from anywhere to anywhere and that's what I really love doing—putting things in their best and proper place, revealing things at the time when they matter most. Often I shift things from the very beginning to the very end (Welty 89).

Welty got the idea of using pins from working on a newspaper and thus used the delete and paste method before the proliferation of computers and achieved a similar result: the ability to test how various sections of her composition appear in relation to one another and thus better choose how to organize and develop her stories. She could in this manner shift her dialogue, characters, descriptive passages, until they fell into the proper place. Revision may be said on one level to be a constant process of trial and error in which writers try out various possibilities, rejecting, accepting, rejecting again and finally arriving at the proper form which lay dormant within the "mind's eye" from the beginning of the work's conception.

The American poet John Berryman also revised in a curious manner: he placed his manuscripts beneath glassine to study them. Berryman began composing three stanzas daily of his poem *Homage to Mistress Bradstreet* but discovered that was too much to try and accomplish so he "got one of those things that have a piece of glassine over a piece of paper, and you can put something in between and see it but not touch it." He would then make a draft of just one stanza and place it beneath the glassine. This allowed him to study the draft and make notes but he would not touch the manuscript itself until he thought he was ready—usually not for several hours. He would then remove his draft, make corrections, put it back beneath the glassine and re-study his text. When he felt satisfied with the draft he would remove and type it and the revision process was complete. He would only write one stanza a day. If he finished in the morning, he would still not look at the stanza again until the following morning. Berryman found the time waiting for his next contact with his manuscript very difficult and would drink whiskey to fill up the time (*Writers at Work,* Fourth Series 314).

For Berryman, making the manuscript physically inaccessible by covering it with a transparent sheet forced him to contemplate his work at a kind of psychological distance which made later revision easier for him. The critical aspect for many writers in the act of revision is *time:* they require the distance that time away from their work allows in order to perceive it in a fresh light. In this respect, many creative writers sometimes may have an advantage over academic writers or journalists who must meet deadlines and thus do not have the luxury of being able to "remove" themselves sufficiently from their work. On the other hand, as we shall see, this time element can also be a liability since authors are tempted to continue to tamper with their work interminably, even after publication. Indeed, it may be wondered sometimes (this point has been raised with regard to W.H. Auden's continual revisions of his poems) whether the earlier versions of a work are ultimately more successful: revision may not always improve.

Thus we can see in the comments of writers themselves the myriad ways they undergo the revision process. It is likely that they are so willing to talk about their individual approaches to revision because in many ways it forms the central aspect of their creative activity. As we have seen, achieving the initial inspiration is in fact the easiest part of their jobs: the hard part is returning to the lonely typewriter or computer screen and facing the long hours of intense labor which revision entails. Examining the drafts of Dylan Thomas's late poem "Elegy" for the death of his father, I was astonished that Thomas—a poet I had always assumed composed easily and in a state of beer-inspired euphoria—had written rows of rhyming words (testing out possibilities) all over the manuscript, had crossed out passages, had begun over and over and over again.

REVISION AND COMPUTERS

With the advent of word processing and computers, the ways scholars study the revision process has dramatically changed. The tracks of revision, so to speak, will now be covered because much of the process will be "erased" by the fact that the writer can now make immediate changes to the text on the computer screen and the corrections will normally not be saved unless the writer saves the computer document, prints it and subsequently revises it by hand (as Charles Bukowski did). For many writers, the change over to computers seemed also to be an abandonment of their devotion to the "old way" of doing things. The shift from pen to typewriter also clearly was momentous for writers and of course brought into being all sorts of changes in style—from e.e. cummings playful use of typographical riffs to perhaps even the staccato dialogue of writers like Ernest Hemingway.

William Burroughs, Charles Bukowski, and Gloria Anzaldua have documented their relationship to word processors. Burroughs, at least in 1987, was still not won over to computers: "Right now word processors seem just too complicated to get into. I guess they would be helpful, save a great deal of time undoubtedly, but at this point the effort involved in learning how to use them just doesn't seem worthwhile" (Burroughs 186). However, both Charles Bukowski and Gloria Anzaldua—although I would consider both to be "Dionysian" "natural" writers whom one might think would abjure technology—wrote and revised their work on the computer. Bukowski actually was initially skeptical regarding the computer, but once he began using the word processor he found it a real spur to writing and used it to compose virtually all of his late work. He told Robert Gumpert in 1991: "The writing's not bad for an old guy I guess and, yeah, maybe now I fear the loss of my soul. When I wrote my first computer poem I was anxious that I would be suffocated by these layers of consumerist suffering. Would old Dostoyevsky have ever used one of these babies? I wondered, and then I said—'hell, yeah!'" (275).

Thus Bukowski voices one of the concerns about the "technologizing" of the writing process. Will the computer take away the "sacred," "natural," elemental aspect of writing, turning what used to be a profound solitary communion with one's soul into another sterile technocratic transaction? Bukowski ended up preferring the computer and found that his output was greatly increased. His typical early practice was to make copies with his printer which he would then revise by hand, sign, and send in for publication. A late four-page manuscript poem entitled "talk" recently offered for sale on eBay illustrates Bukowski's working methods: the poem printed from the computer is heavily revised, including eighty-eight individual handwritten corrections in black marker.

Gloria Anzaldua was asked by Andrea Lunsford: "Do the words seem to come out as well from the ends of your fingers typing as when you were scripting?" Anzaldua responded:

> Yes. I prefer writing directly on the computer, especially the first few drafts when I'm still imagining the story or if I'm writing nonfiction, discovering what I'm trying to say and trying out different directions. With electronic writing I can try out different points of view, scenarios, and conflicts. I like to edit on the computer too, though I need to do the last few edits on paper. When I was at the Norcroft writer's retreat my hard drive crashed and I had to resort to handwriting for four weeks. I was surprised to find that I could achieve a smoother flow by writing on paper. I'd gone there to revise *La Prieta, The Dark One,* a collection of stories. I had nineteen of the twenty-four stories in hard copy, so I was able to revise on paper, but the rest of the time, much to my surprise, I wrote poems and worked on my writing guide—exercises, meditations for writing, the elements of writing and fictive techniques. I also spent a lot of time thinking and writing about composition, composition theory and creativity—things I hadn't planned on doing. I just wanted to do the stories but not having a computer forced me to switch over. Basically I'm a several-projects-simultaneously type of writer. (259)

Anzaldua underscores the differences between writing "on paper" and composing on the computer. She edits with the computer, but then changes to paper for the final revisions. As we have seen with many writers, there is a natural movement from one writing technology to another during the process of receiving the initial idea, drafting, revising and publication. It is quite usual for writers like Anzaldua to move from the computer (where she does her initial writing and revision) to paper for what she terms "the last few edits." Because the computer is still a relatively recent form of writing technology, we do not yet have a complete understanding of the ways it has altered creative writers' revision methods, but it is clear that the influence of computers has been extremely important in the ways imaginative writers do their work today. With spell check, grammatical interventions, thesauruses and other helps to the composition process, we may now never be able to know whether a great writer—like John Keats for example—was in reality a terrible speller (as Keats in fact was) or not.

The Role of Collaborators and Editors

Is the "solitary genius" actually the model which emerges when we study revision, or is it more complicated than that? The issues involved in revision expand when we go beyond the idea of composition as a solitary act and consider the roles of friends, collaborators and editors. Gustave Flaubert wrote in a letter to Louise Colete [July 22, 1852]:

> I am in the process of copying and correcting the entire first part of *Bovary*. My eyes are smarting. [. . .] A week from Sunday I shall read the whole thing to Bouilhet, and a day or two later you will see me. What a bitch of a thing prose is! It is never finished: there is always something to be done over. (682)

Thus Flaubert showed his work to others and wanted their response in order to gauge the effectiveness of his writing and to aid in the revision process. Frequently a close colleague or fellow practitioner takes on the symbolic role of "midwife," helping during the maieutic process of birthing the literary baby. Anais Nin read the typescript of Henry Miller's *Tropic of Cancer* and suggested many substantive changes which Miller implemented.

T.S. Eliot's *The Wasteland* was significantly changed during the revision process due to the influence of Ezra Pound. Pound's revisions and comments can now be studied because *The Wasteland: A Facsimile and Transcript of the Original Drafts Including the Annotations of Ezra Pound* was published in 1971, edited by Eliot's wife Valerie. In passage after passage, Pound makes incisive comments on the typescript. For example in "The Fire Sermon" section, Pound writes on the first page: "Too loose [. . .] rhyme drags it out to diffuseness" (39). Along the first stanza of part 4 of the same section, Pound scribbles "verse not interesting enough as verse to warrant so much of it," and along the second stanza "inversions not warranted by any real exigence of metre" (45). Eliot revised his manuscript accordingly and the book documents incontrovertibly that *The Wasteland* would probably not have become the classic twentieth century poem it did had not Eliot received Pound's help. It is perhaps no accident that Eliot dedicated the poem to Pound—*il miglior fabbro*—"the better craftsman."

An unlikely collaboration developed between the American Trappist monk and writer Thomas Merton and Evelyn Waugh. Merton asked for Waugh's help in revising his autobiography *The Seven Storey Mountain*. Waugh's biographer reports that "Merton allowed Waugh freedom to cut the text and he relished the task; not simply as an exercise of professional skill but as an act of homage; the more he cleaned up the prose, the brighter shone its significance. It took him just a week. He removed about a third, polished what remained and later produced a Foreword" (*Evelyn Waugh* 222).

Once the manuscript has left the writer's study, it often goes to a professional editor, who also may have a role in the revision process. Maxwell Perkins had a deep influence on the shape inchoate massive manuscripts such as Thomas Wolfe's *The Web and the Rock* would ultimately assume. Just as a composer needs instrumentalists and conductors to realize his/her musical score, so too few writers brings a poem, story, novel or play to completion alone. Authors such as T.S. Eliot, as we have seen, acknowledged the central role of Ezra Pound—who in a sense was both collaborator and editor—by dedicating *The Wasteland* to him. In the prefatory acknowledgement pages of many books we witness the omnipresence of collaboration in the commonly expressed words: "And I would like to thank the following people for all the help they have given me in the writing of this book."

REVISION OF PROOFS AND GALLEYS

The omnipresence of the computer during the revision and editing process in modern publishing has minimized the significant moment of proofs and galleys which were important stages for several of the great modern writers such as Joyce, Hemingway and Proust. Once their texts had been set up in galleys, the revision process might—and often did—continue. Ernest Hemingway described the proofs as yet another "chance" to revise following the earlier stages of composition: "I always rewrite each day up to the point where I stopped. When it is all finished, naturally you go over it. You get another chance to correct and rewrite when someone else types it, and you see it clean in type. The last chance is in the proofs. You're grateful for these different chances" (*Writers at Work,* Second Series 222). Seeing his text "clean" in type form allows a kind of distance which as we have seen many writers find extremely useful.

Some writers labor intensively to send off to the printers a correct text. J.R.R. Tolkien, for example, was a perfectionist:

Nothing was allowed to reach the printer until it had been revised, reconsidered and polished—in which respect he was the opposite of C.S. Lewis, who sent manuscripts off for publication with scarcely a second glance at them. Lewis, well aware of this difference between them, wrote of Tolkien: 'His standard of self-criticism was high and the mere suggestion of publication usually set him upon a revision, in the course of which so many new ideas occurred to him that where his friends had hoped for the final text of an old work they actually got the first draft of a new one. (Carpenter 154)

There is naturally a powerful psychological element in the varying ways authors revise their work. Perhaps Tolkien's unwillingness to send off anything but the most polished and sparkling manuscript speaks to a powerful superego which fears criticism and which sets a high bar for performance. Other writers also may simply be under a myriad of personal or professional pressures which make it impossible to revise their work as thoroughly as they might have hoped.

James Joyce entered into a titanic creative struggle when he received the proofs of *Ulysses*. Richard Ellmann described Joyce's work during 1918–1919 on specific episodes of his great novel:

> He was encouraged to make great progress with *Ithaca* and *Penelope*. At the new flat, on June 10, he received from Darantiere the first galley proofs, and by Sept. 7 he had read them through *Scylla and Charybdis*. With Joyce the reading of proof was a creative act; he insisted on five sets, and made innumerable changes, almost always additions, in the text, complicating the interior monologue with more and more interconnecting details. The book grew by one third in proof. Darantiere's characteristic gesture, throwing up his hands in despair, became almost constant when the type had to be recast time after time, and Sylvia Beach was much tried; but Joyce won his point. (527)

Joyce turned proofreading itself into a "creative act" and thus made life thoroughly miserable for his typesetters. Of course, it is an expensive proposition to revise a text once it has been set up in galleys, yet this has not deterred many famous authors from having second thoughts. (Marcel Proust was wealthy enough to afford extensive revisions to the proofs of *A La Recherche du Temps Perdu*). *Ulysses: A Facsimile of the Manuscript,* published in 1975, illustrates the immense problems encountered when the printer Maurice Darantiere of Dijon and his twenty-six non-English-speaking typesetters had to continually reset the text to include Joyce's additions and in the process made additional errors at each stage of the resetting.

Joyce's other gigantic masterwork—*Finnegans Wake*—was an even greater nightmare of revision. David Hayman describes how—beginning in 1924—Joyce revised *one sentence* in *Finnegans Wake* over a fourteen year period: "A study of the thirteen-odd stages of its development should give us a reasonable number of insights into the artistic method and into the meaning of Book III, the section of *Finnegans Wake* to which this sentence belongs" (257). The text appeared in the avant-garde magazine *transition* and Hayman points out that "the second of the above-treated drafts dates from April 1928. During the four years that had elapsed since 1924, nine revisions had been made. Joyce was already working from *transition* magazine page proofs" (275). Hayman methodically follows the revision process and astonishes us with the labors Joyce lavished on a single sentence:

The sixteenth draft, completed in 1936, is the end product of several minor revisions undertaken over a period of seven years. Consequently, these *transition* pages are generously annotated in a variety of Joycean scripts. (Joyce's handwriting varied with the state of his eyesight). [. . .] With the inclusion of Joyce's additions to the second galley proofs of *Finnegans Wake,* our passage lacked but one syllable ('leaves') of the published sentence. (285, 287)

Not only was bringing the book to publication a superhuman labor of revision, but *Finnegans Wake*—composed in Joyce's multi-lingual, pun-filled, lyrical, allusive, fiendishly complex, portmanteau style ("riverrun past Eve and Adam's, from swerve of shore to bend of bay, brings us by a commodius vicus of recirculation back to Howth Castle and Environs")—of course may pose the most insuperable problems of any book in history for scholars attempting to establish an "error-free" edition (*Finnegans Wake* 3). It's hard enough for a typesetter to work from texts in the English language: the Joyce language of the *Wake* is the most amazingly bizarre and elaborate tongue yet invented.

Henry Miller published a revised version in 1956 of his book *The World of Sex* which includes photographs of his corrections and revisions. In rereading the original text (which had appeared in 1940 and had gone out of print), Miller informs us he "began (quite involuntarily) making changes and corrections, never dreaming what I was letting myself in for. If the reader will turn to the reproductions in this volume, he will see for himself with what almost diabolical enthusiasm I plunged into this work of revision" (9). As we have seen, Miller in fact found the revision experience pleasurable and thought that readers might be curious about the ways writers compose. Although he wrote many of the passages of his books in an "inspired" state, it is also clear that his keen enjoyment of revision underscores the creative nature of this stage of the composition process. It appears that it is at this moment—after the work has lain fallow for a period (or in the present case, a sixteen-year interval between original and revision!)—that there is intense joy in finding the right words, style, phrasing or punctuation for what one really wants to say.

It is clear that the added objectivity of seeing the text in printed form allows the writer yet another chance to "re-see" or "re-vise" his or her work. As we saw earlier with the shift in perception occasioned by writing with pen, typewriter or computer, so too the complex process of bringing a manuscript through the galley and proof process create time and distance from the original conception and thus allows and often *forces* a new awareness of the writer's aims and intentions. It may well be that the setting up of the work in type is the final objectification of the work, the final distancing of the live plasma of the artistic organism created in the artist's heart and soul. Now it is *out there,* alive and kicking, the text itself, the hard clean shape of print: cold, objective, almost as if it had been created by someone else. A last chance to say goodbye, to assure a happy delivery to the literary baby, now bravely out there all alone in the world.

Revision after Publication

However, some writers—in particular poets such as Robert Lowell, W.H. Auden, W.B. Yeats and Robert Graves—took one *more* chance and extensively revised their work even after publication. The fact that most lyric poems are relatively short may allow poets the luxury of returning to their printed texts to tinker with them in ways which would be prohibited to the novelist or playwright. Robert Lowell "endlessly" revised his published work (*Writers at Work*, Second Series 350). Lowell also moved lines from one poem to another. A passage at the end of the poem "Cistercians in Germany" from *Land of Unlikeness* was rewritten to form the last lines of "At the Indian Killer's Grave" (349). Lowell revised his poem to John Berryman in four different printed versions: the original version and then subsequent variations were printed in the volumes *History* (1973) and the two editions of *Notebook* (1969, 1970). "Beyond the Alps" is another poem Lowell ceaselessly revised even after publication. He reshaped the poem obsessively over a twenty-year period, altering the original rhymed couplet structure, and deleting it from *Life Studies*. Lowell then revised eight of the forty-two lines of the poem he had omitted and rewrote them into another poem "For George Santayana" (Moore).

Again, we must take into account psychological aspects in this context: Robert Lowell suffered from manic-depression throughout his life and had to be repeatedly institutionalized. He was ultimately treated with lithium which considerably relieved his symptoms (Hamilton). Certainly a good deal of his extreme behavior with respect to revision may be linked to the cycles of his illness. The relationship between psychological types and revision practices should be kept in mind when we study writers' composition practices. Poets throughout history of course have tended to both extremes of bi-polar experience: either ecstatic highs or depressive, suicidal lows. John Berryman— who as we have seen suffered through the revision process by drinking whiskey and observing his poems beneath glassine—was a suicide, as were Hart Crane, Sylvia Plath, Anne Sexton and (most likely) Randall Jarrell. A study of the actual manuscripts of these poets reveals the intense psychological struggle involved in their revision practices. The effort to "get it right" was ultimately a life-or-death struggle.

W.H. Auden also "drastically" (according to his literary executor Edward Mendelson) revised his poems after publication (Spender 249). Auden's obsessive revision practices have been studied by Joseph Warren Beach in *The Making of the Auden Canon*. Beach studied Auden's "textual alterations made in the poems as they appeared in earlier collections and/or in periodicals; excision of passages of some length in the poems reprinted; elimination of entire poems published in earlier collections and/or periodicals" (3). Beach demonstrates Auden's anxious desire to get his poems right, often returning over and over again to rework them. Auden remarked: "I do an enormous amount of revising. I think of that quote from Valéry, 'A poem is never finished, only abandoned.' Some people feel revisions have ideological significance. I revise if I feel the language is prolix or obscure. Your first idea is not always your best" (*The Poet's Craft* 3). Auden here neatly contradicts Allen Ginsberg's formulation, "first thought, best thought."

Auden's *Collected Poems* contained many poems that had been thoroughly revised. An interviewer asked about one of his most famous poems: "In 'September 1, 1939,' you revised one line ('We must love one another or die'), and then omitted the entire stanza in which this line occurs." Auden replied:

> I have scrapped the whole poem. I took out that section, then I decided the whole thing had to go. I will put it this way: I don't think a writer can decide how good or bad something he writes is. What he can tell, though, is whether the poem is authentic, really written in his own hand. I decided this poem is unauthentic as far as I am concerned. It may have certain merits but I should not have written it. (*The Poet's Craft* 3)

When the interviewer asks about the relationship between rejecting whole poems and Auden's conception of his own style, Auden replied:

> You can see in the *Collected Short Poems* what I have removed. It is different from revising poems. When one revises, one is not revising emotions, but reworking the language. But the poems I decided were unauthentic went out. There was something false about them. The others which I have revised a great deal had more a question of language. (*The Poet's Craft* 3–4)

Auden raises an interesting question here regarding the revision of a single poem and the removal of one or more poems from a collected edition. In the second case, the author is "revising" the whole shape of his oeuvre, creating a legacy, making the form in which he wants his work preserved. He is not deciding the aesthetic success or failure of a single line or two, but rather removing entire poems from his *oeuvre* because they no longer adequately represent the self he wishes to pass on to posterity. The ongoing altering and reconceptualizing of a poet's entire corpus can also be seen in Walt Whitman's multiple versions *Leaves of Grass* which he revised as a whole volume several times throughout his career. Yet Auden's revisions were not always considered improvements and many of his admirers ironically preferred the earlier versions of his poems: the writer has satisfied himself, but left his readers unhappy (Carpenter 417–18). As we shall see, this curious situation may be obviated by the possibility of parallel texts which allow the reader to choose his/her own favorite version.

Scholars Study Revision: Process Criticism

As we have seen, the emergence of printing opened up the question of revision to students of creativity. Now there was a multiple trail to follow: not only the original manuscript with its myriad corrections, but the typewritten text (also frequently heavily edited), followed by galleys and proof sheets. And the process did not even cease there, for poets often revised their works *even after they were published*, thus further complicating the idea of a pure, unalloyed absolute text. Modern writers thus have left a tantalizing trail for scholars to follow in their efforts to understand the creative process. For example, Regina Fadiman in her *Faulkner's Light in August: A Description and Interpretation of the Revisions* defines what she calls "process criticism":

> The manuscript provides a clear record of the techniques Faulkner employed to revise the novel. His alterations during the process of composition resulted in a significant shift in the ultimate meaning of the work, for its new form shaped its new content. In a larger sense the manuscript contains a record of the work habits and methods of revision of the artist who is considered by many to be the major American novelist of the twentieth century; it offers, therefore, valuable insights into Faulkner's imaginative genius and into the creative process itself. (ix)

Faulkner's manuscripts demonstrate revisions at each stage of the writing process, from small stylistic details to the rearrangement of entire chapters in his novels. As Faulkner looks again at the draft of his novel, new ideas begin to take shape as he sees new relationships between themes, characters, style, metaphors. New patterns emerge as one reconsiders the work and the writer is then compelled to incorporate these fresh ideas into his new draft: the novel thus undergoes a metamorphosis—a "re-vision"—in the very process of reading one's own words again. It is as if a hidden pattern emerges which heretofore had been obscured. There is a synergy between the text and the author: unexpected connections form in the mind during the contemplation of the work and demand different modes of expression, different ways of solving the problem posed by one's own earlier self.

Helen Gardner in *The Composition of Four Quartets* seeks clues to T.S. Eliot's creativity through a close study of his manuscripts. Although Eliot did not approve of preserving his manuscripts, he donated the drafts of *Four Quartets* to Magdalene College, Cambridge University. Gardner, in her study of the drafts remarks:

Manuscript and typed drafts display both major, substantial changes and minute alterations in phrases, words, and pointing; and, up to the very last moment, in corrected proofs, he can be seen changing his mind, sometimes finding a new word, sometimes reverting to a word he had earlier rejected but now found more satisfactory than its substitute. (3)

Thus just as Fadiman studied Faulkner's multiple revisions, so too Gardner attempts to fathom revision and creativity in Eliot's poetry. Thus throughout his career Eliot both relied on collaboration (as we saw above with Ezra Pound's help with *The Wasteland* published in 1922) and later engaged in extensive revision of *Four Quartets*, the four parts of which were published separately between 1935 and 1941.

Charles Ross has explored D.H. Lawrence's revision methods in the various versions of *Women in Love* in his study *Women in Love: A Novel of Mythic Realism*. Between 1913 and 1919, Lawrence composed a long novel with the tentative title "The Sisters" which eventually was broken up into the two novels, *The Rainbow* and *Women in Love*. Censorship also affected the revision process: following its publication in 1915, *The Rainbow* was deemed "obscene" and suppressed by the police. Lawrence would ultimately censor and "revise" the proofs (6). Other modern writers including James Joyce, Henry Miller, Charles Bukowski, William Burroughs and Vladimir Nabokov had to "revise" their work in order to have it published and to conform to legal standards of propriety. However, they fought and won their cases in court.

Censorship is revision in its most unpalatable form: compelled by the "authorities."

Curtis Bradford studied W.B. Yeats's drafts in order to fathom his ability to create such flawless verse. According to Bradford,

> Yeats's manuscripts and typescripts are extremely interesting to any student of the writing process, for it is nearly always possible to reconstruct from them at least the external aspects of how a poem, play, or essay was put together. One can also watch lines of poems and single sentences of prose emerge from the inchoate as Yeats achieves with immense labor the expression he wants. For Yeats the construction process usually meant adding on: his works accumulated slowly, as a coral reef accumulates. (x)

For Bradford, Yeats's drafts reveal the ways Yeats created his work in a number of genres—poetry, plays and essays. Bradford makes the analogy to a coral reef: so too Yeats's work was built up very slowly over time through a process of accretion and involved substantial and hard revision.

Thus scholars who employ process criticism in their studies of writers such as Faulkner, Lawrence and Yeats attempt to uncover the tracks of the creative mind. They seek to discover the ways revision reveals to us the hidden elements of artistic expression. The author himself/herself clearly often does not know where the trail will lead as they embark on a poem, play or novel, but we can try to reconstruct the process through a careful study of the available manuscripts or printed versions. The manuscripts reveal a constant struggle of give and take between the writer and his/her work, a continual "separating of the chaff and the grain." This process provides a deep sense of accomplishment: order is being brought out of chaos. Yet the fascinating thing is that the writer at the outset may not yet fully (or even partially) know what this order is: it is only through the process of revision that he/she discovers that pattern and structure which was implicit (but not yet fully formulated) in the conception from the beginning.

Wordsworth, Parallel Texts, Nabokov, Poststructuralism, Hypertext and Beyond

A final complexity which emerges from a consideration of literary revision is the question of parallel texts. William Wordsworth affords an intriguing example of the problems involved with a text which exists in various versions. Wordsworth completed *The Prelude: Growth of A Poet's Mind* in 1805–6. He continued to revise the work throughout his lifetime and it was published not long after his death in 1850. Because some readers have preferred one version over the other, Penguin decided to publish both versions in a parallel text format with the 1805–6 version facing the 1850 text so the reader can make a line by line comparison. And the situation gets even more intricate. The editor J.C. Maxwell points out that in addition to the 1805 and 1850 versions we must take into account other variants:

> But if we are thinking in terms, not of revisions but of radically different forms of the whole poem, we must further distinguish three versions; a two-book form completed by 1800, a proposed five-book version which Wordsworth had almost completed early in 1804, when he decided to expand it still further, and the full text as we have it both in 1805 and 1850. (17)

Such a situation illustrates the problems involved when an author leaves alternate versions of his or her work. In this case, the reader can compare and contrast the two alternate versions and in a sense create a *third* version of the text by choosing one version or another at various points in the reading process. The two versions may be said to "cancel each other out" and compel us to become an accomplice in creating the meaning of the work. From here, "reader-response" criticism is not far away: this is a text which cannot exist without the reader.

Vladimir Nabokov's novel *Pale Fire* can be read (at least on one level) as a marvelous parody of the problems of "collaboration," literary interpretation and parallel texts. The novel contains a four part poem entitled "Pale Fire" by John Shade, preceded by a "Foreword" and followed by a "Commentary" and "Index" by his "friend" Charles Kinbote. Kinbote "rewrites" the poem. He invents a preposterous parallel story (concerning the faraway land of Zembla with himself as its exiled King) to serve as his own interpretation of the meaning of the poem: he does not serve the author's text, he bends the text to suit his own preconceived idea of its meaning. Kinbote, the mad editor of Shade's poem, uses the vocabulary of textual criticism and revision—"manuscript," "corrected draft," "fair copy" throughout. He even includes variant readings of "Pale Fire" which he claims Shade has not included, yet we suspect he has himself composed the alternate lines. Thus we as readers must often decide whether Kinbote's readings and emendations are correct or whether he has "revised" the text to suit his own purposes. Nabokov thus has created his own kind of parallel text: he plays with the reader's struggle in interpreting a literary work and sets into motion a number of simultaneously contradictory readings, leaving the ultimate decision concerning the meaning in the reader's hands. To interpret the poem, we may be at every turn relying on the unreliable textual emendations of a madman.

It can be seen how the questions of parallel texts, meaning and authorial intention can quickly turn into philosophical quandaries which remind us of the now old, passé debates about poststructuralism and the new, lively debates about the Internet. Structuralism, which evolved from the work of the Swiss linguist Ferdinand de Saussure, held that there is no necessary connection between word and thing, and that language is essentially arbitrary: we call a tree a tree, but we may as well call it an orange. Thinkers such as the anthropologist Claude Levi-Strauss held that meaning does not exist in some abstract ideal realm, but emerges only from the interrelations of items within a given structure: it is their place in the system which gives them meaning, not any putative significance inhering essentially within the words/objects themselves.

Poststructuralists such as Jacques Derrida have gone a step further and believe that a text "deconstructs itself" and that the systems of oppositions—male/female, good/bad, heaven/earth etc. which the structuralists posit in fact "privilege" one element of the "opposition" in an arbitrary fashion. The poststructuralists end in a place beyond relativism: some call it nihilism, some prefer to see it as a playful game of interpretative activity. Thus with regards to the "correct" text and its myriad revisions and transformations, the poststructuralists might claim that the whole question is a perfect description of their philosophy: there is no final text, no final meaning, no *ousia, telos, arche* (being, end, beginning) as Derrida would have it. "Original text" and "revision" is yet another opposition which deconstructs itself. How can there be revision if there is no text? And how can there be a "stable" text if it can be endlessly revised?

Wordsworth, Nabokov and poststructuralism may make us think of the idea of hypertext. Hypertext is "a document retrieval network that permits the user to access any of a group of linked documents by clicking on a jump maker, or link structure. Each of the documents contained in this network appears in full-text form on the computer screen; once users access one document, they can jump to other documents at will" (*Bedford Glossary of Critical and Literary Terms* 205). It is now possible to construct a labyrinth in cyberspace of millions of different versions of a text, or of a story with alternate endings reminiscent of Jorge Luis Borges's "The Garden of Forking Paths" in which an infinity of possible plot lines proliferate in an infinity of possible directions. And hypertext has also become another tool by which scholars can study revision: they can now link "textual editions and textual variants, not only with one another but also with contextual (including visual) materials" (205). Revision has come a long way indeed. Theseus, the Minotaur and the Labyrinth are perhaps the main figures of postmodern mythology.

We may with justice conclude that revision touches virtually every aspect of the activities of creative writers from ancient times to the advent of cyberspace and the debates of contemporary philosophy and literary theory. Revision dominates the lives of professional authors from the initial inspiration, through incubation and drafting, editing, collaboration and even following the actual publication in printed form and is intimately connected with the creative process itself. Indeed, one might legitimately claim that revision *is* the creative process. Writers are undoubtedly sometimes struck by an initial "inspiration" but just as undoubtedly they must labor long and hard to render their inspiration into coherent, aesthetic and readable form. In literary studies, perhaps we would do well to honor the re-visionary as well as the visionary.

10 Best Classroom Practices

Carol Trupiano

INTRODUCTION

The Process Approach debuted during the 1970s and dramatically changed the way writing is taught. One of its most significant contributions was establishing that writing happens over time and is not a one-step phenomenon. Process Writing put the "re" into writing, showing that re-thinking, re-envisioning, re-organizing, and re-writing are essential and integral parts of writing well. Although Process Writing has traditionally been presented as linear, its recursive "re" nature reveals its cyclical nature. The past thirty years have brought modifications and evolutions to the Process Approach, but many of its central premises and practices remain with us today in large part because they offer writers useful strategies. Practices such as developing a paper over time in multiple drafts and peer workshops are widely accepted and implemented in teaching writing from elementary school through college. This chapter explores some of those time-tested practices, suggests ways writers and teachers can implement them, and highlights the collaborative nature of the revision process.

Despite the widespread acceptance of the need for revision, most beginning writers resist rewriting. Indeed, in his book *The Craft of Revision,* Donald M. Murray makes the point that "any suggestion for a change in a draft is a personal insult" (2). Our writing, he goes on to say, reveals to the world what we know and what we don't know, how we think and how we feel. When we write, and when others read what we have written, we feel exposed and vulnerable. Is it any wonder, then, that inexperienced writers often are the most resistant to the idea of revision? Lacking in skills, knowledge, and self-confidence, beginning writers, or those individuals who perceive themselves as poor writers, think of revision a punishment for not getting it right the first time. The task for instructors is to find ways to break down these barriers, to help *all* writers see revision as an opportunity to uncover what it is they really want to say, and to discover new ways to say it. Revision is, as Wendy Bishop states, a chance to "re-see, review, re-envision, and re-fashion our work" (313).

As I poured through the books, articles, and case studies that dealt with the subject of revision and talked with colleagues about how they use revision in the classroom, I found the possible approaches and methods for revision to be staggering. Looking for those "best practices" in revision proved to be a daunting task, indeed. What I did find was that as varied as the methods and theories were the common denominator was that they all encouraged a collaborative approach. The authoritative method—where the teacher functions as judge and jury, and where students write in isolation, turn in papers for those inevitable red markings and grades, and then move on to the next writing assignment—is no longer in fashion. Instead, the writing process is really best described as the *revision process*. Students are encouraged to talk about their work-in-progress with peers, tutors, and teachers throughout the process, from generating ideas, through the development stage, to the final draft. Students share their writing with other students as well as with their teachers in formal and informal conversations about writing that can be heard and seen in classrooms, in writing centers, in offices, and online.

For this chapter I have chosen a sampling of current representative methods for revising papers. I have divided this chapter into four main categories: Peer Review, Writing Centers and Other Writing Support Programs, Portfolios, and Teacher and Student Conferences. At the end of this chapter there are also training exercises that my colleagues and I have used to prepare our students for peer review. This is by no means an exhaustive list of revision strategies, but it does illustrate some of today's most forward thinking, and, I hope, useful information. Throughout, the aim has been to help teachers help students gain control of their writing by making intelligent decisions when they are revising their own papers.

Peer Review

Peer review can be a beneficial approach in encouraging students to look at their writing and to consider ways they might revise what they have written. Studies suggest that both the student writer and the peer reviewer benefit from these sessions. In one such study involving response groups, Sandra M. Lawrence and Elizabeth Sommers found that with "careful assignment scaffolding combined with substantial training and ample opportunities for peer collaboration," peer response groups became a successful classroom practice (101). Both Lawrence and Sommers teach students who attend a two-year college at a four-year University. Their instructional activities for their study took place in student-centered writing workshops where students discussed readings, works in progress, and other writing concerns. Lawrence and Sommers discovered that in peer response groups first-year college students were able not only to talk effectively about the texts, but also to use their peers' suggestions and feedback to revise their writing profoundly. Moreover, in his article "Teaching Students to Revise: Theories and Practice," Richard C. Raymond discusses how he uses peer evaluation of rough drafts to help direct students away from merely rewriting to revising. He asserts that through peer review students become adept at "diagnosing strengths and weaknesses in writing," which in turn often leads to better-revised papers (49).

In a peer review session, students respond to each other's draft through written comments and discussion, often during class time. However, a problem arises because inexperienced writers frequently lack the language of writing. In her article "Helping Peer Writing Groups Succeed," Wendy Bishop points out that students need to become familiar with the "vocabulary and terminology of the composition community" and identifies this deficiency as one of the causes that peer writing groups fail (121). So that a peer review session doesn't become a mutual admiration encounter ("I like your essay"/ "I like your essay too") or so that the reviewer doesn't come across as a tyrant leaving the student writer defeated, peer reviewers and student writers do best with training and practice. Activities such as group reviews, modeling, and role-playing are useful ways for students to become comfortable showing their own writing to their peers and learning how to comment on other students' writing. (Sample exercises have been included at the end of this section.)

In *The Craft of Revision,* Donald M. Murray supports the use of test readers as a way to "see in our own drafts what we have not seen before" (33). He applies the analogy of actors and directors using dress rehearsals to see how others react to their work to explain why authors share their writing. Writers, too, need feedback from readers who can tell them what works and what needs work. Murray points out that members from a class make good test readers because they face the same tasks, as well as similar concerns and struggles. They know the parameters of the assignment, are juggling similar class/work/family/social schedules, and bring to the table common weaknesses in writing. These shared experiences and challenges create an environment in which ideas can be expressed openly, where peers can candidly talk about the meanings and feelings found in a draft and where further examples or explanations are necessary. These test readers can provide that "extensive, hard-to-take" criticism Murray looks for that helps writers "see new possibilities, new challenges" in their drafts (35).

Murray argues that there are a variety of ways to promote a reading in process that will benefit the writer. He teaches his students how to encourage and control readers' responses by following five basic transactions:

- The writer explains the type of reading he needs and/or his main concern.
- The readers read the draft with the writer's instructions in mind.
- The readers tell the writer what they think works and needs work.
- The writer doesn't defend or explain but does ask follow-up questions that clarify the readers' responses.
- The readers make any other suggestions that they think will help the reader achieve the writer's intention. (40–41)

Murray's approach can easily be adapted for both a one-on-one peer review situation and large or small group responses. For large group responses, Murray has found it helpful to have students read the draft before the meeting. Sometimes he staples several sheets of paper to the draft and passes it around the room so that students can write their responses to the questions, "What works?" and "What doesn't work?" When working with small groups, Murray prefers to build them around the best students in the class so that each group has its own "expert practitioner." These groups stay together for several sessions so that they can follow the process and progress of each other's work. Sometimes groups choose the best paper and will read it to the class, explaining why they chose it (41).

It does take some effort to create a collaborative environment where students feel comfortable enough to respond to Murray's central questions of "what works and what needs work" and are open to receiving suggestions. In "From the Park Bench to the (Writing) Workshop Table: Encouraging Collaboration among Inexperienced Writers," Lawrence and Sommers describe how they devote the first three weeks of their classes to demystifying the response-group process through ice-breaking and training exercises. In order to have successful peer response groups, they use a variety of peer-group configurations before students participate in a peer response session (102). One activity involves putting students in either pairs or groups of four and asking them to interview one another by following certain parameters, such as place of origin, ethnic heritage, particular interests, and views about writing. After the interview, the students introduce the group members to the class. Lawrence and Sommers use this ice-breaking activity to help "students see both their commonalties and their individual differences" (102). This encourages students to realize that there is a great deal they can learn from one another. It also models the types of thinking, listening, and writing they can expect to do in future class sessions. Lawrence and Sommers follow the interview with additional group activities that are intended to build trust among group members and promote collaboration, such as responding to readings, engaging in pre-writing discussions, and practicing writing strategies.

Participating in a number of group activities may not be enough to convince students of the value of group work or to teach them how group response can be used for revision. Lawrence and Sommers argue that instructors need to emphasize the purpose and benefits of peer response groups through discussion and further training exercises. Students need to be reminded how sharing their writing with others gives them the opportunity to see their ideas through someone else's eyes and perhaps gain a new perspective on their work. Other students may provide them with alternative approaches and ways to revise their drafts. This is also the time that instructors can talk about how the best feedback is that which centers around a paper's focus, content development, and organization rather than the surface blunders students are so fond of pointing out such as typographical or spelling errors. Other activities, such as reviewing and analyzing transcripts from actual peer response sessions followed by class discussions, or watching videos of peer response sessions are also ways students can become familiar with how peer groups can function (103).

Establishing a peer group that can operate effectively and efficiently can be challenging. In his book *Small Groups in Writing Workshops,* Robert Brooke, Associate Professor of English at the University of Nebraska-Lincoln, explains that his approach is to let his students actively participate in choosing the members of their group and deciding how that group functions. He states that his overall goal for the small groups in his classes "is for the individual students to come to realize what they need from others to support their writing" (128). This type of decision making means that the student must consider the way in which the group works and assume some responsibility for its success and failure in meeting the student's needs. Brooke encourages this process with suggestions on how to form the groups themselves. Although his goal is to have groups of four or five people that will remain the same for the duration of the semester, he begins with a period of experimentation. For the first three weeks of classes, he encourages students to get into groups with different people each week and to record their impressions of these groups. In week four, he asks each student to make three lists: one list of four to six people the student would absolutely want in the group, a second list of individuals the student wouldn't mind being with in a group, and a third list of people the student does not want in the group under any circumstances. Using these lists, Brooke assembles groups based on the students' preferences (129).

In addition to choosing groups, Brooke points out that students must "develop strategies to guide discussions so they can get the responses they need to keep themselves writing" (132). He suggests that groups divide their time equally among writers, and that each writer should (1) tell the responders what sort of response he or she wants; (2) read the piece aloud; (3) repeat the request for a response, asking direct questions where necessary (132). In the beginning stages students may ask for listening or positive responses ("What do you hear me saying?" "What parts of the piece do you like best?"). As the weeks progress, students ask more direct-task responses ("What parts did you have trouble with?" "What changes would you make?").

Since Brooke wishes his students to make informed choices about their writing, their groups, and the responses they receive, he requires that they write their own responses to their groups at the end of each session (135). Reflection allows students to think about how their group is functioning, how the students' responses are helping them find ideas, and where they might use these responses to revise their work. To help students get in the habit of reflection, Brooke leaves fifteen minutes at the end of each session for this activity. He asks them to respond to Elbow and Belanoff's three process log questions: "What happened?" "What do I think of my writing now?" and "What will I do next?" Brooke then asks volunteers to read their reflections aloud. This gives the class the opportunity to hear the different reactions people have to their group discussions (136).

Instead of group response, Richard C. Raymond uses one-on-one peer review to teach students how to revise. In "Teaching Students to Revise: Theories and Practice," Raymond starts from the premise that revision begins with prevision—what is your purpose and who is your reader. To help students form this prevision, he suggests that instructors provide writing projects rooted in students' interests or work experiences (50). Raymond devotes a class period, either in one large group or several smaller ones, generating ideas on assigned topics. Students may devise their own topics based on their *knowledge* and *experience,* adhering to what they know and what they care about (50). After this activity, Raymond asks his students to use one of the pre-writing techniques they have studied, such as looping, branching, or listing. He then requires them to prepare a written statement of purpose that identifies a reader, describes the reader's assumptions toward the topic, and discusses how these assumptions will affect the content and arrangement of the essay. Each student brings the written statement and a rough draft to class for a peer review session.

In this peer review session, Raymond distributes guidelines for the students to follow. The guidelines are intended to help the peer reviewer detect errors in focus or development and to offer strategies for improvement. Some questions the peer reviewer responds to are as follows:

- Is the thesis preceded by sentences that identify the subject, narrow the focus, and reveal writer's purpose?

- Does each topic sentence tie into thesis? Are examples sufficient and varied?

- What suggestions for improvement would you offer? (51)

After students write and sign their evaluations, Raymond encourages his students to talk one-on-one. He asserts that these discussions help "students become reader-centered, learning to detect the gap between the message intended and the message conveyed" (51).

Once the written and oral evaluations are completed, the students revise their rough drafts. To encourage his students to take the entire process seriously, Raymond requires that they turn in all prewriting, statement of purpose, the rough draft, and the signed evaluation with the second draft. Students who do not participate in the peer review sessions forfeit their right to revise further for a higher grade (51). For those students who do evaluate conscientiously, Raymond asserts, they gain "not only a thoughtful guide to revision," but also "more experience in diagnosing strengths and weaknesses in writing" (52).

A variation of reviewing papers with peers is to set up a small group that includes the instructor. In this process, each student, in turn, has a paper looked at by the group. The teacher, as much as possible, is an equal member of the group. Of course, the teacher may need to take an active role in encouraging the students to ask questions and give opinions. This can be a good learning experience for students because they can see the instructor thinking, questioning and discussing issues about writing in an informal atmosphere in which the student has peer support. It can also be helpful to the instructor because he is able to see what aspects of the revision process with which students are having most trouble. Another advantage for the instructor is that she can meet with more than one student at a time in order to review rough drafts. Further, it may relax the student because he is receiving comments without a grade. Ideally, once the students learn the language of revision, they may be able to function as a peer review group without the instructor.

Overall, students react favorably to these small group sessions. They find that they are able to get more personal attention, and they also appreciate the ideas and suggestions for improvement that the feedback generates.

Peer review, whether one-on-one or in groups, can have a positive impact on how students revise their work. The studies reviewed in this section support the argument that through peer review writing ceases to be a solitary act performed in isolation and becomes, instead, a vital means of communication where ideas, writing concerns, and revision strategies can be freely discussed and examined. Peer review encourages students to participate in the conversation of writing and revision. Through role-playing, modeling, training, and practice, students learn the language of writing. And because of this dialogue with their peers, students also become more aware of their audience—their reader's attitude towards the topic and how it affects the content and arrangement of an essay. Peer review helps students to become aware of their strengths and weaknesses in writing, leading to improved revision.

Writing Centers and Other Writing Support Programs

In both secondary and higher education, writing centers and other writing support programs have played a vital role in assisting students' efforts to become better writers. In her essay "A Unique Learning Environment," Writing Center Director Pamela Farrell-Childers points out that places like writing centers provide a low-risk environment where students are encouraged to "play with language, question the validity of ideas, laugh at their own mistakes, and empathize with each other's frustrations" (112). She also asserts that because tutors do not give grades, students are more likely to engage in a dialogue that does not take place in classroom-teacher conferences. Once students are free from the time constraints of the classroom and the "peer pressure to respond in what students deem to be appropriate ways," they can get down to the business of focusing on such concerns as meaning, process, authorial intention, and audience expectation (121).

Realistically, teachers do not have the time to review carefully every stage of the writing process with every student on every assignment. Writing centers, and other writing support programs, can reinforce and enhance the practice of process writing. They may come in a variety of configurations and subscribe to a myriad of methods or theories, often reflecting, as Farrell-Childers points out, the "philosophy of the institution and the director of the writing center" (111).

An example of an interactive and collaborative program is the Writing Fellows at Brown University. Here, selected undergraduates are trained to help other students improve their writing skills across the curriculum. All Writing Fellows must complete a seminar course on the theory and practice of teaching writing in their first semester with the program. Each Writing Fellow is assigned to approximately 15–20 students in a class where at least two substantial papers are required. The instructor makes participation in the Writing Fellows

Program mandatory. The student submits a first draft of a paper to a Writing Fellow two weeks before it is due. The Writing Fellow focuses her comments on strengths and weaknesses in argumentation, analysis, organization, clarity, and style. The student then has time to reflect on the suggestions, meet with a Writing Fellow, and revise the paper. The student submits the final version along with the annotated first draft. This approach guarantees that all papers have been through at least one revision, and it also allows the professor to see the writing process the student went through to complete the assignment. In some Writing Fellows Programs, a Fellow will often attend several classes, becoming familiar with the students, the assignment, and the instructor's expectations. The instructor allows class time for the Writing Fellow to work with students on the writing assignment, either one-on-one or in small groups. The students may also be required to schedule one or two appointments with a Writing Fellow outside of class. Programs like the Writing Fellows encourage dialogue between peers so that students recognize that process writing leads to better papers.

Another example of a writing support program is the Writing Lab at Purdue University. In her case study "A Multiservice Writing Lab in a Multiversity: The Purdue University Writing Lab," Muriel Harris describes the types of writing the students engage in from freshman composition essays, term papers, lab reports, and doctoral dissertations to job application letters, resumes, and report forms for school contests. Because students come to the lab with diverse writing histories, writing needs, and learning styles, the focus of the Writing Lab is individualized instruction (1). The writing tutors work with students in the developmental course, the regular two-semester composition sequence, honors course, and with students enrolled in English-as-a-second-language courses. Tutors can also expect to work with students from business writing, technical writing, creative writing, and journalism courses.

The tutors in the Writing Lab are divided into three groups: (1) Writing Lab instructors—graduate students; (2) writing consultants—peer tutors; and (3) undergraduate teaching assistants—another group of peer tutors who work with students from the developmental composition program (10). Each group undergoes a separate training program where they are taught the theory and practice of collaborative learning, and general and specific tutoring principles that will assist them as they support students through the writing and revision processes.

Besides using the method of one-to-one interaction with peer tutors, the Writing Lab has found other ways to meet the needs of students. For example, for students who prefer to work on their own and at their own pace, the Writing Lab has a large collection of self-instructional materials in grammar, rhetorical skills, spelling, vocabulary, business writing, and technical writing. For ESL students, the lab offers modules on listening comprehension, pronunciation, conversation skills, and vocabulary. Harris notes that end-of-semester evaluations indicate that ESL students in particular "express great satisfaction at having materials made available that they can study on their own" (16). The Writing Lab also houses a myriad of handouts on spelling, punctuation, usage, diction, revision, proofreading, documentation style, and so on. These handouts can be used in conjunction with verbal explanations and examples, as reference sheets for a student's notebook, or as supplementary materials for instructors' classes (19).

One unique component to Purdue's Writing Lab is what Harris refers to as the *writing room*. Since many of the composition courses are taught in the same building that houses the Writing Lab, students are encouraged to set aside one hour before or after a writing course to do some writing on their own. Students can usually find an empty chair at a table where they can write, as Harris states, "in an atmosphere where people all around them are busy 'talking writing'" (20). The benefits for students are that they have access to the bookshelves of reference material, and they can call on tutors to answer quick questions. Harris says that "students find that the informality and the conviviality of such a setting spurs them on to better writing" (20).

Besides working with students on campus, many of these writing support programs encourage the process of writing in other ways. Some offer online tutoring where students can submit their work and receive feedback from a tutor, often within 48 hours. Students have access to an online resource library, newsletters, and chatrooms. Other schools are involved in outreach programs like the Writing Lab at Purdue, offering a grammar hotline and noncredit courses where people in the community are able to make use of the Writing Lab for grammar review or tutorial response to short writing projects (Harris 21). Some programs, like the one at Medgar Evers College, create a partnership with area high schools, sending their trained tutors into the high schools helping high school students improve their reading and writing skills in their subject-area courses (Greene 42).

As different and as unique as each of these writing centers and writing support programs are, they do share one commonality—all of them use a collaborative approach to supporting student writing and revision. In a low-risk environment, students share their writing with other students who have often undergone specific training in the theory and practice of collaborative learning and in tutoring principles. Students have the opportunity to meet with these specially trained tutors throughout the writing process—from idea-generating sessions, to first drafts, to final versions—sharing writing concerns, revision strategies, and successes along the way. These programs create a space where students can feel liberated from teacher criticism and evaluation and feel free, instead, to experiment with ideas and language as they move through the different stages of writing.

PORTFOLIOS

A benefit of using portfolios as a means for supporting revision is that they allow the students to track their progress as writers. By keeping a record of their drafts and final papers, students are able to see *their* process of writing: what ideas they first generated, how they supported those ideas, what type of feedback they received, what changes they made with each revised draft, and how the final copy of a paper compares to earlier drafts. At various times throughout the semester, particularly at mid-term and end-of-term, instructors can reinforce this benefit by requiring students to submit a written reflection on the steps they took to develop a paper and how these steps influenced their growth as writers.

In their book *Assessing the Portfolio,* Liz Hamp-Lyons and William Condon explore the theory and practice of integrating portfolios in writing programs and how they can be used for assessment purposes. They make the argument that in order to be effective, all portfolios must be built around three basic, but essential, components—collection, reflection, selection (118).

In its simplest forms, portfolios collect just the finished responses to more than one writing assignment. Some portfolios include not only the finished responses, but also earlier drafts. Other portfolios include writing produced under different circumstances, such as in-class assignments, revised writing, papers done collaboratively, and writing addressed to different audiences. Hamp-Lyons and Condon point out, however, that without reflection and selection, all that is left for the student and the instructor is "simply a pile" of texts (119). Using reflective writing, such as a letter to the reader or a cover letter, students have the opportunity to demonstrate the growth they have made as writers. They can explore the processes they have used in their writing, discuss what they found challenging about the writing assignments and how they met those challenges, evaluate where they were successful, decide which skills need further development, and identify future goals. If students are then allowed to have some autonomy in choosing which writing samples to include in the portfolio, they can select those pieces that best represent the progress they have made as writers—they can determine the shape of their portfolios. Without selection, Hamp-Lyons and Condon argue, instructors "would be unable to judge how much the student understands about his or her own strengths and needs as a writer" (120). Furthermore, students would be unable to present their best work or show what they have learned.

The portfolio's characteristic of delayed evaluation enhances this reflection and selection process. Hamp-Lyons and Condon point out that because grading happens at the end of a term, students are motivated to revise their work (34). They have time to put some distance between themselves and their writing, to consider teacher and peer feedback, and to make decisions about their texts in progress. They can decide which papers they like best, which ones have the most potential, and which papers they would most like to develop or revise. Delayed evaluation could possibly encourage students to take risks with their writing that they might not otherwise take. They can practice using a different point-of-view on the same text, or try writing in another genre. And by including these successive and alternative drafts in a portfolio, students will have a more accurate representation of the effort they have put into their writing and a tangible record of their accomplishments.

As Hamp-Lyons and Condon argue, teacher assessment that only looks at final drafts are inadequate, for it does not take into consideration the growth a student goes through while revising. The final grade on a paper tells just a part of the story. The portfolio allows both the teacher and student to look back and reflect upon how the writer approached each assignment, how ideas were generated and developed, and how the student used teacher, peer, and tutor comments to revise her work that lead to the final product.

Teacher and Student Conferences

In her book *Teaching One-to-One: The Writing Conference,* Muriel Harris views teacher and student conferences as "opportunities for highly productive dialogues between writers and teacher-readers" (3). She continues by saying that not only does the one-to-one setting of a conference allow teachers to hear what students have to say about their writing, but it also provides a format in which teachers no longer have to talk about writing in the abstract and can address individual concerns and issues for each writer. Proponents of the one-to-one conference find that it is the most effective and efficient way to meet the needs of each student and to track individual progress as the student moves through the writing process.

In discussing the role of the conference and how it fits in the teaching of writing, Harris points out that by talking with students as they write or prepare to write, teachers reinforce the ideas that writing is a "process of discovery" and "primarily an act of communication" (5). The teacher assists in the process, helping the writer to move through multiple drafts, identifying areas of concern the writer might have, and teaching the writer strategies that she can use to help her navigate through the writing process. During a conference, the teacher encourages exploration by asking the student questions or making subtle suggestions. Using such simple prompts as "Why did you choose this topic?" or "What examples can you give?" the teacher can help the writer to discover ideas or material that has not yet been put into words. As these ideas are refined and reshaped, teachers can use these conferences to explore revision strategies and offer support and encouragement to the student who is feeling overwhelmed by the messy business of revising a paper. Without the one-to-one conference, Harris asserts, students will too often fall back on what they already know how to do, correcting spelling errors or changing a word or two. The personalized instruction of a conference empowers students to "go off on their own with some sense of what should be done," leading to more substantive changes in their writing (8).

Teachers often express concern as to what format to use and how to schedule conferences. There is no best answer to either of these concerns—simplicity and flexibility appear to be what truly matters. Conventional classrooms can quickly be turned into writing workshop settings where small groups of students work on writing assignments together as the teacher walks around the room offering brief comments. Sometimes it may be preferable to have students working alone on writing assignments while the teacher meets with individual writers during class time. Alternatively, teachers may wish to schedule conferences outside of class, either meeting in an office or writing lab. Each of these formats can be effective ways of integrating conferences with the traditional methods of teaching writing. What is important is to create an environment where student and teacher can freely exchange ideas, a give-and-take atmosphere. Sitting side-by-side, or even better, at a round table enables the student and teacher to view the paper together. The teacher takes on the role of supporter participating in the writing process.

The length of the conference depends on the format. If students are engaged in small-group workshops, the teacher might spend a few moments briefly talking with each group. A scheduled conference might last anywhere from fifteen minutes during class time to thirty minutes in a writing lab or office. Beyond thirty minutes, the physical and emotional strains of a conference tend to make students and teachers less productive. If time is a concern, one solution might be group conferences. Some teachers have found that meeting with three or four students at a time is a good way to talk about writing concepts and revision strategies. And because there is safety in numbers, students may feel less intimidated than they would be in a one-to-one conference.

As Harris points out, the question as to when or how often to hold conferences has a simple answer—throughout the semester (50). Conferences can be held occasionally, offered at various times as a student progresses through a paper. Conferences at the prewriting stage can help students explore topics and generate ideas. During early drafts, conferences provide that extra boost students need when they feel they have run out of ideas or have strayed from their original intent. Scheduling conferences before the final draft is due is an excellent way for the teacher to provide reader feedback, crucial during the revision stage of writing. Everyone seems to agree that the one stage where a conference is not particularly profitable is after a final draft. Unless the student is given the opportunity to revise a final draft, a conference after the fact has limited benefits.

The advantage of integrating conferences into a writing program is that it gives both teacher and student the opportunity for an open dialogue about the writing process. The teacher can ask direct questions and help the student to develop ideas, consider alternative approaches, learn revision strategies, and generally offer support. The student benefits by receiving individual attention so his specific needs and writing concerns can be addressed. This open dialogue removes the mystique that surrounds writing, and turns the process of writing into something concrete and tangible that the student can put into application. And by holding conferences periodically throughout the semester, teachers reinforce the idea of open dialogue, providing reader feedback that is essential when students are at the revision stage of writing.

The onus is on instructors and directors of writing programs to find ways to encourage students to revise their work. Those of us in the business of teaching writing must help our students to see revision as an opportunity to grow as writers, as an act of discovery, not as punishment. How best to meet this challenge has been the focus of this chapter. The good news is that innumerable approaches promote revision—methods that can be used both in and out of the classroom. Using peer review, whether one-on-one or in small groups, is a good way to get students familiar with the language of the composition community. And because peers know the parameters of the assignment and share similar experiences and challenges, these sessions take place in an environment where ideas can be expressed openly. Writing centers and other writing support programs reinforce and enhance the practice of process writing by providing tutors who have been trained in the art of collaborative learning, and tutoring principles. Students benefit by receiving outside help with their writing from qualified tutors, self-instructional materials, learning modules, and online assistance. Portfolios support revision by allowing students to track their progress as writers—how they developed ideas, what type of feedback they received on their writing, how they used this feedback for revision, and how the final paper compared with earlier drafts. Finally, teacher and student conferences provide a format in which teachers can address individual concerns and issues for each writer. The teacher can help the student to discover new ideas and material, and can focus on specific revision strategies. The personalized instruction of a conference leads to more meaningful changes in the student's writing.

Each of these categories is based on the collaborative approach. Each encourages dialogue where ideas can be freely expressed, where exploration and experimentation are celebrated, and where the writing process is a shared experience. By incorporating these revision strategies into the teaching of writing, perhaps we can help students to see that "Revision is not the end of the writing process but the beginning" (Murray 1).

Group Review Exercise

This activity requires a student writing sample on an overhead or PowerPoint projection. The sample might be a draft of a short writing assignment or a paragraph or two of a longer assignment. The class looks at the sample and comments on what works and what doesn't work. Here the instructor takes on the role of facilitator. Students often will zero in on surface errors, such as spelling, punctuation, and grammar. The instructor can shift the focus by asking such questions as:

- What is the topic of this paragraph?
- What is the tone?
- Where has the writer used descriptive language?
- Where could the writer use more details?
- What is the writer trying to say?
- What would you like to hear more about?

The benefit of doing a group review is that the students can learn a great deal from hearing a variety of responses. Facing a peer review session, inexperienced students may be reluctant to express their opinions about a piece of writing. Peer reviewers might lack confidence or even the language of how to talk about writing. Student writers might not even know what types of questions they should ask during a review session. In a group setting, however, there appears to be strength in numbers. As some students offer feedback, others seem more willing to express their observations.

Modeling Exercise #1

In the first scenario the instructor takes on the role of the peer reviewer, while a student volunteer presents a short draft that needs revising. (It is preferable that the writing sample is not the student's paper. It is also helpful if the student is given a few minutes before the exercise to look over the writing sample.) The rest of the class watches as the instructor models the process. In an interactive exchange, the instructor and the student discuss the paper. The instructor moves through the writing pointing out specific successes, offering suggestions on improvement, and encourages the student to ask questions. The benefit here is that the students not only learn how to approach and talk about a piece of writing, but they also see first-hand how the instructor evaluates a written assignment. At the end of the modeling session, the instructor invites the rest of the class to comment on what they have just witnessed.

Modeling Exercise #2

(In the following activity the student volunteer is given the opportunity to practice some of the reviewing techniques he or she learned from the first modeling exercise.)

Another variation of this modeling exercise is to have the instructor and student reverse roles. The instructor pretends to be the student while the student becomes the peer reviewer. Using another writing sample, the instructor poses questions and concerns that students might have (or should have) about a writing assignment, such as what ideas need further development and what areas need clarification. Again, as the class watches this interactive exchange, they begin to gain a better understanding of how to focus on a draft that needs revising by learning what questions students should have about their writing and how to respond to those questions as peer reviewers. At the end of this activity, the instructor leads a discussion by asking the students to talk about what they observed. The instructor should also invite the student volunteer to tell the class what it felt like to be the student writer and the peer reviewer.

Role-Playing Exercise #1

The Fishbowl

(Role-playing is similar to modeling, except that the students are the participants and observers while the instructor facilitates the activity.)

In this exercise one student volunteer takes on the role of the peer reviewer while a second student plays the role of the writer. Using a short writing sample supplied by the instructor, the students model what would go on in a peer review session while the rest of the class watches. The student playing the role of the writer reads the paper aloud and asks the peer reviewer for help in specific areas. (It is useful if the instructor gives the students a chance to read the writing sample before engaging in this activity.) For example, the student might express concerns about the paper being too short or sounding too repetitious. The peer reviewer would respond using some of the composition terms and vocabulary the instructor introduced during the modeling sessions. At the end of the review session the rest of the class would report back on what they observed. The instructor might guide the discussion by asking the class the following questions: Were the specific areas for which the student writer asked for help the same areas that you have trouble with when you write a paper? What do you think went well in the session? What would you have done differently?

Role-Playing Exercise #2

One-On-One

For this exercise the instructor breaks the class up into pairs and gives each pair a short writing sample. Once again, one student volunteers to play the role of the student writer while the other is the peer reviewer. (The instructor should encourage the students to take a few minutes to read over the writing sample before beginning the role-playing exercise.) The student writer reads the paper aloud and asks the peer reviewer specific questions about global issues, especially in the areas of development and organization. After giving the students a reasonable amount of time for the first part of this activity, the instructor has the students reverse roles and repeat the process, preferably with a different writing sample. Throughout the session the students apply the terminology and techniques about peer review and the writing process. A class discussion follows this activity where each pair reports back on what happened during their one-on-one peer review session. The instructor might ask the following questions: What did the student writer ask the peer review to focus on? How did the peer reviewer respond to the questions? What was the biggest challenge the peer reviewer faced in trying to help the writer?

11 Practical Guidelines for Writers and Teachers

Cathleen Breidenbach

Attitudes take generations to change. Process writing pedagogy and initiatives over the past thirty years have dramatically changed the way we understand how writers write and how people learn to improve their writing. However those ideas have not trickled down to the average person writing a business letter, to professionals, white-collar workers, or to parents and students studying writing. Many continue to believe that writing well means abiding by a set of rules and using good grammar and mechanics. They have limited awareness that rhetorical decisions writers make about purpose, genre, point of view, audience, tone, and style are central to the effectiveness of any piece of writing.

Often when I attend social gatherings of civilians not involved in the writing business, the getting-to-know-you conversation gets around to the fact that I teach writing. Someone invariably intones with an isn't-it-awful smile, " Why don't they teach kids how to spell and write a proper sentence anymore?" or "Nobody teaches students grammar and punctuation." Vestiges of misguided assumptions that writing is solely about content and correctness persist, and they continue to hobble writers. Consequently attitudes about what constitutes good writing, how to teach people to write well, and the role revising plays in the process are themselves in need of revision. The previous chapter outlines best practices that have found acceptance and are used widely and effectively. What has not yet found a central place in writing and writing curricula is commitment to the rhetorical nature of all good writing—the decisions about content, purpose, tone, genre, and style that effective writers make and revisit when they revise. This chapter will first explore the need for change in attitudes about revision, reflecting on dangers in the enterprise; the second portion suggests practical guidelines so writers and writing teachers can build rhetorical considerations into their revising repertoire.

Revision: A Complex, Intuitive, and Elusive Process

The standard perception that revision is something that happens at the end of the writing process is a good place to start revising ideas about revision.

The standard process approach to revision describes it as linear, but recent research confirms that for most writers, revision is very much a recursive, interwoven, intersecting process. In one revising read-through of a text, experienced writers multitask on a ladder of levels, considering deep revision questions of idea, genre, point of view, audience and tone along with the cosmetic editing of surface details. In the same reading writers may eliminate confusion resulting from words, syntax, or punctuation; modify the representation of idea; assess the very validity of the idea; clean up typos and other minute debris littering the text; adjust rhythm and pacing, hunt for grammar slips, replace lame adjectives and verbs, and tweak for tone—all in one reading.

Experienced writers use an intuitive awareness of what needs changing; however even the most articulate and self-aware writers are hard pressed to explain how their brain synapses fire as their fingers tap at the keyboard making changes. Most would need time to figure out their own revising process because it's so internalized and intuitive they do it almost instinctively. Over time, they have developed what Alice S. Horning refers to in her book *Revision Revisited* as "metarhetorical and metalinguistic awarenesses," (8–9) a set of understandings that informs every keystroke of change for experienced writers. Metarhetorical awareness includes the ways writers are conscious, or mostly conscious, of their own ways of writing, of "the strategies, behaviors, techniques, or approaches" that work for them (Horning 8–9). Metarhetorical awareness is shaped by a writer's personality, proclivities, and experiences writing and revising texts. Horning defines metalinguistic awareness as cognizance of language as language (9). The term encompasses a variety of linguistic features of a text and particularly emphasizes how experienced writers achieve readability by listening to the sounds, flow, and patterns of the words.

If writers themselves struggle to explain what it is they do, it's no wonder there are limited texts available to help writers and teachers of writing. Horning's book *Revision Revisited*, Donald Murray's *The Craft of Revision*, and Meredith Sue Willis's *Deep Revision* offer some of the best analyses of what knowledge writers are tapping into as they revise (Horning) and strategies to help writers of all ages revise their work (Murray, Willis).

The Dangers of Practical Strategies

Unpacking the complex understandings that constitute metarhetorical and metalinguistic awareness and unscrambling the spaghetti threads in the multitasking process of revision to offer practical advice is not only challenging, but fraught with dangers. The divide and conquer philosophy—dividing revision into different types of revision (deep or global revision versus surface or final editing) and into different aspects and strategies seems the only way to see the process with clarity and communicate revising moves to those who would like to do it better. Yet there are dangers in the enterprise. Dividing something complex, with overlapping interdependent aspects into discrete, seemingly autonomous elements for the sake of understanding runs the risk that each element will be understood as actually discrete and separate. Like Humpty Dumpty, the whole of the complicated, interconnecting puzzle may be difficult to put together again. The nature of revision is recursive—not linear—yet when we suggest ways to go about revising, we break down the process into its elements and speak of those elements in sequence. We model the process as if it were linear—a conundrum when we say one thing and do another.

The second danger, akin to the first, is that dividing and structuring the complex revision process to make it easier to understand and implement—to simplify it by looking at the threads of revision one at a time—runs the risk of watering down the process, of making it simplistic, even formulaic. Revision is more than a matter of completing a checklist or following ten sure-fire steps to success. It's a creative process, even a mysterious process—which leads to the third danger, misrepresenting its true nature.

Revision's Secret Identity

Revision suffers from the reputation of being tedious and mechanical, yet Donald Murray insists it's a creative and sometimes inspired process. In an effort to get students to edit at all, then to do it carefully and well, many teachers emphasize that it's hard, necessary work. However, revising can be much more. Bolts of inspiration occasionally come as we revise. More commonly, quiet satisfaction settles upon us as we till fields of words. Sometimes the words we write reveal truths we didn't know we knew; language can create knowledge; revision can facilitate discovery. This business of revising can be revelatory, inspiring, and deeply satisfying. Yet we who have experienced deep satisfaction or moments of inspiration usually keep those experiences to ourselves, sharing only with the initiated and then only sometimes. Would we be exposing ourselves so much if we at least hinted that revision is not always onerous work, that it can be creative and occasionally even exciting? Donald Murray thinks not.

Murray's loose-jointed, experimental (try this and see what it reveals) approach to revision emphasizes its creative possibilities. If more writers regarded revision as creative work with the possibility of surprise (Wherever did that idea come from?) and inspiration (Let's put this with that . . . voila, it works), they'd approach revision with less dread and more anticipation. To be creative, however, revision needs time and freedom from excessive constraint and regimentation. It needs to remain open and loose and walk on the edge of possibilities, trying them on and checking them out. This chapter proposes some practical guidelines to help writers revise. The challenge is to keep the spark of creativity alive in revision, to fan its feeble flame so writers experience revision as possibility, maybe even as an interesting and inspiring part of writing.

The Fallacy of the Natural Writer

Students often divide the world into two kinds of people: those who write well and those, who, like themselves, struggle to get ideas on a page and are "not good at writing." They assume that writing comes easily to publishing writers, writing teachers, journalists, and others naturally facile with language, that such natural writers compose with clarity and grace, that words flow and ideas spring fully formed onto the page. Such assumptions grossly exaggerate the truth that some people *are* more verbal than others. Writing well, however, is a learned skill for everybody, and all writers are lucky if words occasionally come easily and ideas flow well. The truth is writing is a struggle. It's difficult to get a piece started, to find a focus; it's a challenge to grow an idea, flesh it out, give it life. Even knowing when to end and how to end are difficult. But students are reluctant to give up their tidy division of the world into those who write naturally and those who are "not good at it" because it's a convenient explanation for their lack of success. Lack of commitment, lack of persistence, and a reluctance to revise multiple times are more valid explanations for unsuccessful writing than lack of natural ability.

Professional writer Anne Lamott's pithy essay "Shitty First Drafts" gets students laughing at her candid vocabulary and persuades them that professional writers really do turn out lousy writing, just as students do, and that all writers struggle. This excerpt gives the flavor of her argument.

> Now, practically even better news than that of short assignments is the idea of shitty first drafts. All good writers write them. This is how they end up with good second drafts and terrific third drafts. People tend to look at successful writers, writers who are getting their books published and maybe even doing well financially, and think that they sit down at their desks every morning feeling like a million dollars, feeling great about who they are and how much talent they have and what a great story they have to tell; that they take in a few deep breaths, push back their sleeves, roll their necks a few times to get all the cricks out, and dive in, typing fully formed passages as fast as a court reporter. But that is just the fantasy of the uninitiated. I know some very great writers, writers you love who write beautifully and have made a great deal of money, and not one of them sits down routinely feeling wildly enthusiastic and confident. Not one of them writes elegant first drafts. [. . .]
> Very few writers really know what they are doing until they've done it. Nor do they go about their business feeling dewy and thrilled. They do not type a few stiff warm-up sentences and then find themselves bounding along like huskies across the snow [. . .] We all often feel like we are pulling teeth, even those writers whose prose ends up being the most natural

and fluid. The right words and sentences just do not come pouring out like ticker tape most of the time. [...]

For me and most of the writers I know, writing is not rapturous. In fact, the only way I can get anything written at all is to write really, really shitty first drafts.

Lamott's essay provides a rationale for using focused free writes to tap into recesses of the mind where ideas may be fermenting. It encourages writers to stop agonizing and just write a draft. Once they begin, the writing can beget ideas. Writing can help us discover what we want to say, loosen up our verbal muscles, get the words flowing. Lamott's freewheeling essay assures us that even accomplished writers write lame beginnings, garbage middles, and fatuous endings. They sometimes write shitty first drafts. And that's no reason to despair because a draft is a beginning that allows writers to discover what needs to happen next.

Once we've dispelled the fallacy of the natural writer, apprentice writers need to clarify the difference between deep revision and final editing.

The Difference between Deep Revision and Final Editing

Inexperienced writers entertain a host of misconceptions about revision. The most persistent is the belief that revising a piece is the same as final editing. Students have learned to hunt for spelling errors and homonyms, fix grammar mistakes, and repair punctuation problems. They're content to fix errors, put in a few paragraph indentions, root out run-on sentences and consider a paper revised. Unless writing teachers define error fixing as surface editing and differentiate that from what Meredith Sue Willis calls "deep revision," surface editing is what they'll get, because that's the widespread understanding of what it means to revise.

Editing holds an important place in the revision process, no mistake; it's essential to clean up a piece of writing to avoid the irritations and interruptions errors cause, to clean it up so readers notice its deeper merits. But surface editing is not deep revision, and dispelling the misconception that they're more or less the same is a necessary first step in persuading students that surface editing, even when it's meticulously carried out and successful at presenting a piece of writing with a clean shining face, is not enough to solve deeper problems. The ants-at-a-picnic metaphor may help put into perspective the ways editing and revision differ.

The Ants-at-a-Picnic Metaphor

Most people would agree that a picturesque setting, a beautiful day, convivial company, and good food are essentials for a successful and memorable picnic and that ants, when they arrive on the scene, are merely nuisances. Problems with mechanics like grammar, punctuation, and capitalization are similar to the nuisance ants cause at a picnic. A few errors won't spoil a fine piece of writing, but numerous pesky errors, like numerous pesky insects at a picnic, can ruin a perfectly wonderful paper.

A lack of errors, however, doesn't mean a paper is wonderful. This is the piece students often don't understand. The essentials are, just that, essential for success. Capitalization, spelling, grammar, and punctuation facilitate our enjoyment of the essentials. Deep revision deals with the essentials of good writing like choosing a genre and point of view that suit the situation and purpose of a piece of writing; having a clever, fresh idea or a mesmerizing tale to tell; considering readers' expectations, knowledge and opinions, and getting the tone right. Editing is akin to pest control—clearing the piece of bothersome bugs. Making the distinction between deep revision and surface editing is the first step in persuading writers to spend time doing deep revision. Before we can take that step, however, those of us who teach writing need to reform our own tendency to emphasize mechanics over other considerations, or at least reform those practices that lead students to believe mechanics—more than anything else—determines the grades they receive and our evaluation of their writing. Once we've gotten students in the habit of doing no fault writing in the form of focused free writes and shitty first drafts that no one else will see, it's time to break our own misleading habits.

Students often believe that teachers care more about mechanics than they care about content, style, and rhetorical decisions (if they even know what rhetorical decisions might be), because most written comments on papers focus on mechanics far more than on all other considerations. Both teachers and peers can benefit from revising the ways they provide feedback to include a more comprehensive response to a piece of writing that clearly focuses on rhetorical considerations.

Breaking Old Habits: Colorizing Comments

One way to break old habits and get our own practices out into the open is to colorize them. Using different colored pens or pencils for four types of comments makes colorfully obvious whether or not our comments strike a reasonable balance. Writing multicolored notations on papers also gives teachers an incentive to avoid a monochromatic emphasis on mechanics and to expand comments to other considerations, to broaden the palette. Teachers might ask questions about logic and content and indicate places where the paper needs transitions in red. They might name the tone and wonder whether that tone might be too outspoken or barbed to appeal to the paper's audience in green, and underline repetitious sentence structures and excessive state of being verbs in pink. Finally they could note problems with mechanics in blue. The colored comments suggest a plan for revision so students can use the divide and conquer strategy, perhaps dealing first with red issues (content, idea, organization), then exploring green issues (rhetorical decisions, tone, and audience) followed by pink (style and voice), and finally getting to blue (mechanics). Whether teachers use colorized comments, standard proofreading symbols, or smiley faces and exclamation points, some of the comments need to encourage, support, and praise successful language choices and interesting ideas.

Including Good News with the Bad

All writers hunger for appreciation—all writers, no exceptions. As cheerful as rainbow coded papers may look, or as efficient as proofreading symbols may be, notations can be devastating if nearly all comments point to problems, difficulties, inadequacies, and work yet to be done. Writers need to know that despite problems with a piece, they did write something good—something genuinely good. Whether teachers comment on a lovely turn of phrase, a thoughtful idea, a witty image, or a vivid description doesn't matter. What *does* matter is that at least some feedback be positive. "I like the way you. . . . , good point! Vivid verb choice, or I laughed out loud." Praise brings solace to students' fragile and often wounded perceptions of themselves as writers. It gives them something to cling to and be proud of and build upon. A bit of praise and public recognition before the class enables students to sustain hope that the paper, despite its problems, has qualities worth developing.

General pat-on-the-back comments such as "Good Job" or "Well Done" written at the end of the paper may warm writers' egos briefly, but they don't make clear *what* is working in their draft that caused you to approve, or smile, or respond. Why else do writers ask others to read their drafts but to take the piece out of their own heads and see how it fares in the world of readers? Writers need specific comments from readers—their friends and peers in writing groups and workshops. Carol Trupiano offers advice on writing workshops in the previous chapter, Best Practices.

Writers also nervously wait to hear what their teacher will say. Teachers can provide the most useful feedback when they react as just another reader, albeit an experienced one. Offer comments not as final arbiter, not as the only reader who counts because you give the grade, but as an attentive, interested reader willing to go into detail about what you liked and responded to and what caused you difficulty or confusion.

Often writers don't understand what they've written until a reader gives it a name. If a reader says, "I like the sarcastic edge here. It gives the paper personality," the writers may say to themselves, "So that's what I was doing, being sarcastic." That's information about how readers perceive the paper. Information is what writers need. Certainly they love praise in any form, but specific praise that provides information is much more valuable when writers decide what to keep, what to cut, and what to change.

Building Time into the Process

Process writing changed the way most teachers help students develop a paper. It built time into the process: idea generation activities (free writing, mapping, listing) followed by first drafts read in peer workshops, conferences with the teacher, then final editing. Process writing builds in multiple times for writers to revisit and re-envision a paper and to see it from the perspective of different readers.

Donald Murray advises writers to get the paper out of their heads. Peer workshops effectively distance writers from the writing on several levels. First, even during the cerebral activity of composing alone, writers envision an audience of peers reading the paper in a workshop. That envisioning discourages self-centered journal writing and encourages writers to relate to an imagined audience, to explain thoroughly, to define, and include transitions. Then in the actual workshop, writers hear from real readers. The comments of real readers affirm that the paper has a life of its own, speaks for itself, and may even say things the writers had not intended or planned. That sense of the paper as a separate entity is an awareness writers need in order to revise, but it can't happen during the intense, symbiotic relationship most writers have with a paper when it's newborn.

So a second value that comes from building time into the process is the objectivity that happens when papers have time to develop a life of their own apart from the writers. When papers are newborn, they are the product of toil and genius. They *are* the writers and have no independent life of their own. To criticize writers' newborn papers is to criticize the writers. Time remedies this state of temporary insanity. Letting a paper rest a day or so miraculously brings increased perspective and, for most writers, the ability to hear comments. Consequently, building time into the revision process is one of the most significant contributions of process writing pedagogy.

If It's Not a Draft, It's a Revision

The language of process pedagogy refers to *developing* a paper, but *revision* is what's actually taking place. Once writers commit their ideas to the page, all reassessments and adjustments that take place on the way to the final version are essentially revisions. Every stage in the process offers not only opportunities to revise, but expectations that writers will analyze what they've done, experiment with different options, and make changes as a piece develops.

Teachers can extend the process further by offering students the opportunity to revise a piece once or twice, even after it's been graded or after it is officially in the student's portfolio. The carrot, of course, that persuades many students to work on the paper yet again is the possibility of getting a better grade. Teachers hope students feel a sense of accomplishment and pride in their own abilities, and that they hone their own metarhetorical and metalinguistic skills as a result of revision. Teachers should make clear that a clean-up-errors kind of edit will raise the grade only slightly, but a full-fledged revision may result in a significant change in the grade. With this clear distinction, teachers reinforce the difference between surface editing and deep revision. Asking students to include their own editorial assessments with the revision packet (containing the revised paper and drafts) puts the revision ball in their court. They must reflect, in writing, what they thought needed attention, how they came to be aware of a problem (Was it their own intuition? A peer's comment? Reading the paper aloud?). Then they explain what they decided to do to resolve the problem and why they made those decisions. Requiring them to reflect on their own decisions helps them develop awareness of genre, audience, tone, and style and encourages deep revision rather than surface editing.

Risk-Free Revision

If we would encourage students to do deep revision and to experiment when they look at their options for changing a paper, we must acknowledge that the trajectory of revision is not onward and upward in a linear path to paper perfection. Sometimes writers make confusing changes, take detours and bog down in quagmires, change a meek tone to be more assertive and come across as obnoxious and pushy. With the best of intentions, all writers make bad choices from time to time. If we want students to feel they can be adventurous when they revise, that they can try something they've never done before or depart from formulas and conventional protocol, revision must be risk free. We must promise students that even a revision that is worse than the original will never receive a lower grade. If revising a paper creates new problems, comment on those problems, but avoid punishing a student for making a genuine effort. Students who venture into deep revision waters deserve praise for their bravery and for their willingness to experiment even if that experiment moves a paper backward rather than forward. Any scientist will confirm that an experiment that proves the hypothesis false is not a failure because it provides information about what doesn't work. So it is also with revision.

Divide and Conquer—Clusters of Consideration

Once rhetorical decisions take the spotlight, teachers and writers need specific strategies. One such strategy to encourage deep revision and show mechanics as subsidiary to rhetorical decisions is to divide revision into four distinct processes or considerations to be addressed separately. Colorizing comments on papers, as described previously, offers one way to launch a four-part analysis that can be implemented in peer workshops, through individual exercises related to the focus, and in conferences with the teacher. Students might work on a paper four different times between the first draft and the final version, focusing each time on one of the four clusters of consideration below:

- Content
- Rhetorical Decisions
- Style
- Mechanics

Content: Argument, Logic, Narrative, Organization

Having something worthwhile to say is a prerequisite for a worthy piece of writing. There's no point in polishing a piece that has structural flaws, that will need to be pulled apart and re-built because the materials are defective or the blueprint is faulty. So content/substance is a good place to begin revising.

Admittedly substance and style are irrevocably intertwined, and substance without style is as unpalatable as style without substance. A piece that's woefully lacking in style may come off as plodding and dull, as lifeless and boring. Nevertheless, if the idea has merit and warrants exploration—even if it's still but a seed, or if the story taps into something essentially human and true, then the writing, however sketchy and undeveloped, however graceless and raw, contains the necessary potential to become something worthy. So focusing first on content makes sense despite the reality that style usually gets noticed first and is more seductive.

The vocabulary of marketing illustrates the way readers respond to the interplay between content and style. Content is product (its design, function, value, and ability to meet a felt need). Style is marketing (advertising, pricing, promotion, distribution). Razzle dazzle marketing can seduce the public into buying a product—for a while, but if the product doesn't work well or is poorly designed, that product will soon lose market share to better mousetraps. Engaging style (clever, witty, graceful, articulate) can seduce readers into trusting writers' ideas—for a while, but if the logic, argument, or plot contain flaws or misrepresentations, that piece of writing will eventually lose readers' allegiance. It's a matter of trust. Only substantive content, developed with integrity and responsibility, warrants trust. So the first focus in a workshop or conference would do well to look at content.

To help writers revise the content of a draft, simply ask them to articulate their main argument, their main line of reasoning, so they can see more clearly the bones on which the paper is built (or should be built). When they speak aloud or express in writing what they want to communicate (one or two sentence limit), the activity helps them realize the thrust and shape of their own argument.

The explain-while-standing-on-one-foot strategy also accomplishes a distillation and clarification of argument that helps students cut through fluff and digression to realize their core message. Writers are asked to express their main argument while standing on one foot. This standing on one foot can be actual or figurative, but it remains a catchy way to facilitate focus and avoid digression. Most people are not adept at standing on one foot for any length of time without teetering, wobbling, and feeling foolish; consequently, the absurd challenge to declare the point of their essay while standing on one foot necessitates focus, decisiveness, directness, and brevity.

Outlines offer another strategy to help writers discover the structure and development of their argument. When they outline their own essay or list the claims they've made, they see that argument more clearly and can fill out and tighten up the reasoning in the next round of revision.

Whether a piece of writing presents an argument, a personal narrative, or a fictional story, whether it compares and contrasts, defines or describes, there are numerous text books and readers that model and discuss developing content, idea, and argument. There are, however, far fewer books to help writers explore their rhetorical options. Rhetorical decisions are too often absent from writing curricula or are given short shrift. They deserve a central place in any discussion of how writing conveys ideas.

Once the idea/content has received attention as the first area of consideration, it's time to move on to the rhetorical decisions writers make, not just when they're drafting, but as part of reassessing those decisions during revision.

Rhetorical Decisions: Purpose, Genre, Audience, Tone, and Point of View

Those who write professionally make rhetorical decisions based on intuited awareness developed over years of experience. Less experienced writers are seldom aware that they even make such decisions. Helping them focus on rhetorical decisions gives them options as writers and gives them the language to describe how writing works.

> *Purpose:* Deciding what purpose the writers hope to accomplish is a wise first rhetorical decision. Do writers wish to inform, persuade, entertain, appeal to readers emotionally, move readers to action, or accomplish some combination of these purposes? Once writers decide what their intentions are, they can move on to deciding the genre that best suits their purposes.
>
> *Genre:* Usually genre is decided by the teacher and specified in the assignment, "Write a theme that presents an argument," or "Write a personal memoir recounting a significant event that happened when you were ten or eleven years old." Consequently, few inexperienced writers are aware they have choices about form. For starters, teachers can introduce the French term, genre, that has crossed over into English usage to mean type or kind of writing and is used to name standard categories that texts fall into. Because many writers have little experience seeing how form affects the ways readers perceive a piece of writing, genre is virgin territory for many of them.

To help writers focus on genre, teachers can try any one or combination of the following three assignments.

1. Present a topic for writing without indicating what form it is to take, in fact make it clear that choosing the genre is up to the writers. The writers can decide whether to write an academic theme, a letter to the editor, a short story, a personal memoir,

even a poem. Students can discuss what messages these forms convey to readers, what readers expect from given forms, and which form best suits the situation and the writers' purpose(s) and message.

2. The teacher could tell students that all of them in class will write about the same idea/issue/event, but they are to write about it in different (assigned or chosen) genres. Once the short papers are drafted, the class can compare how genre affects what readers expected of the piece because of its form and how the genre itself shaped the message.

3. Students could write a paper in a genre of their choice, then rewrite the paper on the same subject in a different genre—academic essay and personal narrative for instance. To reinforce the focus on genre, a good follow up exercise asks students to write an analysis of the ways form changed their emphasis or content or changed the way readers perceive their message.

Asking how form affects *readers* leads to the importance of knowing the audience, not just knowing generally in the abstract, but in particular and in detail.

> *Audience:* The more precisely writers understand those who will read a piece, the better writers can get their attention, make them laugh or cry or change viewpoints or behavior. The following visualization exercise gets writers to fine tune their thinking about audience, borrowing from exercises fiction writers use to get to know their characters.

Visualizing Henrietta

Situation: You are writing a letter to Mrs. Henrietta Schollenberger (or whatever other fanciful name strikes students' fancy) to inform her that she was not accepted for (fill in the blank here). Students can visualize Henrietta in detail—and most importantly—imagine how she will feel when she receives the rejection letter. The exercise encourages writers to know their readers in particular rather than in the abstract and to visualize and anticipate how readers will respond to the message. Awareness of the audience leads writers to ask the following questions: What can writers assume readers know and what might writers be wise to explain? What ideas are readers likely to resist and what will they probably embrace? What tone will most likely help achieve the purpose with this particular audience?

Another means to encourage writers to focus on audience is to ask students to write adjectives to describe how readers will likely react to the message of the piece. Will readers feel angry, upset, pleased, argumentative, amused, disappointed, worried? Knowing and naming what feelings a piece of writing will likely elicit in readers empower writers to develop a strategy that intensifies or ameliorates those feelings, that uses awareness of audience to accomplish the purpose. When writers ask themselves "How do I want to come across to readers?" they're getting at tone.

> *Tone:* Students refer to tone of voice and attitude when describing how speakers are perceived by those who hear them. Tone prevails in written language too; sometimes it's neutral or mild and sometimes it bristles with attitude. Teachers can help students notice tone by first asking them to name it in texts they read, to find words to describe this attitude.

Next students can declare the tone they intend as a prerequisite for drafting a piece. What adjectives would they like readers to use to describe their text? Would they like to come across as outspoken, well informed, sarcastic, playful, thoughtful, sincere, impassioned, committed? Having to articulate the tone they're aiming for and that suits the situation and purpose helps writers keep focused as they write.

> *Point of View:* Students often assume that point of view is determined by genre, that essays are always written in third person and personal narratives are naturally written in first person. The emerging popularity of new and hybrid genres like the personal nar-

rative essay and creative non fiction have reinstated point of view as a variant of choice. Experimenting with the implications and shadings of meaning that point of view brings to writing opens up possibilities that few inexperienced writers have thought much about.

Implications of Point of View

The *first person point of view,* the pronoun "I" brings a sense of immediacy to the action and feels more personal and candid.

The *third person point of view* backs away from the action or idea and lends perspective and a presumption of objectivity. Students can decide whether they want to be "up close and personal" hence first person, or to back away from events and see with the wide-angle lens of third person point of view. They enjoy contemplating the powers of *third person omniscient point of view* where a godlike observer sees everywhere at once and even sees into characters' minds.

The *second person point of view* pronoun "you" with its finger pointing connotations has a deserved home in directions and step-by-step descriptions. "First you align tab A with slot 1." "You," however, has become the pronoun of choice in casual conversation and creeps regularly into student writings. "*You* know how you feel," students say when they don't really mean you the reader, but themselves. In its easygoing, lazy way, the "generic you," is a convenient pronoun used as if it fits any situation. Unfortunately, it is replacing more exacting pronouns. Some teachers ban the generic you from student writing except in directions, in the most informal writing situations, and in dialogue. The pronoun "you" can also put people on the defensive with its implied finger pointing accusation. It can create division—"you people" as outsiders, unaccepted and unacceptable. The pronoun "we," on the other hand, brings people together, suggests unity, cooperation, and shared destiny.

Since show is better than tell, the following exercises encourage students to realize for themselves the difference point of view can make.

1. Write about an event in first person point of view; then write about the very same event in third person point of view. In what ways does the point of view change things?

2. Give advice to someone about how to look better, write better, or drive better using the pronoun "you." Then give the same advice using "we." Discuss whether readers would likely respond differently to the same advice written from the two points of view?

Style

Good style is often so inconspicuous that readers are unaware of it. It expresses ideas clearly, makes descriptions come alive, energizes the action, and keeps a piece moving. It allows words to strut and dance and enjoy themselves, rather than plod along doing their duty. Problems with style include a host of language practices that are not exactly incorrect, but nevertheless mire a piece of writing in mediocrity. Style problems include redundancies and wordiness; choppy sentences, repetitious sentence beginnings, limited sentence variety; too many state of being verbs, imprecise verbs, excessive use of passive voice, and general bland descriptions to name a few. Many students in college writing classes report that no teacher in their twelve years of previous schooling ever explicitly addressed issues of style. Yet writing that lacks style can never be truly good. Style can quietly exude the inconspicuous competence of clear, well written prose, or it can play with words and images more ostentatiously. Because style is so integral to the way readers perceive a piece of writing, it deserves serious attention, especially during revision. Numerous handbooks on writing effectively address the issues listed above, so teachers have many resources to draw on.

What handbooks don't stress enough is that style problems are best diagnosed by ear, because style, after all, is the music of language. When students make it a practice to *read their own writing aloud* and trust their own sense of what sounds good and what sounds slightly off key, they become increasingly able to hear problems of style. Experienced writers hear words in their heads, in their mind's ear. Inexperienced writers need practice listening for style in written language. To develop students' sense of language as music and their ability to discern good style from mediocre, teachers can try the following exercises:

1. Ask students to *Read aloud* and discuss passages from texts (by published writers and by the students themselves). Choose texts that would cause stylists to smile inwardly at the pleasing rhythm and flow of words, the symmetry and parallelism of phrases and clauses, the aptness of word choices, the exuberance of verbs. Ask students to discuss what they liked and responded to in the passage and what made it good style.

2. Ask students to revise a weak passage with one or two specific style difficulties such as general adjectives rather than concrete, specific adjectives, or generic, bland verbs rather than vivid, action verbs, or short choppy sentences. First someone *reads the passage aloud* allowing students to diagnose the problem by ear; then the teacher passes out a text version of the passage or displays the text on an overhead projector so students (alone or in pairs) can revise the passage by replacing nondescript adjectives with vivid ones; replacing bland verbs with specific, active ones; combining choppy sentences for a more mature, graceful style.

3. Require students as an experiment to *read their own writing aloud* in three different ways and record in a journal what the writing-by-ear experiments revealed.

    a. In quiet and solitude, students can *read the paper aloud* to the walls. Ask them to trust their impressions and to ask, "What do your ears like? What troubles you, just doesn't get off the ground, but merely skitters along. Ask students to *read the paper aloud* to an attentive listener. In this exercise, the listener's comments are only part of the pay off. More important is how students transpose their ears into another and hear their own writing from the perspective of the listener.

    b. Ask students to have someone else *read their papers aloud* to them. When they read their own work, they're likely to read what they meant to say or what they thought they said.

Another reader will read what's actually on the page. The dissonance between what they meant to say and what's actually on the page can alert them to places where the style needs adjustment. When readers stumble over words or visually struggle to follow meaning, those clues can help writers identify places where language is obstructing the idea rather than supporting it.

These exercises focus on hearing what's amiss with style. Style also includes adding flourishes and grace notes of language to the bones of an idea to flesh it out and give it depth and vitality. Metaphors (both short and extended), similes, and stylistic repetition are three stylistic additions that many inexperienced writers have never themselves tried to write. In the interest of experimenting and trying out possibilities, a class can read aloud Dr. Martin Luther King Jr.'s "I Have a Dream" speech so they hear the techniques at work in his language. King relies extensively on metaphors in the speech and uses deliberate stylistic repetition effectively when he says "I have a dream" and "One hundred years ago [. . .]" Once students have heard and identified fine examples of figurative language and stylistic repetition, they can try writing their own. Everyone, even the teacher, can try writing a metaphor and try stylistic repetition (the phrase they choose should be repeated at least three times). Then everyone shares attempts with the class. Some students will write feeble first tries, but others' attempts will have real possibilities and everyone will hear language taking flight in those few attempts that work well. They'll hear the possibilities and realize that figurative language and stylistic repetition are techniques within reach of ordinary writers like themselves.

Voice

Donald Murray says "voice is the quality in writing, more than any other, that makes the reader read on" (65). The terms style, voice, persona, and tone all refer from slightly different angles to the idea of personality that comes through in the writing. The four terms nibble around the central idea of the mind behind the words, the word view of the person that readers know through the text. Spending time with an interesting mind and seeing the world the way writers see it are what engage readers. We've all read texts with scintillating ideas that nevertheless droned on endlessly because writers had no presence in them. We've also read texts on superfluous, overworked topics that nevertheless leapt off the page and made us care, pulled us off the sidelines because the writer was there on the page. Whether friend or adversary, writers with a distinctive voice are people readers can not easily ignore.

Yet many writers, particularly student writers, seldom let their individual voices speak out in their writing. They often write flat, generic, formal prose, thinking that's what the assignment calls for and what the teacher expects. It takes courage for writers to reveal themselves; it's dangerous to expose our foibles, foolishness, convictions, and passions for others to read. Writers don't do it lightly. Yet readers love and respect most those writers with the courage, daring, and generosity of spirit to share their ideas and experiences with readers, to be present in what they write.

Those who teach writing can foster voice in students' writing in several ways:

1. Include assignments in the curriculum in addition to the academic essay with its typically disengaged style. Letters to the editor, journalistic columns, personal narrative essays, and creative non fiction are genres that invite writers to be more present and engaged. Teachers can open up the essay and invite students to dispense with protocols they find cumbersome and to experiment with other forms or combinations of forms. They can read Montaigne and see how the father of the modern essay wrote loose-jointed, free flowing investigations of ideas that were a far cry from the lockstep format that now characterizes the academic essay.

2. Teachers can make the writing classroom a safe place where students' egos will not be bruised by harsh criticism from the teacher or from classmates because by class decree, critiques must be gentle, diplomatic, and constructive. The classroom should be a place that fosters experimenting with possibilities and a place where earnest effort receives support and encouragement. Teachers themselves can do the assignments they give students (some in-class assignments at least) and read their own efforts to the class, not to show superiority, but to show that the teacher's writing is not always wonderful, that all writers struggle to get it right, and that everyone in a community of writers should be willing to take chances and experiment—teachers included.

Mechanics

Dozens of excellent writing handbooks and grammar books teach how to fix errors that typically appear in the work of inexperienced writers. Researchers in writing pedagogy continue to debate whether noting problems on student papers is the most effective way to help students learn, whether teachers should notate at all, and if they do, in what detail. Scholars question whether teachers should even bother to instruct students about language patterns that are fast becoming standard usage (lay taking over for lie, disagreement of pronoun and antecedent, i.e. We should judge *a person* by who *they* are). The verdict is not yet in about which teaching practices result in the most improvement in student writing.

Nevertheless, we who teach writing can expand understanding of revision as more than error fixing and final editing. Teachers can model that repairing errors is not, and should not be, the most important part of revision. To model that deep revision is as important as final editing, teachers can focus on the other three clusters of consideration: content, rhetorical decisions, and style (in any order that suits). The clusters of consideration develop students' awareness and expand their understanding of what choices they have as writers.

This Much We Know Is True—
Writing Teachers Who Write

What is clear is that teachers who themselves write and revise are in closer touch with the frustrations and insecurities writers grapple with and in a better position to speak about revision in practical ways that are helpful to inexperienced writers. If we wish to revise perceptions of what constitutes good writing, good revision, and good teaching, we must emphasize the critical importance of rhetorical considerations—purpose, genre, point of view, tone, voice, audience, and style—and make them part of the repertoire for all writers.

Writers need multiple times to revisit a piece with time off between revision sessions, because good revisions happen over time. One peer workshop between the first draft and the final version may not be enough time to practice deep revision. That one workshop can too easily revert to a hunt for errors at the expense of addressing deep revision issues such as assessing the development and validity of the idea and weighing the effectiveness of writers' rhetorical decisions. Teachers who schedule several weeks to develop and revise a paper enable writers to see their papers more objectively, experiment with their options, and practice deep revision.

When writers reflect (and write down those reflections) on their own choices as writers, they develop the metalinguistic and metarhetorical awareness that professional writers employ when they revise. As less experienced writers become aware of their choices and grasp the interplay of decisions they make, they can depart from the artificial practice of looking at one issue at a time in sequence. Then revision can revert to its true nature as a recursive process happening on many levels at once, a process that is sometimes surprising and revelatory, and consistently challenging and interesting.

Glossary

Cathy McQueen

Case study research: an approach to research entailing close study of a single individual or situation.

Coded teacher feedback: identifying specific types of errors.

Contrastive rhetoric: a branch of linguistics and SLA theory that identifies problems of L2 writers and tries to explain them by referring to the rhetorical strategies typical for their first language.

Convergent data: use of multiple sources or reviews of a body of material in case study research to add validity to data analysis.

Direct teacher feedback: correcting student errors.

EFL (English as a Foreign Language): English as taught in other countries where it has a foreign language status.

Emergent English-Dominant Learners: a sub-category of ESL students. Usually children of immigrants, at least to some extent educated in the US schools, whose oral and cultural competencies in English are close to native and who are not usually recognized as ESL students.

ESL (English as a Second Language) students: students for whom English is not a native language.

Eureka Phenomenon: a seemingly sudden moment of inspiration which has actually been prepared slowly by the unconscious.

Fossilization: making certain language forms, natural for interlanguage, permanent. It usually means that students make the same errors because they have fully internalized interlanguage forms and never learned correct ones.

Hypertext: a document retrieval network allowing access to a group of linked documents.

Indirect teacher feedback: marking student errors without correcting them.

Interlanguage: a stage in English language acquisition, when the student isn't fully proficient, and when there is some confusion between the native language forms and those of the English grammar, syntax, usage etc.

L1 (First Language) writing: writing performed in a student's native language, in this context mostly in English.

L2 (Second Language) writing: writing performed in a student's second language.

LEP (Limited English Proficient) students: another term used for ESL students, mostly naturalized citizens or aliens, by researchers who recognize the stigmatizing connotation of the phrase ESL in some communities.

Metalanguage: knowledge of linguistic and grammatical terminology, ability to talk about language structures and usage.

Metalinguistic awareness: specific knowledge about language that professional writers have and use as they write and revise, information about sounds, words, sentence structures, meanings in the language of the text.

Metarhetorical awareness: refers to writers' knowledge of themselves as writers.

Metastrategic awareness: arises from writers' knowledge of themselves as people, especially in terms of personality type, and the implications of this self-awareness for their approaches to writing.

Myers-Briggs Type Indicator: a personality instrument designed to reveal an individual's preferences on four dimensions of personality; based on the work of psychiatrist Carl Jung.

NES (Native English Speakers) students: students for whom English is a native language.

Novice writers: and others who are learning to write.

Parallel Texts: publishing two versions of the same text by an author next to one another.

Process Criticism: the study of authorial revision in order to understand the creative process.

Professional writers: people who use writing to earn money in one way or another. These might be people whose job title says writer or editor such as novelists, journalists, or copy editors, or those who use writing as a basic part of their work, such as lawyers, public relations people, or members of the clergy.

Satisficing: this term was coined by researcher Linda Flower to describe the process by which writers produce text that isn't wholly satisfactory for some reason, but leave the text in place while they go on working, planning to make additional changes or adjustments at a later time.

SLA (Second Language Acquisition): long and arduous process of learning a foreign language.

TESOL (Teachers of English to Speakers of Other Languages, Inc.): a professional organization affiliating teachers of English as a Second Language. It focuses on all language skills and places no special emphasis on writing.

Textual Criticism: the attempt to establish the authoritative version of a text. Look at Smagorinsky (cited in RR) for a formal definition.

Think-aloud protocol: w they are working, writers talk out loud about the processes, strategies, changes and thinking that they are using; typically, the comments are audio taped and sometimes transcribed for further study and analysis.

TOEFL (Test of English is a Foreign Language): standardized English language test required of all foreign students admitted to the US colleges.

Uncoded teacher feedback: circling of errors.

Visual rhetoric is "an emergent key term being used to describe the attention being devoted to the symbolic and performative dimensions of visual culture, including everything from cartography to photography and from architecture and interior design to public memorials and museums" (*Visual Rhetoric*).

Annotated Bibliography

Alamargot, Denis, and Lucile Chanquoy. *Through the Models of Writing.* Norwell, MA: Kluwer Academic Publishers, 2001. Vol. 9 of *Studies in Writing.* Ed. Gert Rijlaarsdam. 13 vols. 1996–2004.

Reviews the various models of the writing process, starting with Hayes and Flower's initial 1980 model, and analyzes the cognitive basis for writing. The development of expert writing skills is shown to be closely aligned to working memory; in addition, maturity and practice seem to be the main difference between the novice and expert writer. Commentaries by Ronald T. Kellogg and John R. Hayes are also included.

Allal, Linda, Lucile Chanquoy, and Pierre Largy. *Revision: Cognitive and Instructional Processes.* Norwell, MA: Kluwer Academic Publishers, 2004. Vol. 13 of *Studies in Writing.* Ed. Gert Rijlaarsdam. 13 vols. 1996–2004.

Reviews how basic cognitive processes operate during revision, paying particular attention to what seems to activate rewriting activity. Recentstudies are also analyzed, with attention given to how classroom instruction, involving grammar skills, drafting strategies, audience awareness, writing instructions and peer evaluation and so forth, facilitate revision work at various writing levels.

Bishop, Wendy, ed. *Acts of Revision: A Guide for Writers.* Portsmouth, N.H.: Boynton/Cook, 2004.

Bishop's book contains twelve essays, some by Bishop herself, and by Brock Dethier, Alice S. Horning, Hans Ostrom, Melissa Goldthwaite, and others on a range of revision issues. The essays, attractively written for students, contain succinct explanations of issues and theories and many helpful suggestions of things to try. The book is a pleasure to read and is equally useful to teachers as they plan and writers as they work.

Chenoweth, N. Ann, and John R. Hayes. "Fluency in Writing: Generating Text in L1 and L2." *Written Communication* 18.1(January 2001): 80–98.

A new writing model combining elements of two previous ones, by Kaufer et al. (1986) and Hayes (1996), is proposed with three key levels: resource, process and control. In addition, since this think-aloud protocol study showed that writing fluency increases as language skills become more automatic, it is important for teachers to offer many opportunities for inexperienced writers topractice writing strategies.

Cowley, Malcolm. *Writers at Work: The Paris Review Interviews.* New York: The Viking Press, 1960.

This series, edited by Cowley and later by George Plimpton, provides an invaluable source of interviews of well-known writers. Virtually every author speaks of his/her revision practices in some depth and some manuscript pages are reproduced in many of the interviews. The writers reveal the centrality of revision in the creative process.

DiTiberio, John K. and George Jensen. *Writing and Personality: Finding Your Voice, Your Style, Your Way.* Palo Alto, CA: Davies-Black Publishing, 1995.

This book is addressed to the general public; it explains the Myers-Briggs Type Indicator, a personality instrument, in the context of writing tasks of many kinds. The authors discuss strategies for writers to draw on their personality preferences in writing and work around problems through an awareness of these preferences.

Ede, Lisa. *Work in Progress: A Guide to Academic Writing and Revising.* 6th ed. Boston: Bedford/St. Martin, 2004.

Ede presents an approach to the writing process with an emphasis on revision that combines a focus on analyzing rhetorical situations and academic writing. She supplements the introductions to the phases of the writing process with strategies to aid students develop writing skills, including readings for reinforcement and analysis.

Eliot, T. S. The Wasteland: A Facsimile Reproduction and Transcript of the Original Drafts Including the Annotations of Ezra Pound. Ed. Valerie Eliot. San Diego: Harcourt Brace, 1971.

The reproduction of the manuscript of Eliot's poem along with Pound's extensive commentary provides a fascinating glimpse for students into the role of collaboration in the revision process. The book demonstrates incontrovertibly that one of the most famous poems of the twentieth century was "revised" not only by Eliot himself, but by a genius behind the scenes, Ezra Pound.

Ferris, Dana R. Treatment of Error in Second Language Student Writing. Ann Arbor, MI: U of Michigan P. 2002.

As Diane Belcher writes in her introduction to this book, Ferris's goal is to write a "theory-into-practice book, "blending research with a practitioner's experience in the ESL classroom. Based on her conviction that ESL writing and revision processes are essentially different from those of NES students, Ferris argues against neglecting error correction and grammar instruction. She provides specific recommendations regarding the types of teacher feedback most effective for ESL students (indirect, coded and comprehensive) and explains how to incorporate grammar mini-lessons as astrategy helping students develop self-correction skills. While mostly interested in teacher feedback, Ferris believes that peer editing can also be helpful but only if the students are trained and the routine is carefully supervised by the teacher. Ferris's book is very useful for ESL teachers looking for effective classroom pedagogy discussed in the context of research.

Flower, Linda, et al. "Detection, Diagnosis, and the Strategies of Revision." *College Composition and Communication* 37.1 (February 1986): 16–54.

Presents a working model for revision, looking in particular at the cognitive processes used—evaluation and strategy selection—in conjunction with the writer's knowledge of how to detect a problem and then diagnose the best way to correct it.

Flower, Linda, and John R. Hayes. "A Cognitive Process Theory of Writing." *College Composition and Communication* 32(1981): 365–87.

Presents a cognitive process writing model to begin the study of how thinking processes work during the writing process, which includes three basic actions: planning, translating and reviewing.

Glenn, Cheryl, Robert K. Miller, Suzanne Strobeck Webb, and Loretta Gray. *Hodges's Harbrace Handbook.* 15th ed. Boston: Thomson Heinle, 2004.

Provides a template for handbook structure, while including several unique ideas to promote the rationale for revision in student writing.

Halasek, Kay and Nels P. Highberg, Eds. *Landmark Essays on Basic Writing.* Mahwah, NJ: Hermagoras Press/Lawrence Erlbaum, 2001.

A collection of classic essays on basic writers and basic writing, all reprinted from their original sources.

Hjortshoj, Keith. *The Transition to College Writing.* Boston: Bedford/St. Martins, 2001.

The author, a cultural anthropologist who has directed interdisciplinary writing and taught writing at Cornell, helps students understand what college writing is all about. One chapter, "Footstools and Furniture," explains the limitations of the five-paragraph essay. Another, "Rules and Errors," demonstrates the crucial idea that context matters in deciding what's correct. Chapters on college reading, structure of assignments, etc., are equally useful. Though written for students, the book's lucid explanations inform teachers as well.

Hjortshoj, Keith. *Understanding Writing Blocks.* New York: Oxford UP, 2001.

Using his work with writers in writing labs and classes, Hjortshoj investigates the nature of writing blocks. These blocks occur when writers encounter significant new demands, whether in writing a thesis or a first college research paper. They happen when the writer loses control of the recursive aspects of writing, swinging wildly from small concerns to global ones and becoming unable to compose sentence by sentence. Though Hjortshoj is mainly interested in writing blocks for composing, the same process can be seen as writers struggle with revision.

Horner, Bruce, and Min-Zhan Lu. Representing the "Other": Basic Writers and the Teaching of Writing. Urbana: National Council of Teachers of English, 1999.

Basic writing emerged during the 1960s and 1970s and positioned basic writing outside of social, political, and historical contexts. Horner and Lu analyze basic writing discourse and question its possible elimination as mainstreaming programs materialize. They explore relationships between writing and the "author function," challenge the separation of "style" from "content, and confront "textual bias of research in composition." Debates about how best to serve students' needs emerge as the discourse of basic writing is questioned.

Horning, Alice S. *Revision Revisited.* Cresskill, NJ: Hampton Press, 2002.

This volume reviews all of the modern studies of revision done in the lastquarter of the twentieth century and then presents case studies with nine professional writers. Their strategies suggest that professionals have three kinds of awareness and four sets of skills that allow them to revise effectively and efficiently.

Jensen, George H., and John K. DiTiberio. *Personality and the Teaching of Composition.* Norwood, NJ: Ablex, 1989.

This volume is addressed to teachers of composition; it explains the Myers-Briggs Type Indicator, a personality instrument, in the context and teaching learning writing at the college level. This book can help teachers broaden their approach to the teaching of writing and revising in a number of productive ways.

Kuehl, John. Creative Writing and Rewriting: Contemporary American Novelists at Work. New York: Appleton-Century-Crofts, 1967.

An important source for students of revision which includes drafts and published versions of work by Eudora Welty, Kay Boyle, James Jones, Bernard Malamud, Wright Morris, F. Scott Fitzgerald, Philip Roth, Robert Penn Warren, John Hawkes and William Styron. The book allows the student to study the novelist as he/she works through early drafts towards a completed, published work.

Lanham, Richard A. *Revising Prose*. New York: Charles Scribner's Sons, 1979.

Lanham makes writing less intimidating by establish a connection with the reader that allows the several suggestions he proposes to be readily accepted by his audience.

Lawrence, Gordon. *People Types and Tiger Stripes*. (3rd ed.). Gainesville, FL: Center for the Applications of Psychological Type, 1993

This volume explores the relevance of personality preferences for all kinds of teaching and learning, including the teaching of writing and other educational areas. The clear and thorough discussion of personality type can help teachers understand how students' personality preferences and their own affect interaction in the classroom.

Levy, C. Michael, and Sarah Ransdell. *The Science of Writing*. Mahwah, N.J.: Lawrence Erlbaum Associates, 1996.

Looks at cognitive theories and models for writing, at how to gather and analyze data for writing research and at various ways to apply research information to writing instruction for both the novice and expert.

Lindgren, Eva, and Kirk P. H. Sullivan. "The LS Graph: A Methodology for Revitalizing Writing Revision." *Language Learning* 52.3 (Spring 2002): 1–14.

Presents information on LS graphing, which is a system for tracking various writing activities and presenting them in layers within one graph. This kind of graphing allows quick comparisons of different levels of writers during their writing sessions, and can be used to help writers see what writing patterns develop in their revision work.

Madden, David and Richard Powers, eds. *Writers' Revisions*. Metuchen, New Jersey: Scarecrow Press, 1981.

This is an excellent study of literary revision. The first part contains a thorough bibliography of articles and books about writers' revisions. The second part includes extensive commentary by writers about the creative process. This is an essential sourcebook for students seeking to understand the connection between creativity and revision.

McCutchen, Deborah, Mardean Francis, and Shannon Kerr. "Revising for Meaning: Effects of Knowledge and Strategy." *Journal of Educational Psychology* 89.4 (1997): 667–76.

Students make better revisions to meaning if they know their topic well, but they also need to have good reading ability in order to make effective revisions. For inexperienced writers, knowing the location of errors didn't improve overall revision, because this prompting made them focus on local rather than global problems.

Murray, Donald. *The Craft of Revision*, 5th Ed. Boston: Heinle. 2004.

This text belongs on the bookshelf of every serious writer. Its down-to-earth wisdom offers practical strategies and playful discussions about revising gleaned from Murray's lifetime as a journalist, poet, novelist and teacher. Every page is infused with excitement about the writing craft and a sense of writing as discovery and adventure.

Olive, Thierry, and C. Michael Levy. *Contemporary Tools and Techniques for Studying Writing.* Norwell, MA: Kluwer Academic Publishers, 2002. Vol. 10 of *Studies in Writing.* Ed. Gert Rijlaarsdam. 13 vols. 1996–2004.

Offers different research tools and methodology for the study of writing from computer based techniques like S-notation to the triple task approach. Of particular note are discussions of working memory loads and how they affect the writing process.

Otte, George. *Basic Writing.* West Lafayette, IN: Parlor Press, forthcoming.

A survey of basic writing, including discussion of definitions of basic writers and their strengths, weaknesses and challenges.

Palmquist, Mike, and Donald E. Zimmerman. *Writing with a Computer.* Boston: Allyn and Bacon, 1999.

Provides an overview of using computers to facilitate all stages of the writing process, including invention, drafting, collaborating, revising, editing, and document design. Focuses on the use of computer applications within the context of writing; thus, separate sections address time-saving processes, data organization schemes, and how to create a computer-facilitated writing environment. Also provides information about Internet-based research and suggestions for protecting and maintaining the computer.

Raimes, Ann. *Keys for Writers: A Brief Handbook.* Boston: Houghton Mifflin, 2003.

Following the typical pattern of a handbook, Raimes creates effective and thorough explanations of all concepts required by the successful writer. The supplemental materials provided primarily through the associated website offer instructors valuable tools to aid students.

—. "What Unskilled ESL Students Do as They Write: A Classroom Study of Composing." *Landmark essays on ESL Writing.* Eds. Tony Silva and Paul Kei Matsuda. Mahwah, NJ: Hermagoras, 2001. 37–61.

Raimes perceives ESL students as very similar to basic L1 writers, and discusses issues both groups share: limited, rather inflexible planning, focus on surface-level errors, concept of revision as editing, lack on emphasis on changes in content, and little understanding of the audience. However, she does not ignore differences between the two groups and generally sees her ESL students as more committed to in-class writing and less intimidated by error than their L1 counterparts. Typically for the process approach, Raimes perceives her students' L1 literacy as more important than their English language proficiency, but she argues that pedagogical strategies have to be modified to fit ESL students' needs better. Her idea that ESL students need more time for revision has become one of the most quoted passages in the ESL writing research.

Silva, Tony. "Toward an Understanding of the Distinct Nature of L2 Writing: The ESL Research and Its Implications." Silva and Matsuda *Landmark* 191–208.

The article argues against the process theory assumption that ESL writing is practically identical to that of L1 students. Silva discusses revision patterns typical for ESL students and defines them as distinct from those of NES writers. Therefore, he argues for a paradigm shift in the discipline. An opponent of mainstreaming, Silva believes ESL students should be placed in writing classes designed specifically for them and instructed by teachers drawing from both composition theory and second language studies.

Sudol, Ronald A., ed. *Revising: New Essays for Teachers of Writing.* Urbana, ILL. : National Council of Teachers of English, 1982.

Sudol's edited collection contains sixteen scholarly essays divided into two sections: "Background: Theory, History, and Cases," and "Applications." There's also an annotated bibliography. Among the thought-provoking essays are "Revision and Risk" by John Ruszkiewicz and "Teaching Teachers to Teach Revision" by Toby Fulwiler. Consult Sudol's introduction for a cogent explanation of revision's interrelatedness with the rest of writing instruction.

Wallace, David L., et al. "Better Revision in Eight Minutes? Prompting First-Year College Writers to Revise Globally." *Journal of Educational Psychology* 88.4 (1996): 682–88.

How much cognitive ability and technical skill college-level writers have influences their ability to make effective revisions after being prompted to make global changes. This study underscores the need for writers to have the three main components Hayes proposed in his 1996 revision model: good basic reading and writing skills, strong working memory capacity, and a well developed task schema.

Welch, Nancy. Getting Restless: Rethinking Revision in Writing Instruction. Portsmouth, N.H.: Boynton/Cook, 1997.

Welch's book makes for interesting reading as she delves into psychological and postmodern theories to discuss revising with students, including those she's worked with in a writing lab. Welch resists defining revision as falling into line and doing closed-in, unimaginative work. She considers revision as a way to pursue doubts, to open up new questions, and to risk "intervening in a draft's meanings and representations" (135).

Woodruff, Jay. *A Piece of Work: Five Writers Discuss Their Revisions.* Iowa City: University of Iowa Press, 1993.

This volume contains work by Tobias Wolff, Joyce Carol Oates, Tess Gallagher, Robert Coles and Donald Hall. The book includes manuscript pages along with commentary by the writers themselves concerning their revisions. A useful contemporary continuation of the work done by John Kuehl in *Creative Writing and Rewriting.*

Works Cited

Adler-Kassner, Linda. "Structure and Possibility: New Scholarship about Students Called Basic Writers." *College English* 63.2 (Nov. 2000): 229–43.

Adler-Kassner, Linda, and Susanmarie Harrington. *Basic Writing as a Political Act: Public Conversations about Writing and Literacies*. Cresskill, NJ: Hampton P, 2002.

Alamargot, Denis, and Lucile Chanquoy. *Through the Models of Writing*. Norwell, MA: Kluwer Academic Publishers, 2001. Vol. 9 of *Studies in Writing*. Ed. Gert Rijlaarsdam. 13 vols. 1996–2004.

Allal, Linda, Lucile Chanquoy, and Pierre Largy. *Revision: Cognitive and Instructional Processes*. Norwell, MA: Kluwer Academic Publishers, 2004. Vol. 13 of *Studies in Writing*. Ed. Gert Rijlaarsdam. 13 vols. 1996–2004.

Anzaldua, Gloria. *Gloria E. Anzaldua, Interviews/Entrevistas*. Ed. AnaLouise Keating. New York and London: Routledge, 2000.

Arabo, Besma. Personal interview. 4 Dec. 2003.

Arieti, Silvano. *Creativity: The Magic Synthesis*. New York: Basic Books, 1976.

Ashwell, Tim. "Patterns of Teacher Response to Student Writing in a Multiple-Draft Composition Classroom: Is Content Feedback Followed by Form Feedback the Best Method?" *Journal of Second Language Writing* 9.3 (2000): 227–57.

Bazerman, Charles. "Comments from Bazerman." E-mail to Anne Becker. 19 July 2004.

—. Email to Alice Horning and Jeanie Robertson. 11 Sept. 2004.

Beach, Joseph Warren. *The Making of the Auden Canon*. Minneapolis: U of Minnesota P, 1957.

Bean, John C. "Computerized Word-Processing as an Aid to Revision." *College Composition and Communication* 34 (1983): 146–48.

Bedford, Sybille. *Aldous Huxley: A Biography*. New York: Knopf/Harper & Row, 1973.

Berg, Catherine E. "The Effects of Trained Peer Response on ESL Students' Revision Types and Writing Quality." *Journal of Second Language Writing* 8.3 (1999): 215–41.

—. "Preparing ESL Students for Peer Response." *TESOL Journal* 8.2 (1999): 20–25.
Berlin, James A. *Rhetoric and Reality: Writing Instruction in American Colleges, 1900-1985.* Carbondale, IL: Southern Illinois UP, 1987.
Berthoff, Ann E. "Recognition, Representation, and Revision." *The Allyn and Bacon Sourcebook for College Writing Teachers.* 2nd ed. Ed. James McDonald. Boston: Allyn and Bacon, 2000. 142–52.
Berzsenyi, Christyne A. "Comments to Comments: Teachers and Students in Written Dialogue about Critical Revision." *Composition Studies/Freshman English News* 29.2 (Fall 2001): 71–92.
Bishop, Wendy, ed. *Acts of Revision: A Guide for Writers.* Portsmouth, NH.: Boynton/Cook, 2004.
—. "Helping Peer Writing Groups Succeed." *Teaching English in theTwo-Year College* 15.2 (1988): 120–24.
—. *On Writing: A Process Reader.* Boston: McGraw-Hill, 2004.
—. "Revising Out and Revising In." Bishop, *Acts* 13–27
Bolter, Jay David, and Richard Grusin. *Remediation: Understanding New Media.* Cambridge, MA: MIT Press, 1999.
Borges, Jorge Luis. *Conversations with Jorge Luis Borges.* Ed. Richard Burgin. Jackson: U of Mississippi P, 1998.
Bower, Laurel. "Student Reflection and Critical Thinking: A Rhetorical Analysis of 88 Portfolio Cover Letters." *Journal of Basic Writing* 22.2 (2003): 47–65.
Boyd, Brian. *Vladimir Nabokov: The American Years.* Princeton: Princeton UP, 1991.
Bradford, Curtis. *Yeats at Work.* New York: The Ecco Press, 1965.
Brater, Enoch. *The Essential Samuel Beckett: An Illustrated Biography.* London: Thames and Hudson, 2003.
Brockman, Elizabeth Blackburn. "Revising Beyond the Sentence Level: One Adolescent Writer and a 'Pregnant Pause.'" *English Journal* (May 1999): 81–84.
Brooke, Robert, Ruth Mirtz, and Rick Evens. *Small Groups in Writing Workshops.* Urbana: National Council of Teachers of English, 1994.
Bukowski, Charles. *Sunlight Here I Am: Interviews & Encounters 1963–1993.* Ed. David Stephen Calonne. Northville: Sun Dog Press, 2003.
Burroughs, William S. *Conversations with William S. Burroughs.* Ed. Allen Hibbard. Jackson: UP of Mississippi, 1999.
Carbone, Nick. "Radical Revision Exercises." Bedford/St. Martin's Workshops on Teaching with Technology, 2002. 12 February 2006 <http://bcs.bedfordstmartins.com/workshops>.
Carpenter, Humphrey. *J.R.R. Tolkien.* New York: Ballantine, 1977.
—. *W.H. Auden: A Biography.* Boston: Houghton Mifflin, 1981.

Carroll, Lee Ann. *Rehearsing New Roles: How College Students Develop as Writers.* Carbondale, IL: Southern Illinois UP, 2002.

Chanquoy, Lucile. "How to Make it Easier for Children to Revise Their Writing: A Study of Text Revision from 3rd to 5th Grades." *British Journal of Educational Psychology.* 71 (2001): 15–41.

Chenoweth, N. Ann, and John R. Hayes. "Fluency in Writing: Generating Text in L1 and L2." *Written Communication* 18.1 (January 2001): 80–98.

Choy, Penelope, and Dorothy Goldbart Clark. *Basic Grammar and Usage.* 6th ed. Boston: Thomson Heinle, 2002.

Cioran, E.M. *Drawn and Quartered.* New York: Arcade Publishing, 1998.

Collier, Richard M. "The Word Processor and Revision Strategies." *College Composition and Communication* 34 (1983): 149–55.

Conner, Angela M., and Margaret R. Moulton. "Motivating Middle School Students to Revise and Edit." *English Journal* (September 2000): 72–78.

Connor, Ulla. *Contrastive Rhetoric: Cross-Cultural Aspects of Second Language Writing.* Cambridge Applied Linguistics Series. Cambridge: Cambridge UP, 1996.

Connor, Ulla, and Mary Farmer. "The Teaching of Topical Structure Analysis as a Revision Strategy for ESL Writers." Kroll, *Second* 126–39.

Connors, Robert J. *Composition-Rhetoric: Backgrounds, Theory, and Pedagogy.* Pittsburgh, PA: U of Pittsburgh P, 1997.

Cook, Abigail, Amie Goldberg, and Michael Russell. "The Effect of Computers on Student Writing: A Meta-analysis of Studies from 1992 to 2002." *Journal of Technology, Learning, and Assessment* 2.1 (1993). 12 February 2006 <http://www.bc.edu/research/intasc/jtla/journal/v2n1.shtml>.

Cowley, Malcolm. *Writers at Work: The Paris Review Interviews.* New York: The Viking Press, 1960.

Crafton, Robert. "Promises, Promises: Computer-Assisted Revision and Basic Writers." *Computers and Composition* 13.3 (1996): 317–26.

Cresswell, Andy. "Self-Monitoring in Student Writing: Developing Learner Responsibility." *ELT Journal* 54.3 (2000): 235–44.

Crowley, Sharon. *Composition in the University: Historical and Polemical Essays.* Pittsburgh, PA: U of Pittsburgh P, 1998.

Dethier, Brock. "Revising Attitudes." Bishop, *Acts* 1–12.

Diaute, Collete A. "The Computer as Stylus and Audience." *College Composition and Communication* 34 (1983): 134–45.

Dillard, Annie. *The Writing Life.* New York: Harper Perennial, 1989.

DiTiberio, John K., and George Jensen. *Writing and Personality: Finding Your Voice, Your Style, Your Way.* Palo Alto, CA: Davies-Black Publishing, 1995.

Ede, Lisa. *Work in Progress: A Guide to Academic Writing and Revising.* 6th ed. Boston: Bedford/St. Martin, 2004.

Elbow, Peter. *Writing with Power: Techniques for Mastering the Writing Process.* New York, Oxford UP, 1981.
Elbow, Peter, and Pat Belanoff. *Being a Writer: A Community of Writers Revisited.* Boston: McGraw-Hill, 2003.
Eliot, T.S. *The Wasteland: A Facsimile Reproduction and Transcript of the Original Drafts Including the Annotations of Ezra Pound.* Ed. Valerie Eliot. San Diego: Harcourt Brace, 1971.
Ellmann, Richard. *James Joyce.* New York: Oxford University Press, 1959.
Fadiman, Regina. *Faulkner's Light in August: A Description and Interpretation of the Revisions.* Charlottesville: U of Virginia P, 1975.
Faigley, Lester. *The Brief Penguin Handbook.* New York: Longman, 2003.
Farrell-Childers, Pamela. "A Unique Learning Environment." *Intersections.* Ed. Joan A. Mullin, and Ray Wallace. Urbana: National Council of Teachers of English, 1994. 111–19.
Fathman, Ann K., and Elizabeth Whalley. "Teacher Response to Student Writing: Focus on Form and Content." Kroll, *Second* 178–90.
Faulkner, William. *Lion in the Garden: Interviews with William Faulkner.* Ed. James B. Meriwether and Michael Millgate. Lincoln: U of Nebraska P, 1968.
Ferris, Dana. "One Size Does Not Fit All: Response and Revision Issues for Immigrant Student Writers." *Generation 1.5 Meets College Composition: Issues in the Teaching of Writing to U.S. Educated Learners of ESL.* Ed. Linda Harklau, Kay M. Losey, and Meryl Siegal. Mahwah, NJ: Erlbaum, 1999. 143–57.
—. "Responding to Writing." Kroll, *Exploring* 119–40.
—. *Treatment of Error in Second Language Student Writing.* Ann Arbor, MI.: U of Michigan P, 2002.
Ferris, et al. "Teacher Commentary on Student Writing" Descriptions and Implications." *Journal of Second Language Writing* 6.2 (1997):155–82.
Fitzgerald, Jill. "Research on Revision in Writing." *Review of Educational Research* 57.4 (1987): 481–506.
Fitzgerald, Sallyanne. "Basic Writing in One California Community College." *Conference on Basic Writing. Basic Writing e-Journal* 1.2 (Winter 1999). 25 May 2004. <http://www.asu.edu/clas/english/composition/cbw/bwe_fall_1999.html>.
Flaubert, Gustave. "Letters to Louise Colete," *Past to Present: Ideas that Changed Our World.* Ed. Stuart and Terry Hirschberg. Upper Saddle River: Pearson Education, 2003. 682.
Flower, Linda. *Problem-Solving Strategies for Writing in College and Community.* Fort Worth, TX: Harcourt Brace College Publishers, 1998.
Flower, Linda, et al. "Detection, Diagnosis, and the Strategies of Revision." *College Composition and Communication* 37.1 (February 1986): 16–54.

Flower, Linda, and John R. Hayes. "A Cognitive Process Theory of Writing." *College Composition and Communication* 32 (1981): 365–87.

Fulwiler, Toby, and Alan Hayakawa. *The Blair Handbook.* 4th ed. Upper Saddle River, NJ: Pearson Education, 2003.

Gardner, Helen. *The Composition of Four Quartets.* London: Faber and Faber, 1978.

Ginsberg, Allen. *Howl: Original Draft Facsimile, Transcript and Variant Versions.* Ed. Barry Miles. New York: HarperPerennial, 1986.

Glenn, Cheryl, Robert K. Miller, Suzanne Strobeck Webb, and Loretta Gray. *Hodges' Harbrace Handbook.* 15th ed. Boston: Thomson Heinle, 2004.

Goldstein, Lynn. "For Kyla: What Does the Research Say About Responding to ESL Writers." Silva and Matsuda, *Second* 3–89.

Grabe, William. "Notes Toward a Theory of Second Language Writing." Silva and Matsuda, *Second* 39–57.

Graff, Gerald. "Disliking Books at an Early Age." Bishop, *On Writing* 137–45.

Graves, Robert. *Robert Graves Papers,* Special Collections, Southern Illinois University Library, Collection 64, 1917–1962.

—. *Conversations with Robert Graves.* Ed. Frank L. Kersnowski. Jackson: UP of Mississippi, 1989.

Green, Brenda M. "The Writing Center at Medgar Evers College: Responding to the Winds of Change." *Writing Centers in Context.* Ed. Joyce A. Kinkead, and Jeanette G. Harris. Urbana: National Council of Teachers of English, 1993. 28–44.

Gussow, Mel. *Conversations with and about Beckett.* New York: Grove Press, 1996.

Haar, Catherine. Email to Alice Horning and Jeanie Robertson. 12 Sept. 2004.

Hacker, Douglas J., et al. "Text Revision: Detection and Correction of Errors." *Journal of Educational Psychology* 86.1 (1994): 65–78.

Halasek, Kay and Nels P. Highberg, eds. *Landmark Essays on Basic Writing.* Mahwah, NJ: Hermagoras Press/Lawrence Erlbaum, 2001.

Hamilton, Ian. *Robert Lowell: A Biography.* New York: Random House, 1982.

Hamp-Lyons, and William Condon. *Assessing the Portfolio.* New Jersey: Hampton Press, 2000.

Harklau, Linda. "Generation 1.5 Students and College Writing." *Digest.* October 2003. 11 March 2004 <http://www.cal.org/resources/digest/0305harklau.html>.

Harris, Joseph. "Revision as a Critical Practice." *College English* 65.6 (2003): 577–92.

—. "Student Writers and Word Processing: A Preliminary Evaluation." *College Composition and Communication* 36 (1985): 323–30.

Harris, Muriel. "A Multiservice Writing Lab in a Multiversity: The Purdue University Writing Lab." *Writing Centers in Context*. Ed. Joyce A. Kinkead, and Jeanette G. Harris. Urbana: National Council of Teachers of English, 1993. 1–27.

—. *Teaching One-to-One: The Writing Conference*. Urbana: National Council of Teachers of English, 1986.

—. "Working with Individual Differences in the Writing Tutorial." (pp.). *Most Excellent Differences: Essays on Using Type Theory in the Composition Classroom*. Ed. Thomas Thompson. Gainesville, FL: Center for the Application of Psychological Type, 1996. 90–100

Hawisher, Gail E. "The Effects of Word Processing on the Revision Strategies of College Freshmen." *Research in the Teaching of English* 21 (1987): 145–59.

Hayman, David. "From *Finnegans Wake*: A Sentence in Progress," in *Bibliography and Textual Criticism: English and American Literature, 1700 to the Present*. Ed. O.M. Brack, Jr. and Warner Barnes. Chicago: U of Chicago P, 1969.

Heilker, Paul. "Revision Worship and the Computer as Audience." *Computers and Composition* 9.3 (1992): 59–69.

Hewett, Beth L. "Characteristics of Interactive Oral and Computer-Mediated Peer Group Talk and its Influence on Revision." *Computers and Composition* 17.3 (2000): 265–88.

Hill, Charles A., David L. Wallace, and Christina Haas. "Revising On-line: Computer Technologies and the Revising Process." *Computers and Composition* 9.1 (1999): 83–109.

—. *Understanding Writing Blocks*. New York, Oxford UP, 2001.

Hirvela, Alan. "Collaborative Writing Instruction and Communities of Readers and Writers." *TESOL Journal* 8.2 (1999): 7–12.

Hjortshoj, Keith. *The Transition to College Writing*. Boston: Bedford/St. Martins, 2001.

Holman, C. Hugh, and William Harmon. *A Handbook to Literature,* Sixth Edition. New York: MacMillan, 1992.

Horner, Bruce, and Min-Zhan Lu. *Representing the "Other": Basic Writers and the Teaching of Basic Writing*. Urbana, IL: National Council of Teachers of English, 1999.

Horning, Alice S. *Revision Revisited*. Cresskill, N.J.: Hampton Press, Inc., 2002.

—. "The Connection of Writing to Reading: A Gloss on the Gospel of Mina Shaughnessy." *College English* 40 (1978): 264–68.

—. *Teaching Writing as a Second Language*. Carbondale, IL: Southern Illinois U P, 1987.

—. "The Trouble with Writing is The Trouble with Reading." *Journal of Basic Writing* 6.1 (1987): 36–47.

Hyland, Fiona. "The Impact of Teacher Written Feedback on Individual Writers." *Journal of Second Language Writing* 7.3 (1998): 255–86.

Jacobs, George M., et al. "Feedback on Student Writing: Taking the Middle Path." *Journal of Second Language Writing* 7.3 (1998): 307–17.

Jensen, George H., and John K. DiTiberio. *Personality and the Teaching of Composition*. Norwood, NJ: Ablex, 1989.

Johns, Ann M. "ESL Students and WAC Programs: Varied Populations and Diverse needs." *WAC for the New Millennium: Strategies for Continuing Writing-Across-The-Curriculum Programs*. Ed. Susan H. McLeod, et al. Urbana, IL: National Council of Teachers of English, 2001. 141–64.

Joyce, James. *Ulysses: A Facsimile of the Manuscript*, commentary by Harry Levin and Clive Driver. New York: Octagon Books, 1975.

—. *Finnegans Wake*. New York: The Viking Press, 1972.

Kies, Daniel. "On Using the Computer as a Writing Tool." *The HyperTextBooks*. 2004. <http://papyr.com/hypertextbooks/engl_101/computer.htm#Revising>.

Klonoski, Edward. "Using the Eyes of the PC to Teach Revision." *Computers and Composition* 1.1 (1994): 71–78.

Koch, Kenneth. *The Modern Library Writer's Workshop: A Guide to the Craft of Fiction*. New York: The Modern Library, 2003.

Krapels, Alexandra Rowe. "An Overview of Second Language Writing Process Research." Kroll, *Second* 37–56.

Kroll, Barbara, ed. *Exploring the Dynamics of Second Language Writing*. Cambridge Applied Linguistics Series. Cambridge: Cambridge UP, 2003.

—, ed. *Second Language Writing: Research Insights for the Classroom*. Cambridge Applied Linguistics Series. Cambridge: Cambridge UP, 1990.

Kuehl, John. *Creative Writing and Rewriting: Contemporary American Novelists at Work*. New York: Appleton-Century-Crofts, 1967.

Kutz, Eleanor, and Hepzibah Roskelly. *An Unquiet Pedagogy: Transforming Practice in the English Classroom*. Portsmouth, NH: Boynton/Cook, 1991.

Lacklicker, William B. "A Basic Introduction to Basic Writing Programs Structures: A Baseline and Five Alternatives." *Conference on Basic Writing. Basic Writing e-Journal* 1.2 (Winter 1999). 25 May 2004. <http://www.asu.edu/clas/english/composition/cbw/bwe_fall_1999.html>.

Lamott, Anne. *Bird by Bird*. New York: Random House, 1994.

Langan, John. *Sentence Skills with Readings*. 2nd ed. Boston: McGraw-Hill, 2001.

Lawrence, D.H. *The Complete Poems*, ed. Pinto, Vivian de Sola Pinto and Warren Roberts. Harmondsworth: Penguin,1978.

Lawrence, Gordon. *People Types and Tiger Stripes*. (3rd ed.). Gainesville, FL: Center for the Applications of Psychological Type, 1993.

Lawrence, Sandra M., and Elizabeth Sommers. "From the Park Bench to the (Writing) Workshop Table: Encouraging Collaboration among Inexperienced Writers." *Teaching English in the Two-Year College.* 23.2 (1996): 101–9.

Leki, Illona. "Coaching from the Margins: Issues in Written Response." Kroll, *Second* 57–68.

—. *Understanding ESL Writers: A Guide for Teachers.* Portsmouth, NH: Boynton, 1992.

Levy, C. Michael, and Sarah Ransdell. *The Science of Writing.* Mahwah, N.J.: Lawrence Erlbaum, 1996.

Lindemann, Erika. *A Rhetoric for Writing Teachers,* Third Edition. New York: Oxford UP, 1995.

Lindgren, Eva, and Kirk P. H. Sullivan. "The LS Graph: A Methodology for Revitalizing Writing Revision." *Language Learning* 52.3 (Spring 2002): 1–14.

Lowes, John Livingston. *The Road to Xanadu: A Study in the Ways of the Imagination.* Boston: Houghton Mifflin, 1927.

Lunsford, Andrea A. *The St. Martin's Handbook.* 5th ed. Boston: Bedford/St. Martin, 2003.

Lutz, Jean A. "A Study of Professional and Experienced Writers Revising and Editing at the Computer and with Pen and Paper." *Research in the Teaching of English* 21 (1987): 398–421.

Madden, David, and Richard Powers, eds. *Writers' Revisions.* Metuchen, New Jersey: Scarecrow Press, 1981.

Mahoney, Denis, Richard L. Martin, and Ron Whitehead. *A Burroughs Compendium: Calling the Toads.* Antwerpen: Ring Tarigh, 1998.

Marcus, Stephen. "Real-time Gadgets with Feedback: Special Effects in Computer- Assisted Instruction." *The Computer in Composition Instruction: A Writer's Tool.* Ed. William Wresch. Urbana, IL: National Council of Teachers of English. 1984. 120–30.

Matsuda, Paul Kei. "Second Language Writing in the Twentieth Century: A Situated Historical Perspective." Kroll, *Exploring* 15–29.

Matsuhashi, Ann, and E. Gordon. "Revision, Addition and the Power of the Unseen Text." *The Acquisition of Written Language: Response and Revision.* Ed. Sarah Freedman. Norwood, NJ: Ablex, 1985. 226–49

McCutchen, Deborah, Mardean Francis, and Shannon Kerr. "Revising for Meaning: Effects of Knowledge and Strategy." *Journal of Educational Psychology* 89.4 (1997): 667–76.

Metzger, Bruce M., and Michael D. Coogan. *The Oxford Companion to the Bible.* Oxford: Oxford UP, 1993.

Micciche, Laura R. "Making a Case for Rhetorical Grammar." *College Composition and Communication* 55.4 (2004): 716–37.

Miller, Henry. *My Life and Times.* Chicago: Playboy Press, 1972.

—. *The World of Sex.* New York: Grove Press, 1965.

Monroe, Jonathan, ed. *Writing and Revising the Disciplines.* Ithaca, NY: Cornell UP, 2002.

Moore, Anthony. "Obsessed with Writing." Review of *Collected Poems* by Robert Lowell. January 2004. 12 February 2006 <http://www.cprw.com/members/Moore/lowell.htm>.

Moran, Mary Hurley. "Connections Between Reading and Successful Revision." *Journal of Basic Writing* 16.2 (1997): 76–89.

Murfin, Ross, and Supryia M. Ray, eds. *The Bedford Glossary of Critical and Literary Terms*, Second Edition. Boston: Bedford/St. Martin's, 2003.

—. "Internal Revision: A Process of Discovery." *Research on Composing: Points of Departure.* Eds. Charles R. Cooper and Lee Odell. Urbana, ILL: National Council of Teachers of English, 1978. 85–103.

—. *The Craft of Revision.* 5th ed. Boston: Heinle, 2004.

Murray, Penelope, ed. *Genius: The History of an Idea.* Oxford: Basil Blackwell, 1989.

Nabokov, Vladimir. *Strong Opinions.* New York: McGraw-Hill, 1973.

—. *Pale Fire.* G.P. Putnam, 1962.

Nelson, Gayle N., and Joan G. Carson. "ESL Students' Perceptions of Effectiveness in Peer Response Groups." *Second Language Writing* 7.2 (1998): 113–31.

New, Elizabeth. "Computer-Aided Writing in French as a Foreign Language: A Qualitative and Quantitative Look at the Process of Revision." *Modern Language Journal* 83.1 (1999): 80–97.

Newton, Stephen. "Teaching, Listening, and the Sound of Guns." *Conference on Basic Writing. Basic Writing e-Journal* 4.1 (Spring 2002). 5 Mar. 2004. <http.//www.asu.edu/clas/english/composition/cbw/bwe_spring_2002.html>.

Nietzsche, Friedrich. *The Birth of Tragedy Out of the Spirit of Music.* Trans. Shaun Whiteside. London: Penguin, 1993.

Olive, Thierry, and C. Michael Levy. *Contemporary Tools and Techniques for Studying Writing.* Norwell, MA: Kluwer Academic Publishers, 2002. Vol. 10 of *Studies in Writing.* Ed. Gert Rijlaarsdam. 13 vols. 1996–2004.

Owston, Ronald D., Sharon Murphy, and Herbert H. Wideman. "The Effects of Word Processing on Student Writing in a High Computer Access Environment." Technical Report 91–93. York, Ontario: York University Centre for the Study of Computers in Education, 1991.

Pack, Robert, and Jay Parini. *Writers on Writing.* Hanover and London: Middlebury College P, 1991.

Packard, William, ed. *The Poet's Craft: Interviews from The New York Quarterly.* New York: Paragon House Publishers, 1987.

—. *The Craft of Poetry: Interviews from the New York Quarterly.* New York: Doubleday, 1974.

Patrick, Catherine. *What is Creative Thinking?* New York: Philosophical Library, 1955.

Peck, Wayne C. "The Effects of Prompts on Revision: A Glimpse of the Gap Between Planning and Performance." *Reading to Write: Exploring a Cognitive and Social Process.* Ed. Linda Flower, et al. Oxford: Oxford UP, 1990. 156–69.

Perkins, D.N. *The Mind's Best Work.* Cambridge: Harvard UP, 1981.

Perl, Sondra. "The Composing Processes of Unskilled College Writers." 1979. *Cross-Talk in Comp Theory: A Reader.* Ed. Victor Villanueva. Urbana, IL: National Council of Teachers of English, 1997. 17–42

Pizzolato, Jane Elizabeth. "Developing Self-Authorship: Exploring the Experiences of High-Risk College Students." *Journal of College Student Development* 44.6 (2003): 797–812. 28 Jan. 2004. <http://muse.jhu.edu/journals/journal_of_college_student_development>.

Plimpton, George. *Writers at Work: The Paris Review Interviews,* Second Series. Harmondsworth: Penguin, 1977.

—. *Writers at Work: The Paris Review Interviews,* Third Series. New York: The Viking Press, 1968.

—. *Writers at Work: The Paris Review Interviews,* Fourth Series. Harmondsworth: Penguin, 1977.

Polio, Charlene, Catherine Fleck, and Nevin Leder. "'If I Only Had More Time:' ESL Learners' Changes in Linguistic Accuracy on Essay Revisions." *Journal of Second Language Writing* 7.1 (1998): 43–68.

Powell, Lawrence Clark. *The Manuscripts of D.H. Lawrence: A Descriptive Catalogue.* Foreword by Aldous Huxley. New York: Gordon Press, 1972.

Raimes, Ann. *Keys for Writers: A Brief Handbook.* Boston: Houghton Mifflin, 2003.

—. "What Unskilled ESL Students Do as They Write: A Classroom Study of Composing." Silva and Matsuda, *Landmark* 37–61.

Randsell, Sarah, and Marie-Laure Barbier. "An Introduction to New Directions for Research in L2 Writing." Randsell and Barbier 1–10.

—, eds. *New Direction for Research in L2 Writing.* Doprdrecht: Kluwer, 2002.

Raymond, Richard C. "Teaching Students to Revise: Theories and Practice." *Teaching English in the Two-Year College.* 16.1 (1989): 49–58.

Reid, Stephen. *Purpose and Process: A Reader for Writers,* 5th ed. Upper Saddle River, NJ: Pearson Education, 2004.

Reynolds, Thomas H., and Curtis Jay Bonk. "Facilitating College Writers' Revisions within a Generative-Evaluative Computerized Prompting Framework." *Computers and Composition* 13.1 (1996): 93–108.

Robey, Cora L., Cheryl K. Jackson, Carolyn M. Melchor, and Helen M. Maloney. *New Handbook of Basic Writing Skills.* 5th ed. Boston: Thomson Heinle, 2002.

Roca de Larios, Julio, Liz Murphy and Javier Marin. "A Critical Examination of L2 Writing Process Research." Randsell and Barbier 11–47.

Ross, Charles L. *The Composition of The Rainbow and Women in Love: A History*. Charlottesville: U of Virginia P, 1979.

Scardamalia, Marlene, and, Carl Bereiter. "Development of Dialectical Processes in Composition." *Literacy, Language and Learning: the Nature and Consequences of Reading and Writing*. New York: Cambridge UP, 1985. 307-29.

Schor, Sandra. "An Alternative to Revising: The Proleptic Grasp." *Journal of Basic Writing* 6.1 (1987): 48–54.

Shafer, Gregory. "Using Letters for Process and Change in the Basic Writing Classroom." 1999. *Teaching Developmental Writing: Background Readings* 2nd ed. Ed. Susan Naomi Bernstein. Boston: Bedford/St. Martins, 2004. 61–69

Sharples, Mike. *How We Write: Writing as Creative Design*. London: Routledge, 1989.

Shaughnessy, Mina P. *Errors and Expectations: A Guide for the Teacher of Basic Writing*. New York: Oxford UP, 1977.

Silko, Leslie Marmon. *Conversations with Leslie Marmon Silko*. Ed. Ellen L. Arnold. Jackson: UP of Mississippi, 2000.

Sharples, Mike. "Revising." *How We Write: Writing as Creative Design*. London: Routledge, 1999. 102–11.

Silva, Tony. "Toward an Understanding of the Distinct Nature of L2 Writing: The ESL Research and Its Implications." Silva and Matsuda, *Landmark* 191–208.

Silva, Tony, and Paul Kei Matsuda, eds. *Landmark Essays on ESL Writing*. Mahwah, NJ: Hermagoras, 2001.

—, eds. *On Second Language Writing*. Mahwah, NJ: Lawrence Erlbaum, 2001.

Smagorinsky, Peter. "Think-Aloud Protocol Analysis: Beyond the Black Box." *Speaking About Writing: Reflections on Research Methodology*. Ed. Peter Smargorinsky. Thousand Oaks, CA: Sage Publications, 1994. 3–19.

Sommers, Nancy. "Revision Strategies of Student Writers and Experienced Adult Writers." *College Composition and Communication* 31(1980): 378–87.

—. "Revision Strategies of Student Writers and Experienced Adult Writers." *The Writing Teacher's Sourcebook*. Washington, DC: National Institute for Education. (ERIC Document Reproduction Service No. ED 220 839).

Spender, Stephen, ed. *W.H. Auden: A Tribute*. New York: Macmillan, 1975.

Stannard, Martin. *Evelyn Waugh: The Later Years 1939–1966*. New York: W.W. Norton, 1992.

Sternglass, Marilyn S. *Time to Know Them: A Longitudinal Study of Writing and Learning at the College Level.* Mahwah, NJ: Lawrence Erlbaum, 1997.

Strickland, Bill, ed. *On Being A Writer.* Cincinnati: Writer's Digest Books, 1989.

Sudol, Ronald A. "Applied Word Processing: Notes on Authority, Responsibility, and Revision in a Workshop Model." *College Composition and Communication* 36 (1985): 331–35.

—. *Revising.* Urbana, IL: National Council of Teachers of English, 1982.

Tedlock, E.W., Jr. *The Frieda Lawrence Collection of D.H. Lawrence Manuscripts: A Descriptive Bibliography.* Albuquerque: University of New Mexico Press, 1948.

Tone, Bruce, and Dorothy Winston. "Why Don't Computers Encourage Revision?" ERIC Clearinghouse on Reading and Communication Skills Bloomington IN. Computer-Assisted Writing Instruction. ERIC Digest Number 2, 1988. [ED 293 130]

Troyka, Lynn Q. "Defining Basic Writing in Context." *A Sourcebook for Basic Writing Teachers.* Ed. Theresa Enos. New York: Random House, 1987. 2–15.

—. "How We Have Failed the Basic Writing Enterprise." *Journal of Basic Writing* 19.1 (2000): 113–23.

—. *Quick Access: Reference for Writers.* 3rd ed. Upper Saddle River, NJ: Prentice Hall, 2001.

Truscott, John. "The Case for 'The Case Against Grammar Correction in L2 Writing Classes': A Response to Ferris." *Journal of Second Language Writing* 8.2 (1999): 111–22.

Tuzi, Frank. "The Impact of E-Feedback on the Revisions of L2 Writers in an Academic Writing Course." *Computers and Composition* 21.2 (2004): 217–35.

Van den Bergh, Huub, and Gert Rijlaarsdam. "What Revisions Can Tell about Writing Processes." Presentation at the Third International IAIMTE Conference on the Learning and Teaching of Language & Literature. July 10–13, 2001. Amsterdam, the Netherlands.

Wallace, David L., et al. "Better Revision in Eight Minutes? Prompting First-Year College Writers to Revise Globally." *Journal of Educational Psychology* 88.4 (1996): 682–88.

Wallas, G. *The Art of Thought.* New York: Harcourt Brace, 1926.

Weiss, Jason. *Writing at Risk: Interviews in Paris with Uncommon Writers.* Iowa City: U of Iowa P, 1991.

Welch, Nancy. *Getting Restless: Rethinking Revision in Writing Instruction.* Portsmouth, N.H.: Boynton/Cook, 1997.

Welty, Eudora. . *Conversations with Eudora Welty.* Ed. Peggy Whitman Prenshaw. Jackson: UP of Mississippi, 1984.

Willis, Meredith Sue. *Deep Revision: A Guide for Teachers, Students, and Other Writers.* New York: Teachers & Writers Collaborative, 1993

Wilson, Paige, and Teresa Ferster Glazier. *The Least You Should Know about English Writing Skills.* 8th ed. Boston: Thomson Wadsworth, 2005.

Winterowd, W. Ross. With Jack Blum. *A Teacher's Introduction to Composition in the Rhetorical Tradition.* Urbana, IL: National Council of Teachers of English, 1994.

Woodruff, Jay. *A Piece of Work: Five Writers Discuss Their Revisions.* Iowa City: U of Iowa P, 1993.

Wordsworth, William. *The Prelude: A Parallel Text.* Ed. J.C. Maxwell. Harmondsworth, Penguin: 1976.

Wynn, Sherry. Personal interview. 2 Dec. 2003.

Wysocki, Anne Frances. "With Eyes that Think, and Compose, and Think: On Visual Rhetoric. *Teaching with Computers: An Introduction.* Ed. Pamela Takayoshi and Brian Huot. Boston: Houghton Mifflin, 2003. 182–201.

Yagelski, Robert. "The Role of Classroom Context in the Revision Strategies of Student Writers." *Research in the Teaching of English* 29 (1995): 216–38.

Index

ACT score, 51, 60
adjectives, 77, 198, 212, 215;
    concrete, 42, 46, 102, 192,
    215; general, 4, 7, 16, 50, 54,
    68, 72, 80, 83, 85–86, 99, 117,
    121, 127–28, 132–33, 148,
    150–51, 187, 214–15, 224;
    specific, 6, 13, 22, 26, 28–29,
    34, 36, 40–42, 45–47, 50–51,
    54, 56, 77–78, 82, 86–89, 90,
    91, 93–97, 100, 108, 111, 112,
    117, 119, 124, 126, 135, 166,
    187–88, 192–95, 205, 208,
    215, 220–21, 225
Adler-Kassner, Linda, 52
Aeschylus, 145
Alamargot, Denis, and Lucile
    Chanquoy, *Through the Models
    of Writing*, 34–35, 223
Alamargot, Denis, 34–35, 38, 223
Allal, Linda, 38–39, 41–43, 46,
    223
Allal, Linda, Lucile Chanquoy,
    and Pierre Largy, *Revision;
    Cognitive and Instructional
    Processes*, 38, 223
Anzaldua, Gloria, 162–63
apparatus criticus, 145
Arabo, Besma, 72, 74–75, 79, 85
Archimedes, 146
argument, 8, 21, 71, 99, 111,
    119–20, 184, 186, 188, 201,
    209–10
Arieti, Silvano, 146

Aristotle, 15
Ascorti, Katia, 42
Ashwell, Tim, 76
Asimov, Isaac, 146
Auden, W.H., 144, 149, 161, 168,
    169, 170
audience, 3, 8, 11, 32, 35–36, 47,
    60, 80–83, 86, 87, 89–92,
    95, 97–99, 106, 112, 119–20,
    124, 126, 129, 132, 136, 141,
    185, 197–98, 204, 206, 207,
    211–12, 218, 223, 228, 230
awarenesses, 158, 166, 171; meta-
    linguistic, 36, 53, 55, 57, 67,
    74, 76, 118–19, 123, 127–28,
    135, 138, 158–59, 173, 183,
    198–99, 207, 219; metarhe-
    torical, 36, 53, 54, 55, 59, 76,
    118, 123, 127–28, 135–36,
    138, 158, 172, 182, 184–87,
    198–99, 207, 219; metastrae-
    gic, 36, 53, 56–57, 76, 118,
    123, 127–28, 134–35, 138,
    158–59, 173, 181-83, 187
Bach, J.S., 149
Baddeley, Alan D., 31
basic writers, 50, 53, 58, 227
Bazerman, Charles, 51
Beach, Joseph Warren, 169–70
Bean, John C., 103
Becker, Anne, 14, 18
Beckett, Samuel, 158
Bereiter, Carl, 26, 28
Berg, E. Catherine, 82–83

Berlin, James A., 14; *Rhetoric and Reality*, 14
Berryman, John, 159–61, 169
Berthoff, Ann, 54, 61
Berzsenyi, Christyne A., 43
Bishop, Wendy, 11, 17, 21–22, 24, 98–99, 178–79, 223; *Acts of Revision*, 11, 21–22, 98, 223; *A Guide for Writers*, 11, 21, 223; *On Writing*; *A Process Reader*, 24
Bolter, Jay David, 112
Bonk, Curtis Jay, 104
Borges, Jorge Luis, 7, 154–56, 176
Boscolo, Pietro, 42
Bower, Laurel, 55
Bowers, Fredson, 145
Boyle, Kay, 147, 227
Bradford, Curtis, 173
Brater, Enoch, 158
Breidenbach, Cathleen, 8, 20, 197
Brooke, Robert, 182; Small Groups in Writing Workshops, 182
Bukowski, Charles, 153, 156, 162, 172
Burroughs, William S., 154, 162, 172

Calonne, David, 19
Carbone, Nick, 105, 111
Carson, Joan G., 79, 80
case studies, 7, 98, 117–18, 120–22, 158, 178, 227
Catullus, 145
CDO process, 27, 28
Chanquoy, Lucile, 34–35, 38–39, 42–43, 45, 46, 223
Chenoweth, N. Ann, 36, 37, 224
Choy, Penelope, 93
Choy, Penelope and Dorothy Goldbart Clark: *Basic Grammar and Usage*, 93

Cioran, E.M., 144
Clark, Dorothy Goldbart, 93
clusters of consideration, 208, 218; content, 8, 50, 54–55, 58–59, 61, 68– 69, 72–77, 83, 108–14, 119–20, 124, 133, 171, 181, 183, 185, 197, 202–04, 208, 209, 211, 218, 227, 230; mechanics, 9, 12, 16, 69, 88, 141, 197, 203–04, 208; rhetorical decisions, 8, 197, 203–04, 208–10, 218; style, 3, 4, 8, 11, 60, 98–99, 105–06, 111, 113, 142, 154–55, 162, 167–68, 170, 172, 186–87, 197, 203–04, 207–208, 214–18, 227
Coleridge, Samuel Taylor, 150
Colete, Louise, 164
collaboration, 36, 53, 58–59, 80, 82, 85, 91, 107, 109–10, 119, 123–24, 128, 136, 138, 142, 160, 164–65, 172–74, 176, 179, 181, 183, 225
collaborative action, 53, 58–59
collaborative revision, 42, 111, 114
Collier, Richard M., 103
componential skills, 41
composition history, 14
computers and revision, 102, 178
Condon, William, 188, 189; *Assessing the Portfolio*, 188
Conner, Angela, 40
Connor, Ulla, 84
Connors, Robert J., 15; *Composition–Rhetoric; Backgrounds, Theory, and Pedagogy*, 15
content, 8, 32, 34, 39–50, 54, 55, 58–61, 68, 69, 72–77, 83, 108–14, 119–20, 124, 133, 171, 181, 183, 185, 197, 202–04, 208–11, 218, 227, 230; argument,, 8, 21, 71, 99,

111, 119, 120, 184, 186, 188, 201, 209–10; logic, 8, 77, 150, 204, 209; narrative, 8, 12, 42, 47, 209, 211, 212, 217; organization, 8, 12, 15, 41, 50, 52, 68, 84, 92, 106, 111, 112, 119, 123, 133, 181, 186, 195, 204, 222, 229
context, 16, 37, 50, 52, 58, 60, 72, 85–86, 90–91, 95, 98, 112, 113, 119–20, 129, 136, 160–61, 169, 174, 221, 224–29
convergent data, 122, 164
Cook, Abigail, 103
Cooper, Charles R., and Lee Odell, 11; *Research on Composing*; *Points of Departure*, 11
corpus linguistics, 77
Couzijn, Michel, 43–44, 47
Cowley, Malcolm, 151, 224
Crafton, Robert, 103
Crane, Hart, 169
creative writers, 132, 136, 138, 143, 150, 161, 163, 176, 178
creativity and revision, 132–34, 142, 228
Cresswell, Andy, 83
Crowley, Sharon, 20; Composition in the University; Historical and Polemical Essays, 20
Cummings, e.e., 162

Deep Revision, 199, 202
Derrida, Jacques, 175
Dethier, Brock, 22, 98, 223
Diaute, Collete A., 103
Dillard, Annie, 138
"discovery draft," 186
DiTiberio, John, *Personality and the Teaching of Composition*, 56, 123, 129, 134, 139, 166, 181, 187, 224, 227

Divide and Conquer, 208
document design, 7, 106, 109, 113, 229
drafting strategies, 39, 47, 223

Ede, Lisa, 99; *Work in Progress*, 99, 224
Eklundh, Kerstin S., 45
Elbow, Peter, 3, 12, 183; *Writing with Power*, 12
Elbow, Peter, and Pat Belanoff: *Being a Writer; A Community of Writers Revisited*, 12
Eliot, T.S., 164–65, 172, 225
English as a Foreign Language (EFL) study, 66
English Language Institute (ELI), 64
error log, 92
Euripides, 145

Fadiman, Regina, 171, 172
Faigley, Lester, 96–97, 100; *The Brief Penguin Handbook*, 96
Farmer, Mary, 84
Farrell–Childers, Pamela, 185
Fathman, Ann K., 69, 73
Faulkner, William, 7, 151, 171–72
feedback, 104, 108; coded, 77, 204, 225; comprehensive, 77, 204, 225; direct, 51, 54–55, 61, 77, 79–80, 110, 135–38, 150, 179, 182, 192; indirect, 77, 84, 225; selective, 77; uncoded, 77
feeling preference, 129, 174
Ferris, Dana, 66, 70–81, 225; Treatment of Error in Second Language Student Writing, 70, 225
First Language (L1), 63
Fitzgerald, F. Scott, 147, 227
Fitzgerald, Jill, 12, 15

Flaubert, Gustave, 164
Fleck, Catherine, 69, 70
Flower, *et al.*, 28, 29, 30, 38
Flower, Linda, 11, 14, 25–31, 38, 137, 195, 222–26; cognitive model of revision, 11; *Problem–Solving Strategies for Writing in College and Community*, 12
fossilization, 64, 67, 73, 75
Freud, Sigmund, 146

Galbraith, David, 39
Gardner, Helen, 172
Gardner, Howard, 146
Generation 1.5, 51, 67
genre, 8, 36, 38, 41, 48, 53, 58–60, 86, 96–97, 114, 119, 120, 124, 129, 136, 138, 142, 151, 158, 160–61, 173, 184, 189, 197–98, 203, 207, 210–12, 218
Ginsberg, Allen, 154, 170
Glazer, Teresa Ferster, 93
Goldberg, Amie, 103
Goldstein, Lynn, 78
Gordon, 54, 139, 228
Grabe, William, 86
Graff, Gerald, 24
Graham, Steve, 40
grammar: minilessons, 73, 75, 77
grammar checking software, 93
grammatical structures, 55
Graves, Robert, 7, 145, 157, 168
group reviews, 179
Grusin, Richard, 112

Haar, Catherine, 3, 5, 10, 61
Haas, Christina, 103
Hamp–Lyons, Liz, 188–89; *Assessing the Portfolio*, 188
Handbooks, 6, 56, 60, 88, 91, 93, 94, 99, 121, 214, 218
Harrington, Susanmarie, 52

Harris, Joseph, 13, 14, 56–57, 103, 187, 190–191
Harris, Karen R., 40
Harris, Muriel, 13, 14, 56–57, 103, 186–87, 190–91; *Teaching One–to–One*; *The Writing Conference*, 190
Harrison, Jim, 149
Hawisher, Gail E., 103
Hawkes, John, 147, 227
Hayes, *et al.*, 28, 37
Hayes, John, 25, 26, 28–38, 223–26, 231
Hayman, David, 167
Heath, Shirley Brice, 19
Heilker, Paul, 106
Hemingway, Ernest, 149, 162, 165
Heuristic, 91, 92, 94, 99, 125
Hewett, Beth, 104, 110
Hill, Charles A., 103
Hirvela, Alan, 85
Hjortshoj, Keith, 17, 22; *The Transition to College Writing*, 17, 226; *Understanding Writing Blocks*, 22, 226
Hodges Harbrace Handbook, 89, 90, 91, 93
Holliway, David R., 40
Homer, 144, 152
Horace, 145
Horner and LU, 58, 227
Horning, Alice S., 3, 4, 6, 13–14, 21, 23, 36, 37, 39, 50, 52, 56– 57, 76, 117, 198, 199, 223, 227; *Revision Revisited*, 4, 6, 7, 13, 21, 24, 36, 39, 53, 56, 58, 60, 117–21, 127, 129, 135–138, 198, 199, 227
Huizinga, Johan, 146
Huxley, Aldous, 7, 157, 159
Hyland, Fiona, 71
hypertext, 142, 176

ice–breaking activity, 181
immigrant ESL students, 66
individual tutoring, 85
inspiration, 9, 142–43, 146–47, 150–59, 161, 176, 200, 220
interface, 103
interlanguage, 64, 67, 73, 220
international ESL students, 66

Ionesco, Eugene, 155
"Jabberwocky," 161
Jackson, Cheryl K., 93
Jacobs, George M. et al., 79–82
Jarrell, Randall, 169
Jensen, George, 56, 123, 129, 134, 138, 166, 181, 187, 224, 227; *Personality and the Teaching of Composition*, 56, 224
Johns, Ann, 66
Jones, James, 147, 227
journalism's heuristic, 168
Joyce, James, 143, 147, 165–68, 172, 231
Jung, C.G., 146, 152

Kaplan, Robert, 84
Keats, John, 142, 164
Kellogg, Ronald T., 31, 33, 35, 39, 44, 223
Kerouac, Jack, 154
Kies, Daniel, 104
King, Martin Luther, 216
Klonoski, Edward, 103
Koch, Kenneth, 147
Kollberg, Py, 45
Krashen, Stephen, 73
Kris, Ernst, 146
Kuehl, John, 147, 231
Kutz, Eleanor, 20
Kutz, Eleanor, and Hepzibah Roskelly, *An Unquiet Pedagogy: Transforming Practice in the English Classroom*, 20

Lamott, Anne, 11, 138, 201, 187, 202; *Bird by Bird: Some Instructions on Writing and Life*, 11
Langan, John, *Sentence Skills with Readings*, 93
Lanham, Richard A., 98, 228; *Revising Prose*, 98, 228
Largy, Pierre, 38–39, 42, 43, 46, 223
Lawrence, D. H., 56, 152, 156–57, 172, 173, 179, 181, 226, 228
Lawrence, Gordon, 56, 139, 152, 156–57, 172–73, 179, 181, 188, 226, 228
Lawrence, Sandra M., 56, 152, 156–57, 172–73, 179, 181, 226, 228
layout, 4, 18, 21, 74, 97, 104, 113–24, 141, 208, 222
Leki, Illona, 64–68, 70–72, 75, 86
Levi–Strauss, Claude, 175
Levy, C. Michael, 44, 228, 229
Levy, C. Michael, and Sarah Ransdell, *The Science of Writing: Theories, Methods, Individual Differences, and Applications*, 31
Lewis, Sinclair, 159
Limited English Proficient (LEP) learners, 66
Lindgren, Eva, 45
literacy practices, 53
logic, 8, 77, 150, 204, 209
long–term memory, 25, 26, 30–37, 48
Losey, Kay M., 67
Lowell, Robert, 149, 168, 169
Lowes, John Livingston, 150
Lutz, Jean A., 103

MacArthur, Charles A., 40
Madden, David, 147

Malamud, Bernard, 147, 227
Marcus, Stephen, 103
Maritain, Jacques, 146
Matsuda, Paul Kei, 64, 230
Matsuhashi, 54
Maxwell, J.C., 174
McCutchen, Deborah, 40
mechanics, 9, 12, 16, 69, 88, 141, 197, 203–04, 208
media, 50, 96, 103, 104, 112–14, 122
Melchor, Carolyn M., 93
Mendelson, Edward, 169
Merton, Thomas, 165
metalanguage, 66
metalinguistic awareness, 36, 55, 57, 118–19, 123, 127, 128, 135, 138, 198–99
metaphor, 12, 13, 15, 21, 103, 128, 203, 216
metaphorical language, 11
metaphorical thinking, 14
metaphors, 5, 11–12, 15, 21, 125, 128, 137, 154, 172, 216
metarhetorical awareness, 53–55, 59, 118, 123, 127–28, 135–36, 138, 219; writing portfolio, 54
metastrategic awareness, 56, 57, 118, 128, 134–35, 138
Miller, Henry, 7, 151–54, 159, 164, 168, 172, 226
Miller, Robert K., 89, 101
modeling, 82, 179, 185, 194–95
Monroe, Jonathan (ed.), *Writing and Revising the Disciplines*, 20
Montaigne, 217
Moran, Mary, 61
Morris, Wright, 147, 227
Moulton, Margaret R., 40
Murphy, Sharon, 103
Murray, Donald M., 3, 7, 11, 21, 97–98, 137, 152, 177, 179–81, 186, 193, 199–200, 229; *The*

Craft of Revision, 7, 21, 97, 177, 179, 199, 229; *The Craft of Revision*, 5th ed., 7, 21, 97, 177, 179, 199, 229
Myers–Briggs Type Indicator (MBTI), 56, 128, 130, 134, 138

Nabokov, Vladimir, 7, 144, 148–49, 159, 172, 174, 176
narrative, 8, 12, 42, 47, 209, 211, 212, 217
Native English Speaking (NES) students, 63; NES, 63–65, 73, 221, 225, 230
natural writer, 8, 200, 202; fallacy of, 202
Nelson, Gayle L., 79, 80
new media, 112, 114
New, Elizabeth, 76
Nietzsche, Friedrich, 146, 150
Nin, Anais, 164
novice writers, 159, 185, 187–88

O'Hara, John, 151
Olive, Thierry, 44, 229
online discussion lists, 111
Oostdam, Ron, 40
organization, 8, 12, 15, 41, 50, 52, 68, 84, 92, 106, 111–12, 119, 123, 133, 181, 186, 195, 204, 222, 229
Owston, Ronald D., 103

Pack, Robert, 147
Packard, William, 147
palimpsest, 145
Parini, Jay, 147
Patrick, Catherine, 146
Peck, Wayne C., 21
peer editing, 17, 78, 90–92, 225
peer response, 40–41, 47, 79, 80–83, 179, 181; training, 8,

24, 56, 66, 73, 81–85, 131, 139, 178–181, 185–88
peer response groups, 179, 181
peer review, 5, 8, 40, 59, 79–85, 90–91, 97, 109–11, 115, 126, 170, 178–79, 183–84, 192–95; instructor, 43, 46, 88, 93, 94, 97, 104, 106–09, 112–13, 126, 184, 186, 189, 193–95; large group responses, 180; one-on-one peer review, 180, 183, 196; online, 110; peer group, 23, 42, 182; peer review session, 5, 8, 79, 90, 179, 183–84, 193, 195; small group responses, 180
Perl, Sondra, 57
personality type, 39, 56–57, 76, 118, 129, 139, 150, 159, 174–76, 185, 221, 228
Piolat, Annie, 38, 44
plagiarism, 68, 87
Plath, Sylvia, 169
Plato, 152
Plimpton, George, 147, 224
point of view, 8, 96, 197, 198, 203, 212–14, 218; first person, 212–14; second person, 91, 213; third person, 212–14; third person omniscient, 213
Polio, Charlene, 69, 70
portfolios, 8, 54, 55, 107, 138, 188; collection, 4, 21, 67, 131, 163, 187–88, 226, 231; reflection, 8, 18, 32, 104, 107, 114, 123, 183, 188–89; selection, 110, 188–89, 225
poststructuralism, 142, 175, 176
Pound, Ezra, 164, 165, 172, 225
PowerPoint, 94, 112, 193
Powers, Richard, 147, 228
process pedagogy, 17, 206
professional writers, 4, 6, 7, 29, 38, 53–58, 60–61, 117–21, 127, 128, 130, 135–39, 165, 201, 219, 221, 227
Proust, Marcel, 167

Raimes, Ann, 64, 69–70, 72, 80, 93, 94, 100, 230; *Keys for Writers*, 93, 100, 230
Rank, Otto, 146
Ransdell, Sarah, 44, 228
Raymond, Richard C., 179, 183
read aloud, 216
recommendations: pivotal moment, 61
reflective writing, 55, 138, 189
Reid, Stephen, *Purpose and Process; A Reader for Writers*, 99
remediation, 112–14
research writing, 161
reviewing strategies: detect/rewrite, 30; diagnose/revise, 30
revision: after publication, 142, 147, 149, 161, 168, 169; best practices, 20, 178, 197; collaborative approach, 178, 188, 193; collaborative environment, 181; collaborators, 42, 147, 164; computers, 44–45, 102, 104, 132, 147, 149, 160–63, 229; editors, 62, 91, 126, 136, 142, 145, 147, 164, 222; galleys, 142, 144, 147, 150, 158, 165, 167, 171; parallel texts, 142, 171, 174–75; planning, 26, 28–35, 43–44, 46, 48, 50, 65, 97, 128, 132–33, 135, 137, 222, 226, 230; prevision, 183; process criticism, 142, 171, 173; proofs, 142, 144, 147, 158, 165–67, 172; revision process, 4–10, 13, 29, 31, 40, 46, 50, 71, 78, 83, 89–91, 94, 97, 104, 108,

110, 113, 115, 122, 143, 149, 150–56, 158, 160–61, 164–65, 167, 169, 172, 177–78, 184, 187, 199, 202, 206, 225; tools, 8, 36, 53, 56, 58, 60, 88, 94, 100, 103–04, 106–07, 109, 119, 121, 136, 138–39, 149, 229–30; with computers, 7, 16, 38, 44–46, 60, 77, 85, 96, 102–04, 106, 110, 112, 114, 121, 123, 127–29, 132, 135, 139, 142, 147, 149, 153, 158, 161–65, 168, 176, 229

revision notes, 61

revision process: detection, 28–29, 31, 38; diagnosis, 28–29, 31, 38, 46

Reynolds, Thomas H., 104

rhetoric, 22, 98, 106, 107, 224; contrastive, 11, 84

rhetorical analysis, 4

rhetorical decisions, 8, 197, 203–04, 208–10, 218; audience, 3, 8, 11, 32, 35–36, 47, 60, 80–83, 86–87, 89, 90–92, 95, 97–99, 106, 112, 119–120, 124, 126, 129, 132, 136, 141, 185, 197–98, 204, 206, 207, 211, 212, 218, 223, 228, 230; genre, 8, 36, 38, 41, 48, 53, 58–60, 86, 96–97, 114, 119–20, 124, 129, 136, 138, 142, 151, 158, 189, 197–98, 203, 207, 210–12, 218; point of view, 8, 96, 197–98, 203, 212–214, 218; purpose, 3, 8, 12, 16–17, 22, 29, 40–41, 47, 60, 79, 82, 89–92, 94, 97, 98, 124, 126, 159, 181, 183–84, 197, 203, 210–12, 218; tone, 8, 11, 19, 70, 90, 92, 119, 148, 193, 197–98, 203, 204, 207, 212, 216, 218

Rijlaarsdam, Gert, 31, 33, 43, 44, 46, 47, 223, 229

Rimbaud, Arthur, 156

Robey, Cora L., 93

role–playing, 179, 185, 195

Ross, Charles, 172

Roth, Philip, 147, 227

Rothenberg, Albert, 146

Rouiller, Yviane, 42

rule–governed, 52

Russell, Michael, 103

Sappho, 145

Saroyan, William, 130, 153

"Satificing," 185

Scardamalia, Marlene, 26, 28

Schor, Sandra, 55

Second Language (L2): L2, 63–68, 70, 72–73, 83, 85, 86, 220, 221, 224, 230

Second Language Acquisition (SLA), 63, 74, 84, 220, 222

self–monitoring, 83, 84

sentences, 5, 11, 39, 84, 88, 90, 92, 106, 121, 125, 154, 173, 183, 201, 202, 214–15; short choppy, 215

Sexton, Anne, 169

Shafer, Gregory, 58

Sharples, Mike, 147

Siegal, Meryl, 67

Silko, Leslie Marmon, 158–59

Silva, Tony, 65, 68–69, 86, 230

Silva, Tony, 65, 230

similes, 216

skills: collaboration, 36, 53, 58–59, 80, 85, 91, 107, 110, 119, 123–24, 128, 136, 138, 142, 165, 172, 174, 176, 179, 181, 225; genre, 8, 36, 38, 41, 48, 53, 58–60, 86, 96, 97, 114, 119–20, 124, 129, 136, 138, 142, 151, 158, 160, 166, 171,

Index 253

173, 186–87, 189, 197–98, 203, 207, 210–12, 218; text and context, 36, 53, 58, 60, 120, 124, 129, 136, 138; tools, 8, 36, 53, 56, 58, 60, 88, 94, 100, 103–04, 106–07, 109, 119, 121, 136, 138–39, 149, 229, 230
Smagorinsky, Peter, 118, 158, 222
Sommers, Elizabeth, 179, 181
Sommers, Nancy, 20, 21, 60
Sophocles, 145
St. Martin's Handbook, 92
Sternglass, Marilyn: *Time to Know Them*, 51, 54
student writers, 157
stylistic repetition, 216
Styron, William, 147, 227
Sudol, Ronald A., 103, 117, 137, 186; *Revising: New Essays for Teachers of Writing*, 10, 231
Sullivan, Kirk P. H., 228
Szczepanski, Jay, 98

task schema, 31–32, 36, 37, 40, 43, 46, 48, 49, 231
task schema model, 31, 40, 48
teacher and student conferences, 190, 192; one-to-one conference, 190–91; small-group workshops, 191
Teachers of English to Speakers of Other Languages (TESOL), 64–65, 87, 222
Tedlock, E.W., 157
Test of English as a Foreign Language (TOEFL), 66, 86, 222
test readers, 179
text tracking: JEdit, 44, 45; LS graphing, 44–45, 228; S–notation, 44–45, 229; text transformations, 41, 44, 46; Trace–It, 44, 45
textbooks: readers, 99–100
textual criticism, 145, 175
The Blair Handbook, 94
think–aloud protocol, 7, 44, 45, 118, 122, 124, 134, 224
think–aloud protocols, 7, 44–45, 158, 163–64, 166, 168, 172, 177, 179–80, 182
Thoreau, Henry David, 19
Tolkien, J.R.R., 166
Tone, Bruce, 103
tools for revision, 160, 162, 174, 184
Torrance, Mark, 39
training exercises, 178, 181
Troyka, Lynn, 94; *Quick Access*, 94, 101
Trupiano, Carol, 8, 20, 97, 177, 205
Truscott, John, 72–73
Tuzi, Frank, 104, 110

Valéry, Paul, 170
van der Bergh, Huub, 31, 33, 46
Van Gelderen, Amos, 40
verbs, 92, 106, 198, 204, 214, 215; bland, 214–15; vivid, action, 215
Virgil, 145, 152
visual, 4, 96, 105, 107–08, 112–13, 176, 222
Visualizing Henrietta, 211
voice, 17, 91, 95–96, 98, 106, 204, 212, 214, 216–18

Wallace, David, 103
Wallas, G., 146, 150
Warren, Robert Penn, 147, 227
Waugh, Evelyn, 165
Welch, Nancy, *Getting Restless; Rethinking Revision in Writing Instruction*, 19, 231

Welty, Eudora, 147, 149, 159–60, 227
Whalley, Elizabeth, 69, 73
Wideman, Herbert H., 103
Willis, Meridith Sue, 199, 202
Wilson, Paige, and Teresa Ferster Glazer, *The Least You Should Know about English Writing Skills*, 93
Winchester, Dorothy, 103
Winterowd, W. Ross, 15, 19; *Introduction to Composition in the Rhetorical Tradition*, 15
Wolfe, Thomas, 165
word processing, 7, 32, 60, 82–83, 92–93, 102–10, 114–15, 121, 128, 131–32, 135, 140, 161, 164
word processing software, 92, 102
Wordsworth, William, 148, 174, 176
working memory, 30–36, 38, 44, 45, 47–48, 223, 229, 231
working memory functions, 32; central executive, 31–32, 48; phonological loop, 31–32; visuo–spatial sketchpad, 31–32
working memory model, 31
World Wide Web (Web), 7, 94, 96, 97, 104, 110–11, 165
writing centers, 8, 85, 178, 185, 188; tutors, 8, 56–57, 85, 178, 185–88, 192; Writing Fellows, 185; Writing Lab, 186, 187; writing support programs, 185–88, 192
writing expertise, 3, 4, 8, 10, 13, 24, 26, 32, 34–36, 38, 40–41, 43, 45, 47–49, 70, 78, 81–85, 105, 111, 120–21, 124–25, 131–32, 143, 152, 162, 179, 185–86, 188–89, 192, 194, 214, 218–19, 223, 225
writing models: process–based, 25, 29, 32–38, 44, 48
writing process, 4, 25, 35, 45–46, 55, 102, 128, 135, 137, 139; planning, 26, 28–35, 43, 44, 46, 48, 50, 65, 97, 128, 132, 133, 135, 137, 222, 226, 230; reviewing, 26, 28, 30–32, 38, 40, 43, 48–49, 55, 92, 181, 184, 194, 226; translating, 26, 30–32, 35, 36, 41–43, 48, 226
writing skills, 5, 27–28, 30, 93, 94; evaluation, 26, 29, 32, 37, 40, 83, 95, 98, 99, 179, 184, 188–89, 203, 223, 225
Wysocki, Anne, 113–14
Yagleski, Robert, 103–04
Yeats, W. B., 149, 168, 173
Zamel, Vivian, 64, 71, 73, 76
Zhang, Shuqiang, 79–80

Contributors

Anne Becker is a special instructor and the coordinator for journalism and communication internships at Oakland University. She has taught freshman composition at OU since 1981, and supervised the internship program since 1984. She also teaches an introductory public relations course. Her classroom and research interests focus on problem-solving approaches to writing; she is also interested in how computer technology impacts writing instruction. Another area of interest involves non-profit public relations activities, especially publications editing and design. Her postsecondary degrees include a BA in English from the University of Michigan and an MA in English from Oakland University.

Cathleen Breidenbach (BA in English-University of Michigan, MA in English-Oakland University, completed PhD coursework in English and Composition Studies-Wayne State University) has taught writing courses at Oakland University for fourteen years, testing over those years ways to communicate to students that the time-consuming process of composition is not only an art but a logical and cyclical serious of decisions, trial runs, re-decisions, and re-trials they can learn to do and do well.

David Stephen Calonne has taught composition and literature courses at the University level for twenty-one years and has published three books and many articles. He has a BA in Ancient Greek from the University of California at Los Angeles and a PhD in English from the University of Texas at Austin. In graduate school at Texas, he studied the history of Rhetoric with James Kinneavy and literary theory with Gayatri Chakravorty Spivak. His training in traditional humanistic disciplines as well as modern theoretical approaches informs his teaching of writing. His particular interest in the teaching of writing lies in engaging students with deep reading and thinking. Calonne has published *William Saroyan: My Real Work is Being* (Chapel Hll and London: University of North Carolina Press, 1983); *The Colossus of Armenia: G.I. Gurdjieff and Henry Miller* (Ann Arbor, MI: Roger Jackson, 1997); and *Charles Bukowski: Sunlight Here I Am/Interviews and Encounters 1963–1993* (Northville, MI: Sundog Press, 2003).

Douglas Eyman, Senior Editor of *Kairos: A Journal of Rhetoric, Technology, and Pedagogy*, is currently pursuing graduate studies in the Professional Writing and Digital Rhetoric Program at Michigan State University. He has served on the board of directors of the Alliance for Computers and Writing and as a member of NCTE's Instructional Technology Committee; he is currently a member of the CCCC Committee on Computers in Composition and Communication. Douglas has also served as the Web Manager for Teaching English in the Two Year College online and taught online courses for the Graduate Center at Marlboro College and the Community College of Southern Nevada.

Catherine Haar received her doctorate in English from the University of Maryland in 1994, with a dissertation on the narrative art of six Old English long religious poems. She has taught composition at Oakland University in Rochester Hills, Michigan, since 1987, and before that at colleges in Maryland. She regularly teaches Basic Writing, Composition I, and Composition II, and occasionally has taught College Reading and an upper-level course, Writing for Human Services Professionals. In Composition II, she's offered themed courses on issues in higher education and concepts of adventure. She writes book reviews for a College Board web site, AP Central, she's presented papers at the Conference on College Composition and Communication, and she's co-authored a program handbook for a local community college.

Alice Horning directs the Rhetoric Program at Oakland University and is a professor of Rhetoric and Linguistics. Her research interests focus on the nature of readable text from theoretical and practical perspectives. On the theoretical side, she is chiefly interested in the psycholinguistic aspects of text processing and those features of text form and structure that facilitate readability. On the practical side, she is interested in how readers and writers meet effectively in text. She has published several books on the nature of texts and on human literacy, including, most recently, *Revision Revisited* (Hampton Press, 2002).

Kasia Kietlinska, who was born and raised in Poland, got her MA degree in English Language and Literature at the University of Gdansk, Poland, in 1978. She worked as an assistant professor at the University of Gdansk and as an ESL teacher, interpreter, and press liaison for the Solidarity Trade Union until she came to the U.S. as a political refugee in 1983. She completed her graduate work at the University of Michigan, in Ann Arbor (ABD in English Language and Literature) in 1988. Since 1989, Kasia has worked as a rhetoric instructor at Oakland University, teaching a variety of composition courses.

Robert Lamphear earned his Bachelor of Arts degree in English from Wayne State University, where he began his graduate study and was able to begin teaching composition on a fellowship. Due to life changes, including the birth of his youngest daughter, he completed his Master of Arts in English at Oakland University. After teaching at Oakland Community College for several years, concurrent with a career in Information Technology, he obtained a position with Oakland University teaching rhetoric. Robert recently earned his second Master of Arts degree in Humanities, which he teaches at Oakland Community College and Baker College. Currently, he attends Oakland University to pursue a third MA in linguistics with a focus on TESL.

Catherine McQueen received her B.S. from the University of Michigan, and her MA from Oakland University, and currently is teaching the Rhetoric sequence at Oakland University. She has authored in-house publications for Oakland Community College which were designed to assist ESL students with comprehension issues in specific coursework. Her ongoing research focuses on the nuances of language and how these impact both the author and reader in terms of basic comprehension along with other, more subtle concerns including readability, impact and imagery.

Colleen A. Reilly is an assistant professor of English at the University of North Carolina Wilmington. Her teaching and research interests include professional writing, writing and technology, distance learning, writing about science, electronic publication, citation analysis, and gender, sexuality, and technology.

Jeanie Robertson teaches composition, reading, and study skills with primary focus on Basic Writing and Composition I and II courses. She has taught composition courses for eighteen years at various colleges and universities (currently full time at Oakland University in Rochester, Michigan) where she encourages students to explore new ideas and ways to communicate them. Her research interest includes classroom observations on how reading and writing interact and influence effective communication. She has a BA and a MA in English from Oakland University.

Carol Trupiano received a BA and MA in English from Wayne State University. She has been teaching composition for four years. For ten years she was the Assistant Coordinator of the Writing Fellows Program at Macomb Community College where she trained students in the methods of peer tutoring. During this time she developed a particular interest in the impact the training had on the peer tutor's own writing. Through her association with the Writing Fellows Program, she participated in outreach programs with high schools and created a training manual for high school teachers and students who want to develop a tutoring program that promotes writing across the curriculum through the use of peer tutors.

www.ingramcontent.com/pod-product-compliance
Lightning Source LLC
Chambersburg PA
CBHW021755230426
43669CB00006B/86